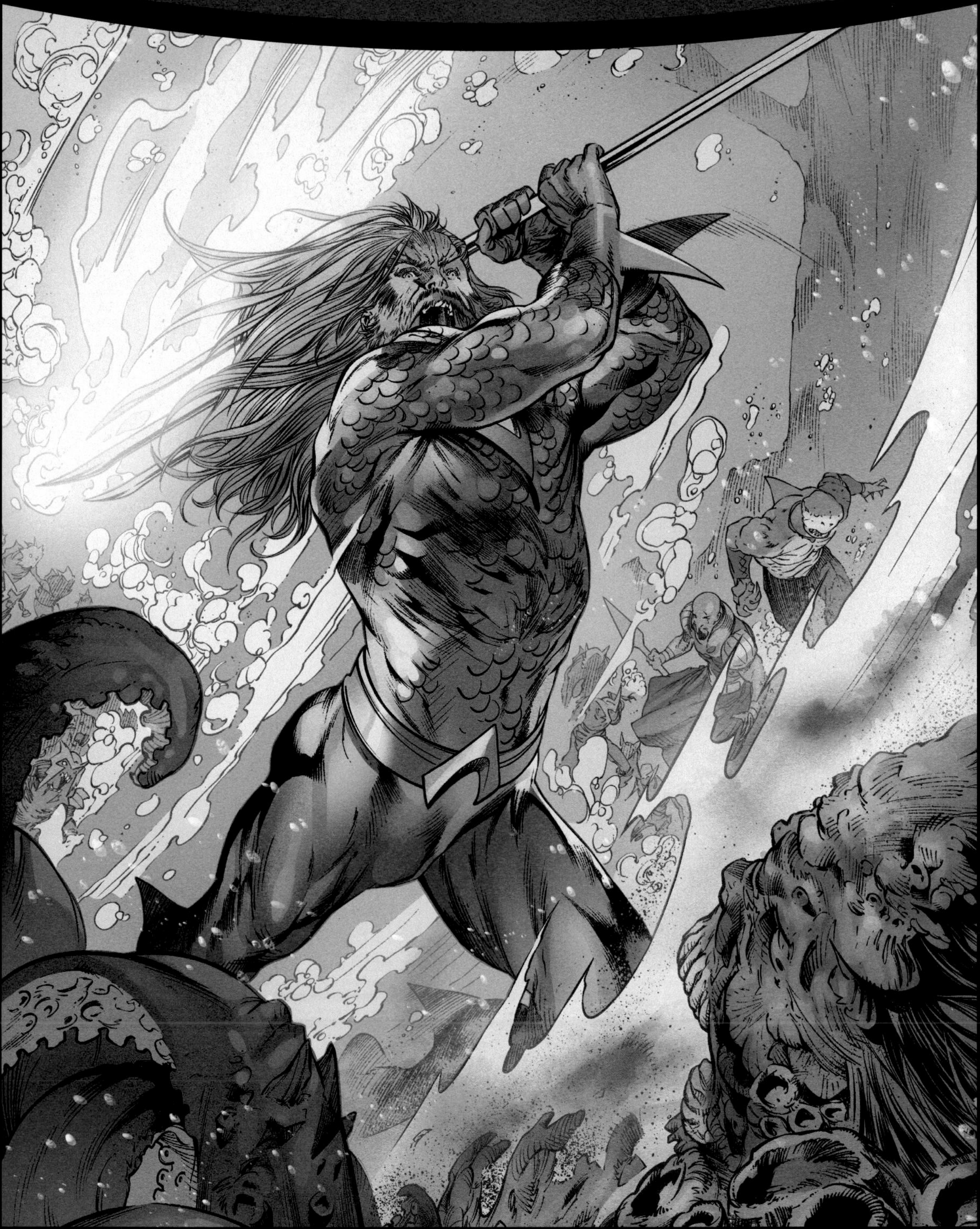

AQUAMAN

VOL.6 KINGSLAYER

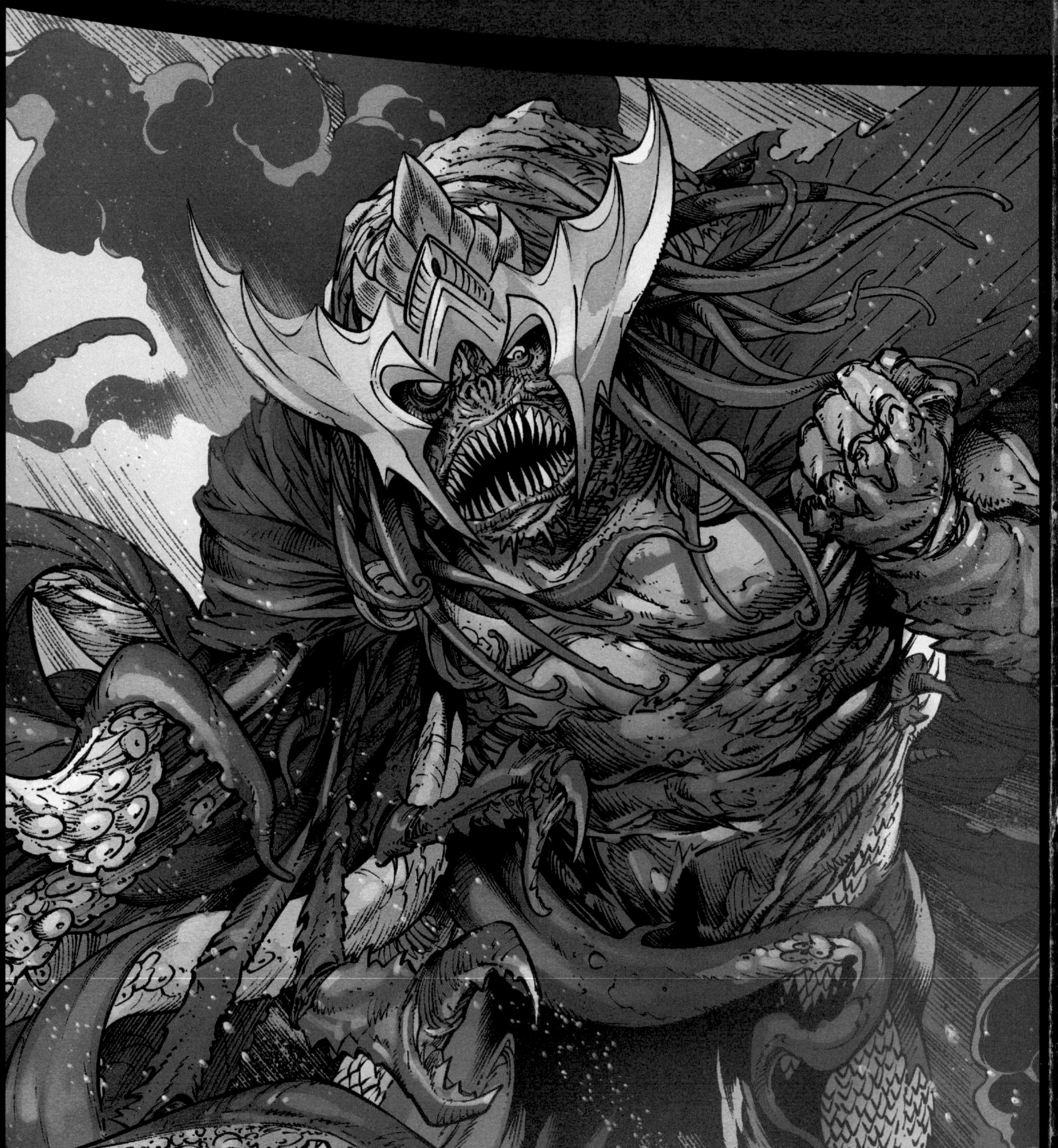

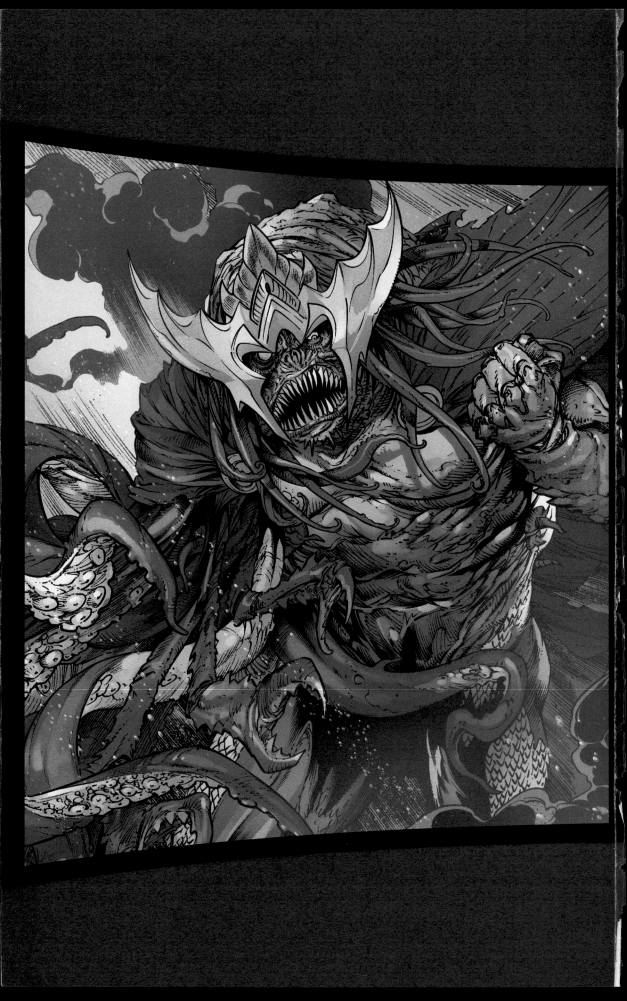

AQUAMAN
VOL. 6 KINGSLAYER

DAN ABNETT
writer

RICCARDO FEDERICI
KELLEY JONES
ROBSON ROCHA
DANIEL HENRIQUES
DANNY MIKI
artists

SUNNY GHO
MICHELLE MADSEN
colorists

STEVE WANDS
TRAVIS LANHAM
letterers

JOSHUA MIDDLETON
collection cover artist

AQUAMAN created by **PAUL NORRIS**

ALEX ANTONE Editor – Original Series ✳ **ANDREA SHEA** Assistant Editor – Original Series
JEB WOODARD Group Editor – Collected Editions ✳ **TYLER-MARIE EVANS** Editor – Collected Edition
STEVE COOK Design Director – Books ✳ **SHANNON STEWART** Publication Design

BOB HARRAS Senior VP – Editor-in-Chief, DC Comics ✳ **PAT McCALLUM** Executive Editor, DC Comics

DAN DiDIO Publisher ✳ **JIM LEE** Publisher & Chief Creative Officer
AMIT DESAI Executive VP – Business & Marketing Strategy, Direct to Consumer & Global Franchise Management
BOBBIE CHASE VP & Executive Editor, Young Reader & Talent Development ✳ **MARK CHIARELLO** Senior VP – Art, Design & Collected Editions
JOHN CUNNINGHAM Senior VP – Sales & Trade Marketing ✳ **BRIAR DARDEN** VP – Business Affairs
ANNE DePIES Senior VP – Business Strategy, Finance & Administration ✳ **DON FALLETTI** VP – Manufacturing Operations
LAWRENCE GANEM VP – Editorial Administration & Talent Relations ✳ **ALISON GILL** Senior VP – Manufacturing & Operations
JASON GREENBERG VP – Business Strategy & Finance ✳ **HANK KANALZ** Senior VP – Editorial Strategy & Administration
JAY KOGAN Senior VP – Legal Affairs ✳ **NICK J. NAPOLITANO** VP – Manufacturing Administration
LISETTE OSTERLOH VP – Digital Marketing & Events ✳ **EDDIE SCANNELL** VP – Consumer Marketing
COURTNEY SIMMONS Senior VP – Publicity & Communications ✳ **JIM (SKI) SOKOLOWSKI** VP – Comic Book Specialty Sales & Trade Marketing
NANCY SPEARS VP – Mass, Book, Digital Sales & Trade Marketing ✳ **MICHELE R. WELLS** VP – Content Strategy

AQUAMAN VOL. 6: KINGSLAYER

DC Comics, 2900 West Alameda Ave., Burbank, CA 91505
Printed by LSC Communications, Kendallville, IN, USA. 11/9/18. First Printing.
ISBN: 978-1-4012-8543-2

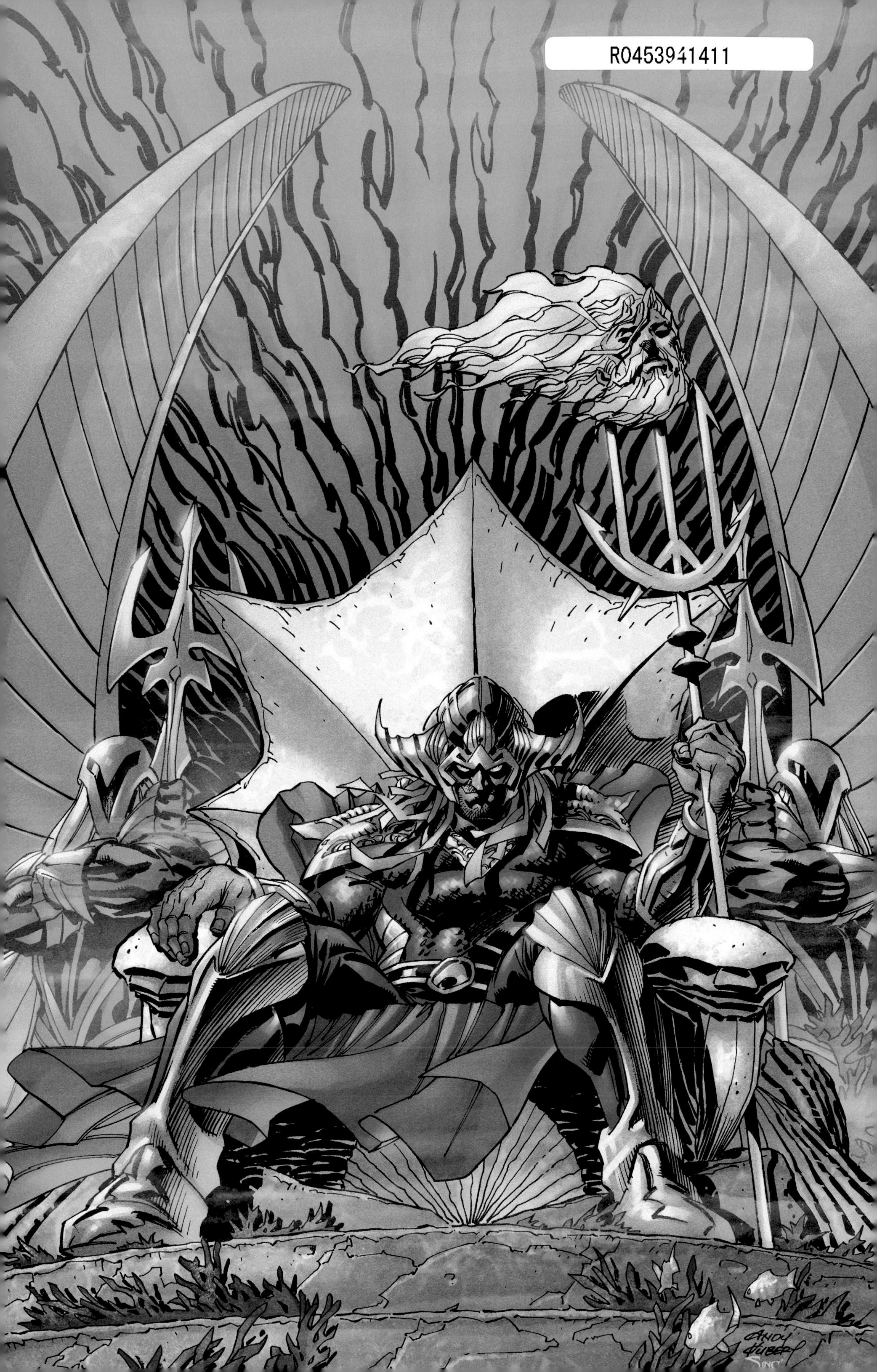

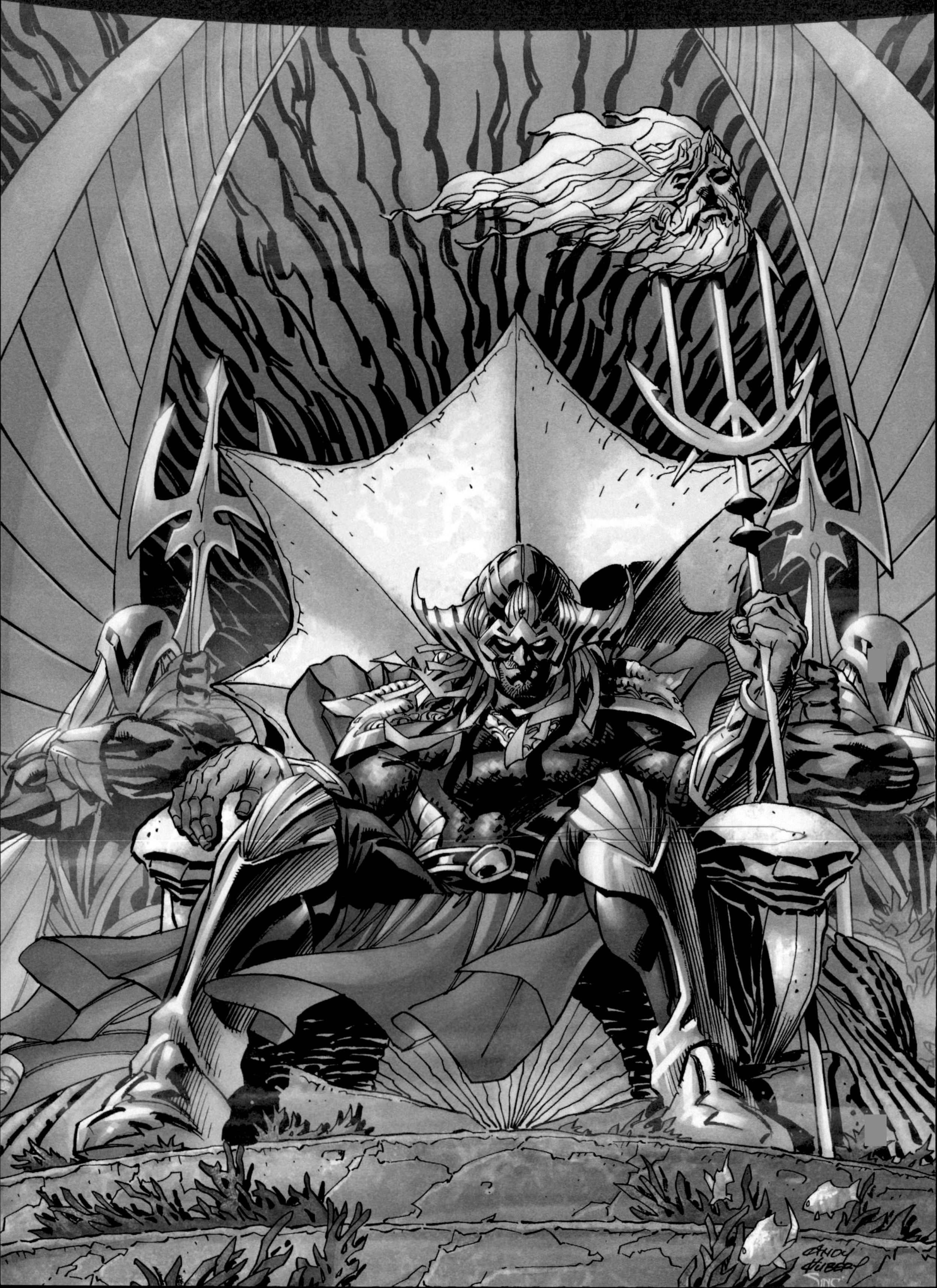

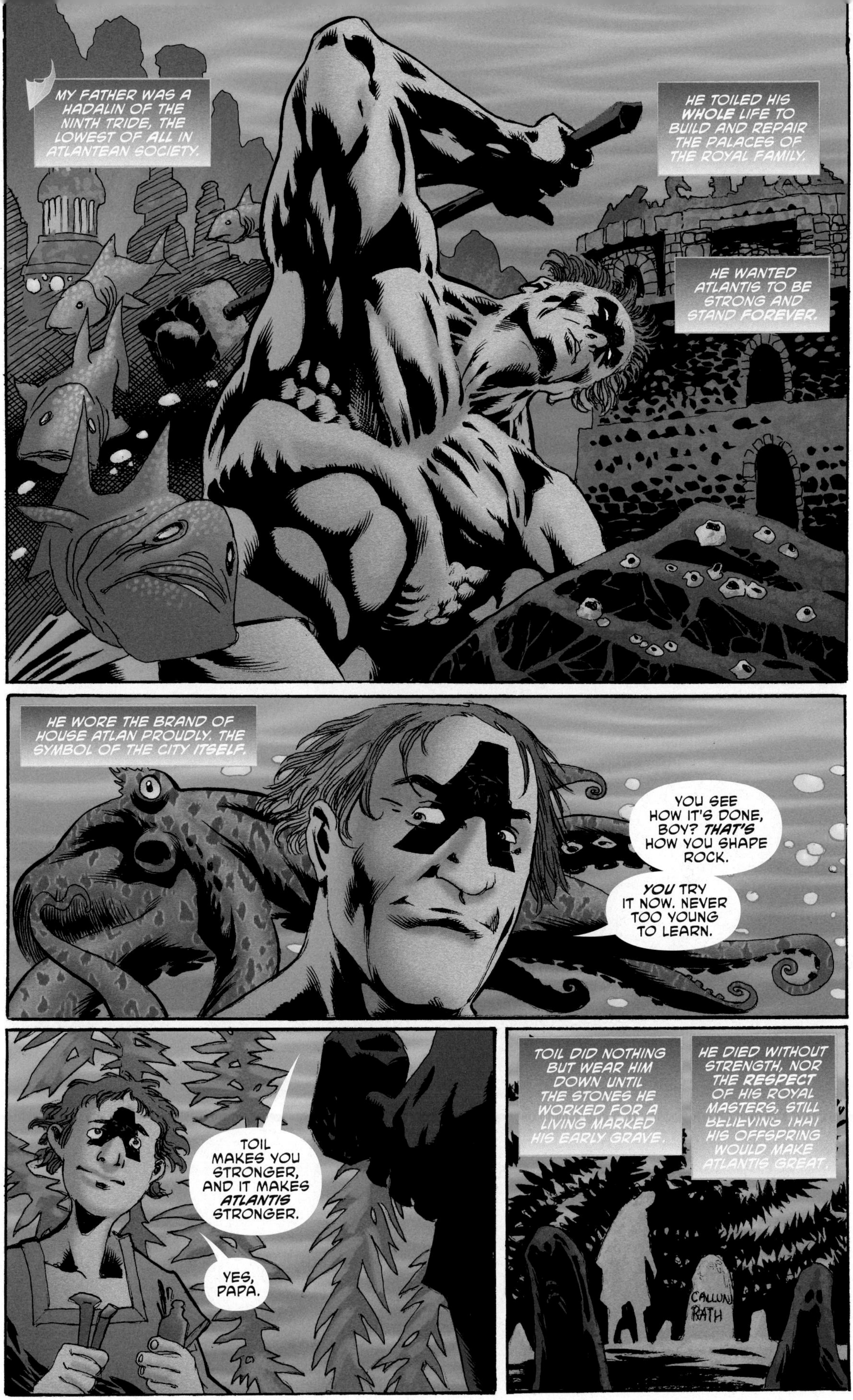
MY FATHER WAS A HADALIN OF THE NINTH TRIDE, THE LOWEST OF ALL IN ATLANTEAN SOCIETY.
HE TOILED HIS WHOLE LIFE TO BUILD AND REPAIR THE PALACES OF THE ROYAL FAMILY.
HE WANTED ATLANTIS TO BE STRONG AND STAND FOREVER.
HE WORE THE BRAND OF HOUSE ATLAN PROUDLY. THE SYMBOL OF THE CITY ITSELF.
YOU SEE HOW IT'S DONE, BOY? THAT'S HOW YOU SHAPE ROCK.
YOU TRY IT NOW. NEVER TOO YOUNG TO LEARN.
TOIL MAKES YOU STRONGER, AND IT MAKES ATLANTIS STRONGER.
YES, PAPA.
TOIL DID NOTHING BUT WEAR HIM DOWN UNTIL THE STONES HE WORKED FOR A LIVING MARKED HIS EARLY GRAVE.
HE DIED WITHOUT STRENGTH, NOR THE RESPECT OF HIS ROYAL MASTERS, STILL BELIEVING THAT HIS OFFSPRING WOULD MAKE ATLANTIS GREAT.
CALLUM RATH

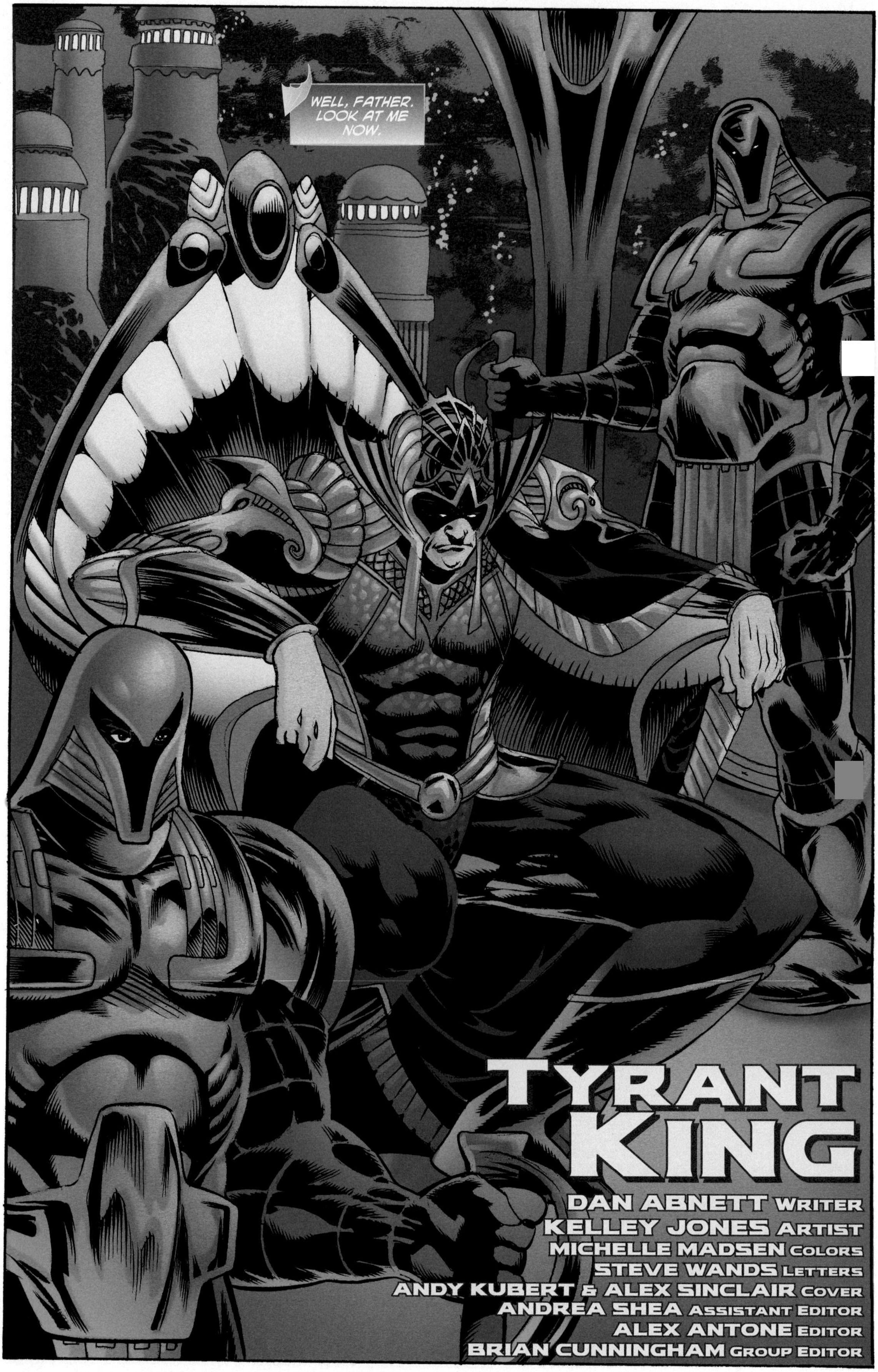
WELL, FATHER. LOOK AT ME NOW.
TYRANT KING
DAN ABNETT WRITER
KELLEY JONES ARTIST
MICHELLE MADSEN COLORS
STEVE WANDS LETTERS
ANDY KUBERT & ALEX SINCLAIR COVER
ANDREA SHEA ASSISTANT EDITOR
ALEX ANTONE EDITOR
BRIAN CUNNINGHAM GROUP EDITOR

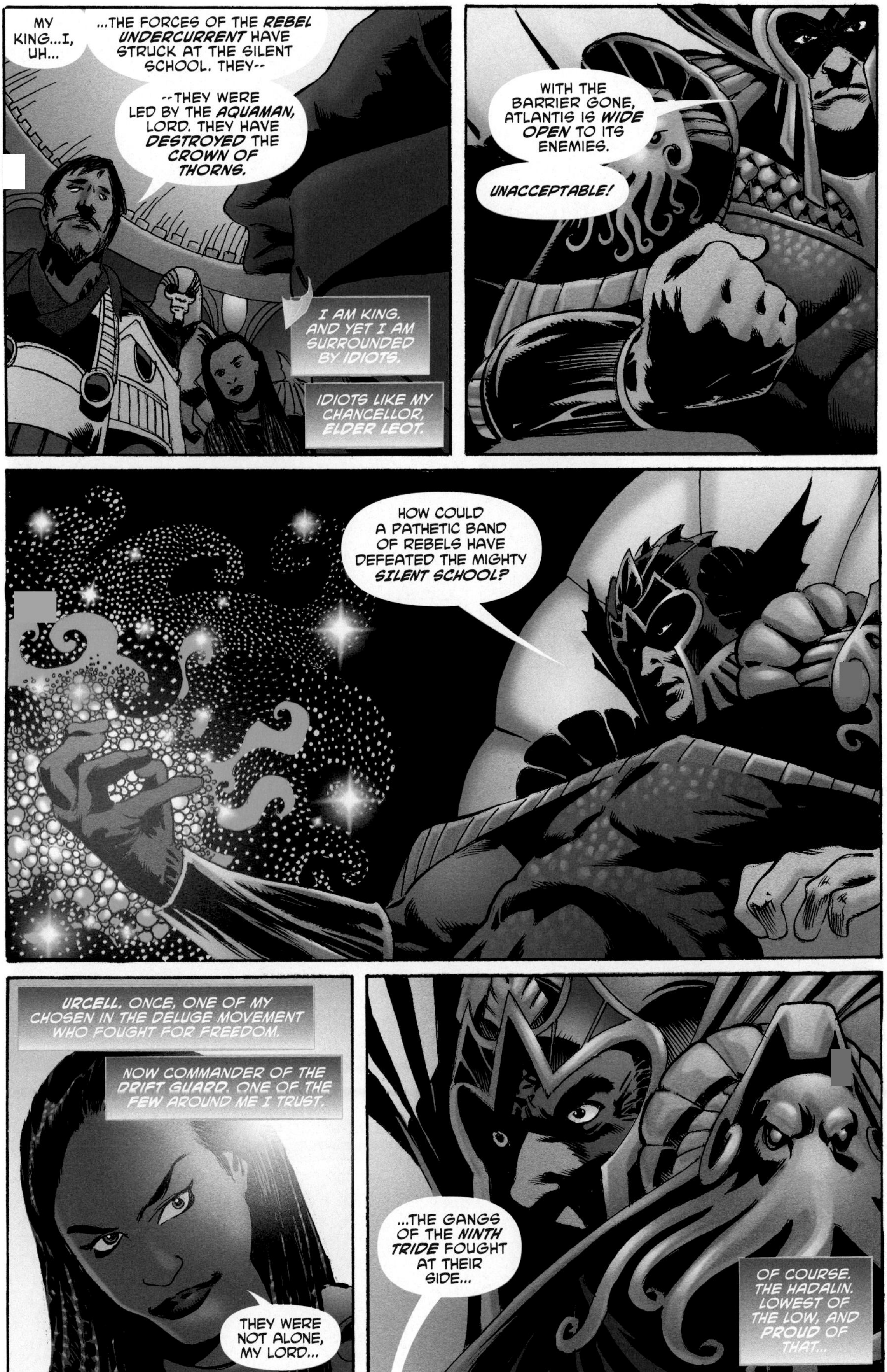
MY KING...I, UH...
...THE FORCES OF THE REBEL UNDERCURRENT HAVE STRUCK AT THE SILENT SCHOOL. THEY--
--THEY WERE LED BY THE AQUAMAN, LORD. THEY HAVE DESTROYED THE CROWN OF THORNS.
I AM KING. AND YET I AM SURROUNDED BY IDIOTS.
IDIOTS LIKE MY CHANCELLOR, ELDER LEOT.
WITH THE BARRIER GONE, ATLANTIS IS WIDE OPEN TO ITS ENEMIES.
UNACCEPTABLE!
HOW COULD A PATHETIC BAND OF REBELS HAVE DEFEATED THE MIGHTY SILENT SCHOOL?
URCELL. ONCE, ONE OF MY CHOSEN IN THE DELUGE MOVEMENT WHO FOUGHT FOR FREEDOM.
NOW COMMANDER OF THE DRIFT GUARD. ONE OF THE FEW AROUND ME I TRUST.
THEY WERE NOT ALONE, MY LORD...
...THE GANGS OF THE NINTH TRIDE FOUGHT AT THEIR SIDE...
OF COURSE. THE HADALIN. LOWEST OF THE LOW, AND PROUD OF THAT...

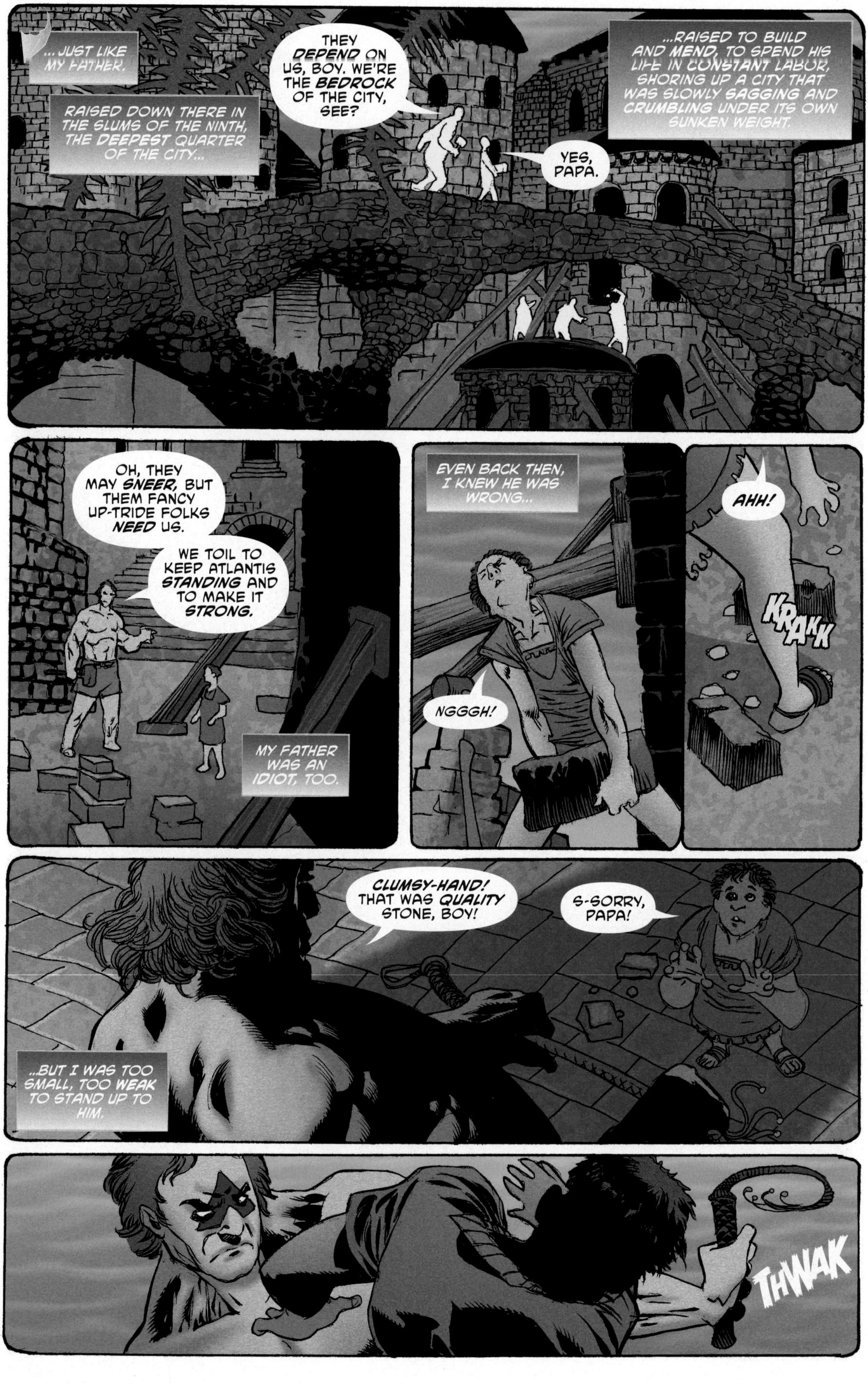
...JUST LIKE MY FATHER.
RAISED DOWN THERE IN THE SLUMS OF THE NINTH, THE DEEPEST QUARTER OF THE CITY...
THEY DEPEND ON US, BOY. WE'RE THE BEDROCK OF THE CITY, SEE?
YES, PAPA.
...RAISED TO BUILD AND MEND, TO SPEND HIS LIFE IN CONSTANT LABOR, SHORING UP A CITY THAT WAS SLOWLY SAGGING AND CRUMBLING UNDER ITS OWN SUNKEN WEIGHT.
OH, THEY MAY SNEER, BUT THEM FANCY UP-TRIDE FOLKS NEED US.
WE TOIL TO KEEP ATLANTIS STANDING AND TO MAKE IT STRONG.
MY FATHER WAS AN IDIOT, TOO.
EVEN BACK THEN, I KNEW HE WAS WRONG...
NGGGH!
AHH!
KRAKK
CLUMSY-HAND! THAT WAS QUALITY STONE, BOY!
S-SORRY, PAPA!
...BUT I WAS TOO SMALL, TOO WEAK TO STAND UP TO HIM.
THWAK

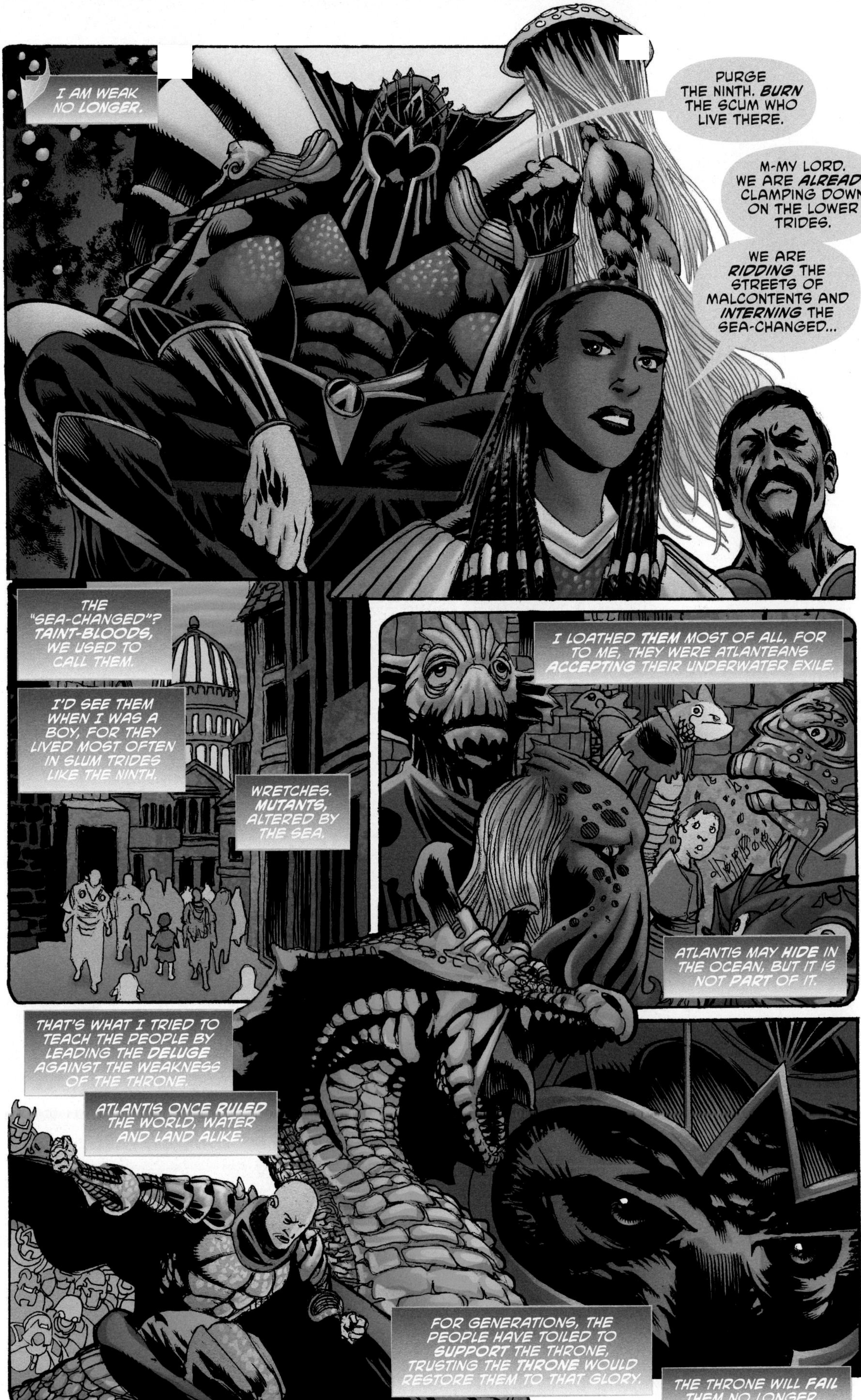
I AM WEAK NO LONGER.
PURGE THE NINTH. BURN THE SCUM WHO LIVE THERE.
M-MY LORD. WE ARE ALREADY CLAMPING DOWN ON THE LOWER TRIDES.
WE ARE RIDDING THE STREETS OF MALCONTENTS AND INTERNING THE SEA-CHANGED...
THE "SEA-CHANGED"? TAINT-BLOODS, WE USED TO CALL THEM.
I'D SEE THEM WHEN I WAS A BOY, FOR THEY LIVED MOST OFTEN IN SLUM TRIDES LIKE THE NINTH.
WRETCHES. MUTANTS, ALTERED BY THE SEA.
I LOATHED THEM MOST OF ALL, FOR TO ME, THEY WERE ATLANTEANS ACCEPTING THEIR UNDERWATER EXILE.
ATLANTIS MAY HIDE IN THE OCEAN, BUT IT IS NOT PART OF IT.
THAT'S WHAT I TRIED TO TEACH THE PEOPLE BY LEADING THE DELUGE AGAINST THE WEAKNESS OF THE THRONE.
ATLANTIS ONCE RULED THE WORLD, WATER AND LAND ALIKE.
FOR GENERATIONS, THE PEOPLE HAVE TOILED TO SUPPORT THE THRONE, TRUSTING THE THRONE WOULD RESTORE THEM TO THAT GLORY.
THE THRONE WILL FAIL THEM NO LONGER...

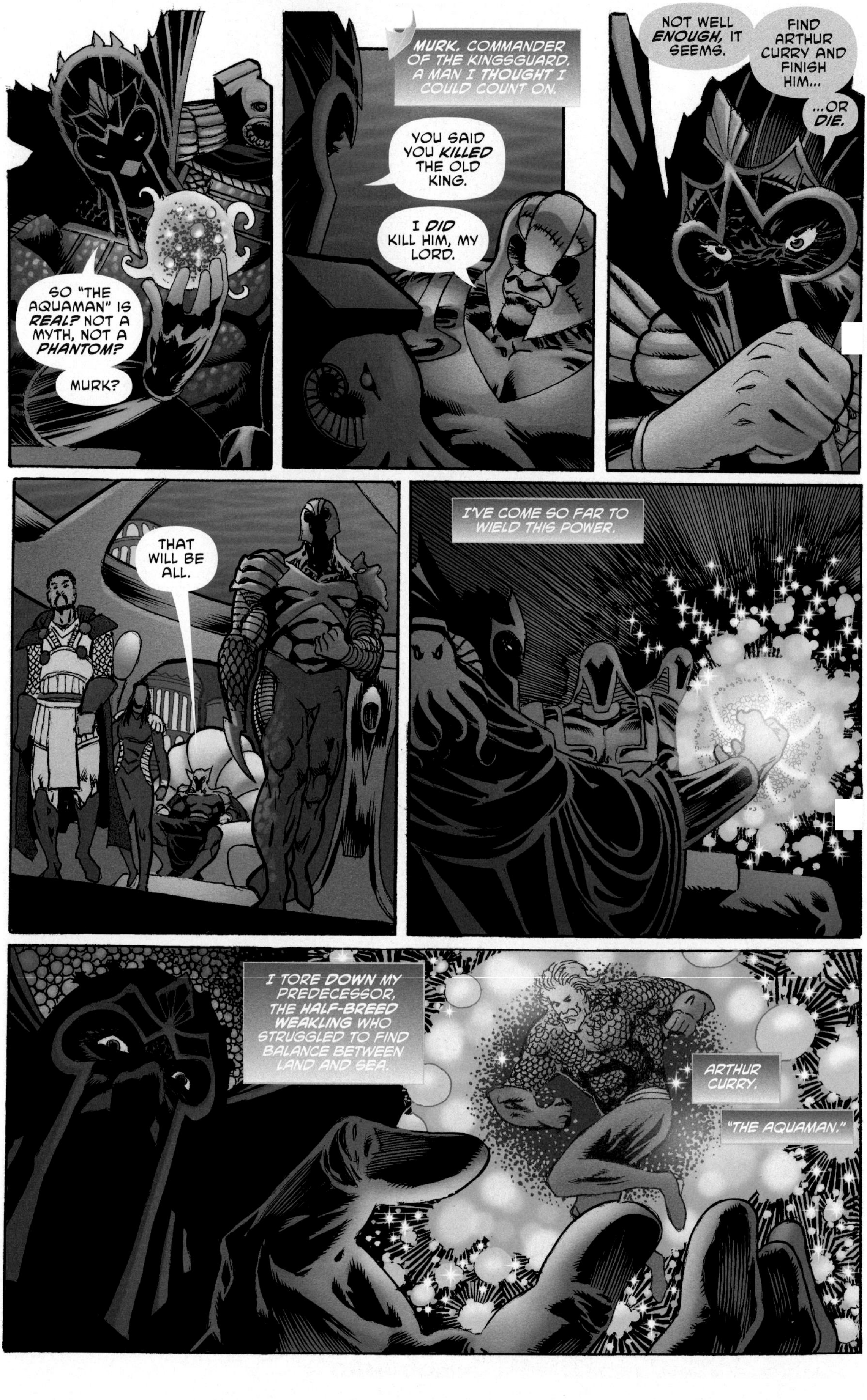
SO "THE AQUAMAN" IS REAL? NOT A MYTH, NOT A PHANTOM?
MURK?
MURK. COMMANDER OF THE KINGSGUARD. A MAN I THOUGHT I COULD COUNT ON.
YOU SAID YOU KILLED THE OLD KING.
I DID KILL HIM, MY LORD.
NOT WELL ENOUGH, IT SEEMS.
FIND ARTHUR CURRY AND FINISH HIM...
...OR DIE.
THAT WILL BE ALL.
I'VE COME SO FAR TO WIELD THIS POWER.
I TORE DOWN MY PREDECESSOR, THE HALF-BREED WEAKLING WHO STRUGGLED TO FIND BALANCE BETWEEN LAND AND SEA.
ARTHUR CURRY.
"THE AQUAMAN."

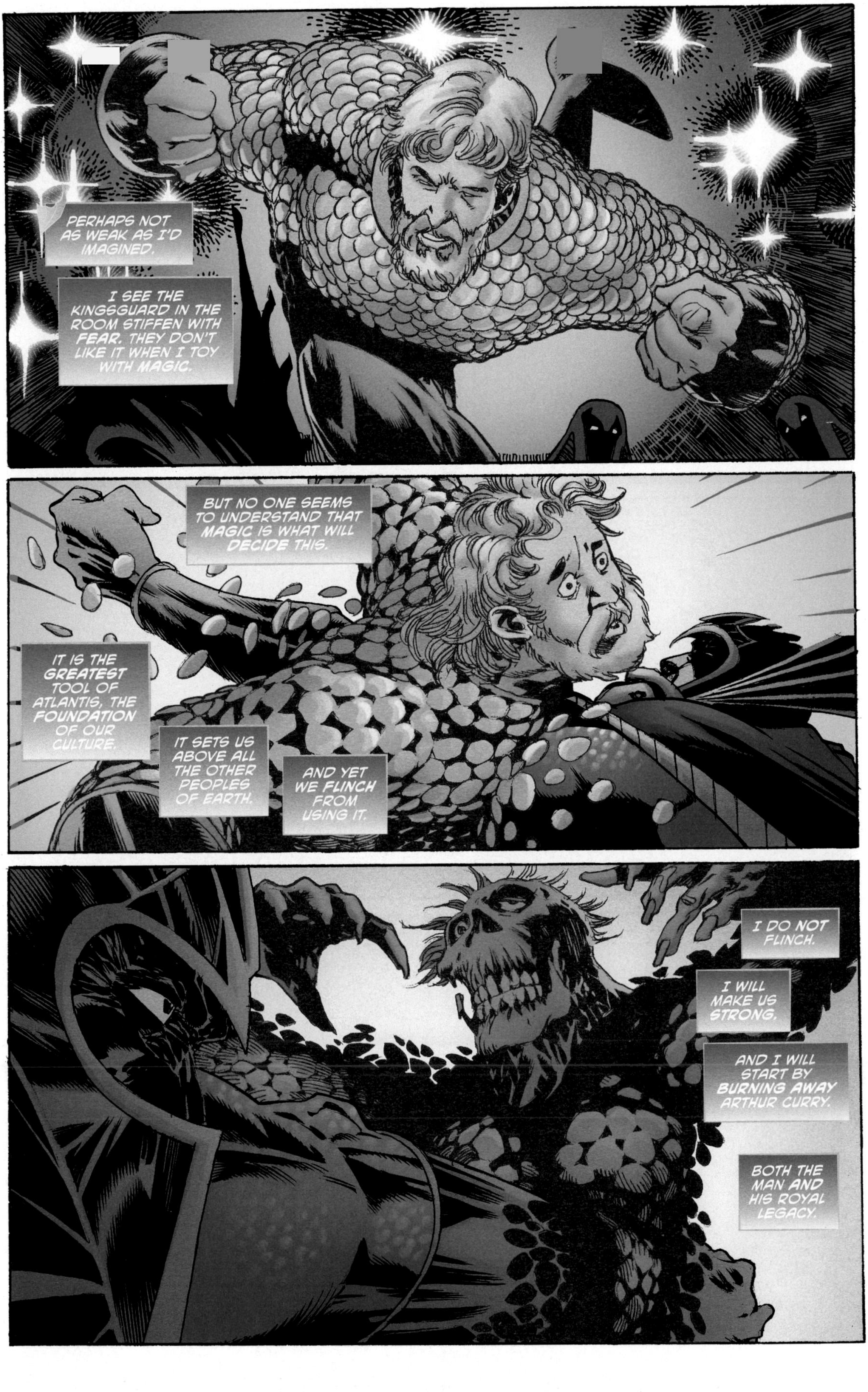
PERHAPS NOT AS WEAK AS I'D IMAGINED.
I SEE THE KINGSGUARD IN THE ROOM STIFFEN WITH FEAR. THEY DON'T LIKE IT WHEN I TOY WITH MAGIC.
BUT NO ONE SEEMS TO UNDERSTAND THAT MAGIC IS WHAT WILL DECIDE THIS.
IT IS THE GREATEST TOOL OF ATLANTIS, THE FOUNDATION OF OUR CULTURE.
IT SETS US ABOVE ALL THE OTHER PEOPLES OF EARTH.
AND YET WE FLINCH FROM USING IT.
I DO NOT FLINCH.
I WILL MAKE US STRONG.
AND I WILL START BY BURNING AWAY ARTHUR CURRY.
BOTH THE MAN AND HIS ROYAL LEGACY.

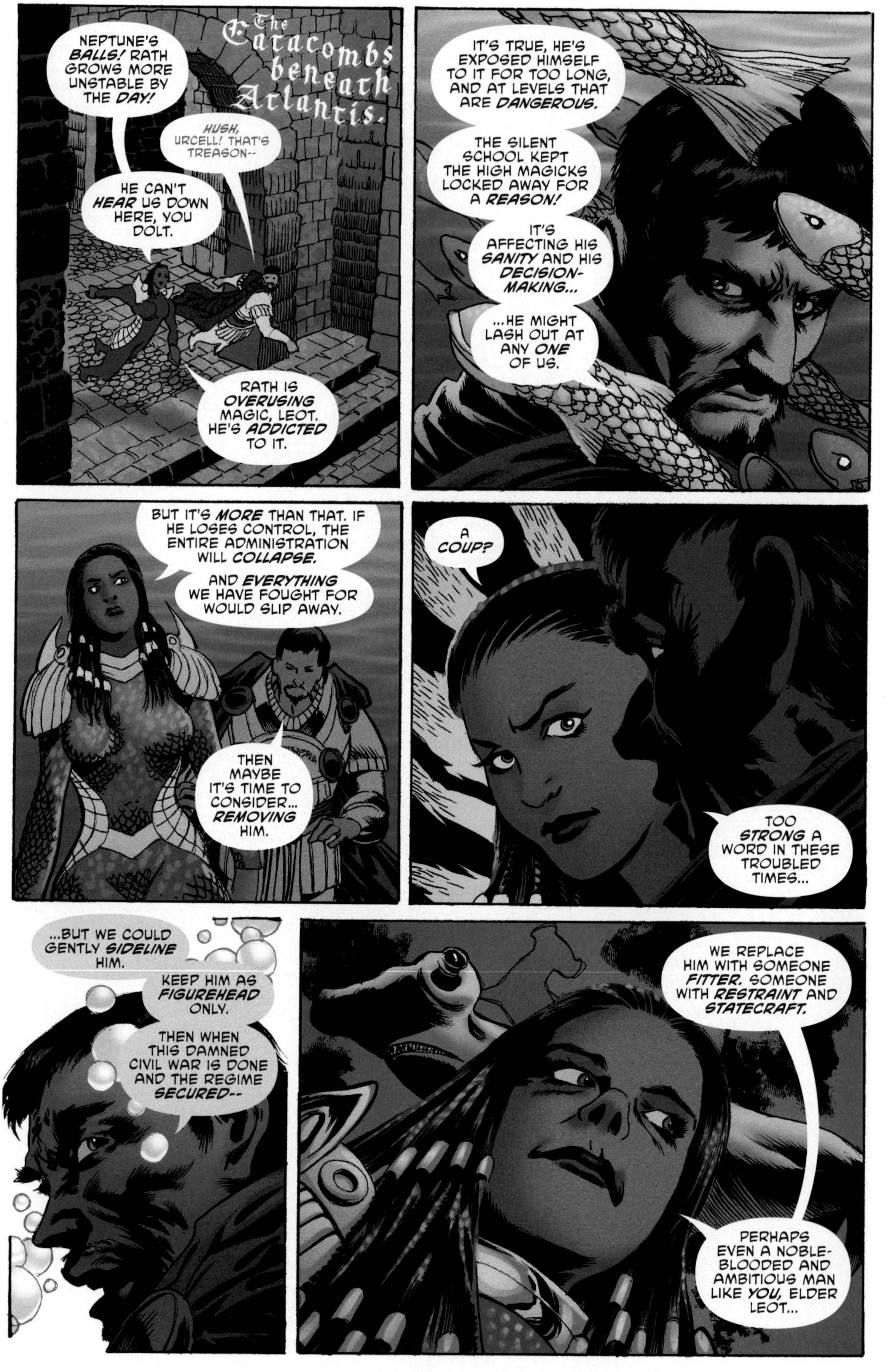
The Catacombs beneath Atlantis.
NEPTUNE'S BALLS! RATH GROWS MORE UNSTABLE BY THE DAY!
HUSH, URCELL! THAT'S TREASON--
HE CAN'T HEAR US DOWN HERE, YOU DOLT.
RATH IS OVERUSING MAGIC, LEOT. HE'S ADDICTED TO IT.
IT'S TRUE, HE'S EXPOSED HIMSELF TO IT FOR TOO LONG, AND AT LEVELS THAT ARE DANGEROUS.
THE SILENT SCHOOL KEPT THE HIGH MAGICKS LOCKED AWAY FOR A REASON!
IT'S AFFECTING HIS SANITY AND HIS DECISION-MAKING...
...HE MIGHT LASH OUT AT ANY ONE OF US.
BUT IT'S MORE THAN THAT. IF HE LOSES CONTROL, THE ENTIRE ADMINISTRATION WILL COLLAPSE.
AND EVERYTHING WE HAVE FOUGHT FOR WOULD SLIP AWAY.
THEN MAYBE IT'S TIME TO CONSIDER... REMOVING HIM.
A COUP?
TOO STRONG A WORD IN THESE TROUBLED TIMES...
...BUT WE COULD GENTLY SIDELINE HIM.
KEEP HIM AS FIGUREHEAD ONLY.
THEN WHEN THIS DAMNED CIVIL WAR IS DONE AND THE REGIME SECURED--
WE REPLACE HIM WITH SOMEONE FITTER. SOMEONE WITH RESTRAINT AND STATECRAFT.
PERHAPS EVEN A NOBLE-BLOODED AND AMBITIOUS MAN LIKE YOU, ELDER LEOT...

YOU SEE?

NOW EVEN MY *FRIENDS* TURN AGAINST ME.

BUT I HAVE ONE *ALLY* REMAINING. MY *OLDEST* FRIEND.

KADAVER. IT'S BEEN A LONG TIME.

DO YOU KNOW WHY I SENT FOR YOU?

IT'S ABOUT THAT *DREAM* WE SHARED WHEN WE WERE BOYS BACK IN THE NINTH...

"...WHEN WE USED TO GAZE UP AT THE SPIRES OF THE HIGH TRIDES.

"AND I WOULD TELL YOU THAT ONE DAY, THOSE MIGHTY TOWERS WOULD *RISE UP* OUT OF THE OCEAN AGAIN AND RULE THE *WHOLE WORLD.*

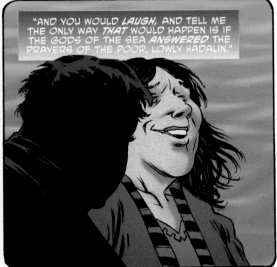

"AND YOU WOULD *LAUGH,* AND TELL ME THE ONLY WAY *THAT* WOULD HAPPEN IS IF THE GODS OF THE SEA *ANSWERED* THE PRAYERS OF THE POOR, LOWLY HADALIN."

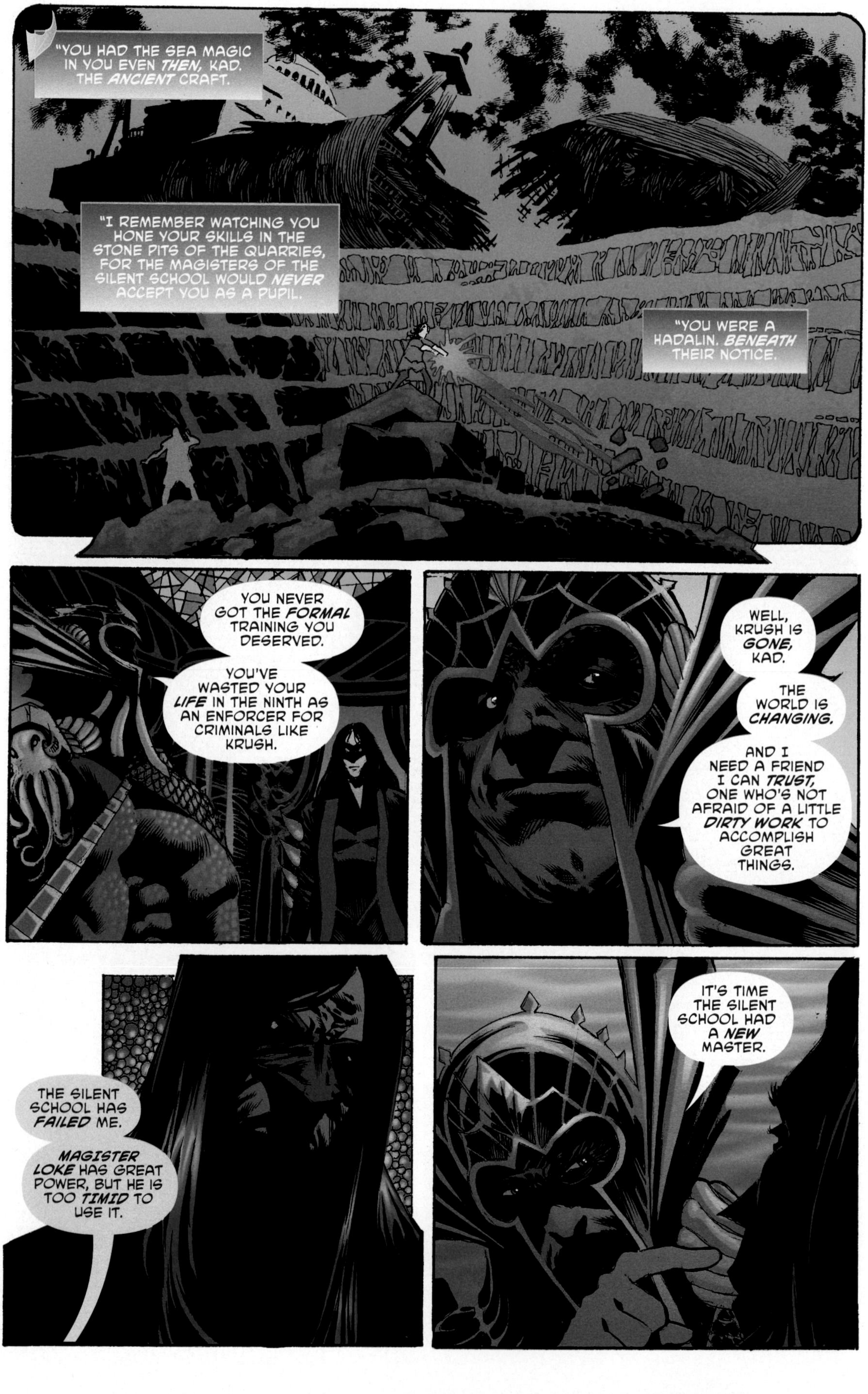
"YOU HAD THE SEA MAGIC IN YOU EVEN THEN, KAD. THE ANCIENT CRAFT.
"I REMEMBER WATCHING YOU HONE YOUR SKILLS IN THE STONE PITS OF THE QUARRIES, FOR THE MAGISTERS OF THE SILENT SCHOOL WOULD NEVER ACCEPT YOU AS A PUPIL.
"YOU WERE A HADALIN. BENEATH THEIR NOTICE.
YOU NEVER GOT THE FORMAL TRAINING YOU DESERVED.
YOU'VE WASTED YOUR LIFE IN THE NINTH AS AN ENFORCER FOR CRIMINALS LIKE KRUSH.
WELL, KRUSH IS GONE, KAD.
THE WORLD IS CHANGING.
AND I NEED A FRIEND I CAN TRUST, ONE WHO'S NOT AFRAID OF A LITTLE DIRTY WORK TO ACCOMPLISH GREAT THINGS.
THE SILENT SCHOOL HAS FAILED ME.
MAGISTER LOKE HAS GREAT POWER, BUT HE IS TOO TIMID TO USE IT.
IT'S TIME THE SILENT SCHOOL HAD A NEW MASTER.

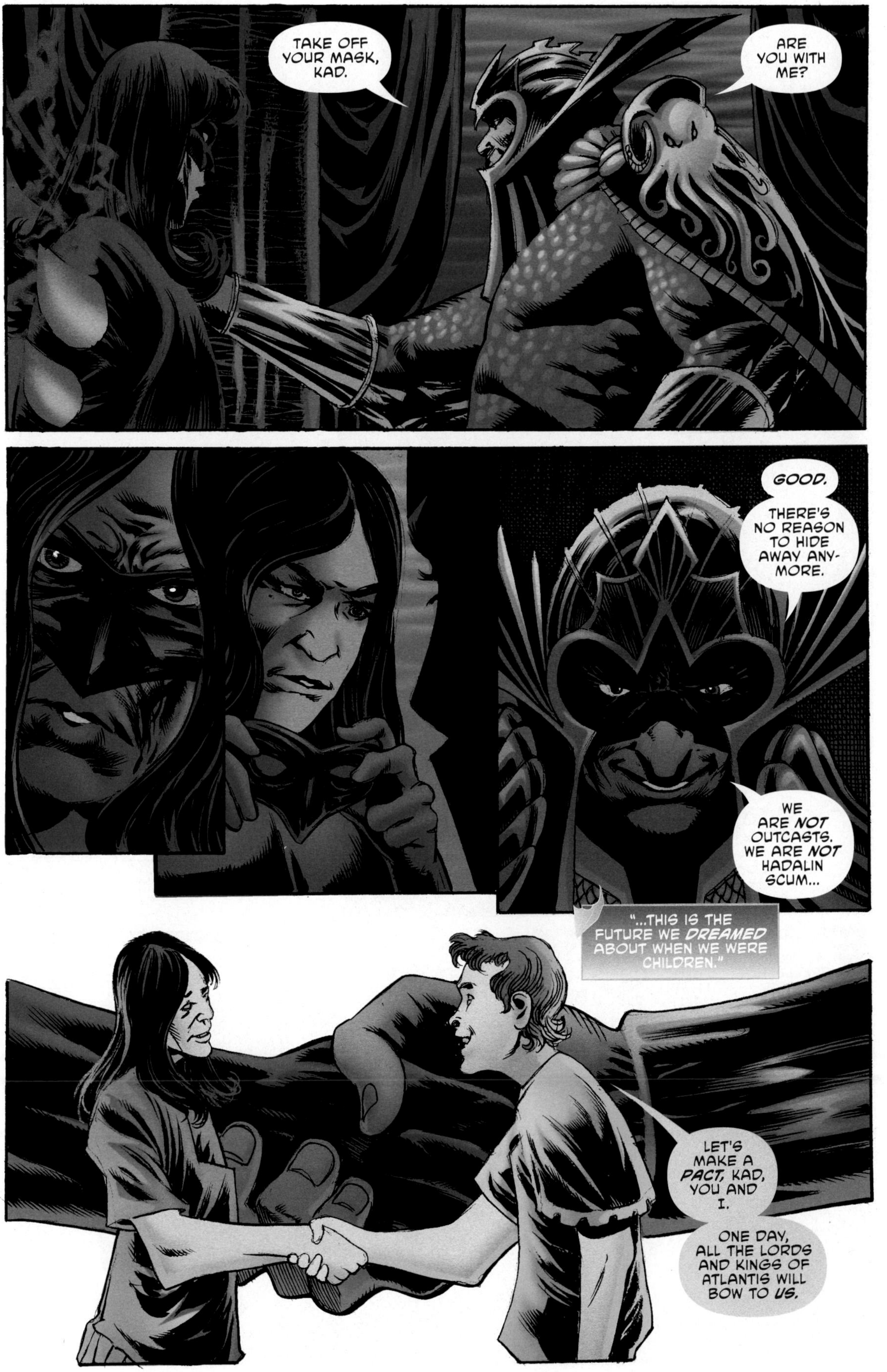
TAKE OFF YOUR MASK, KAD.
ARE YOU WITH ME?
GOOD.
THERE'S NO REASON TO HIDE AWAY ANY-MORE.
WE ARE *NOT* OUTCASTS. WE ARE *NOT* HADALIN SCUM...
"...THIS IS THE FUTURE WE *DREAMED* ABOUT WHEN WE WERE CHILDREN."
LET'S MAKE A *PACT,* KAD, YOU AND I.
ONE DAY, ALL THE LORDS AND KINGS OF ATLANTIS WILL BOW TO *US.*

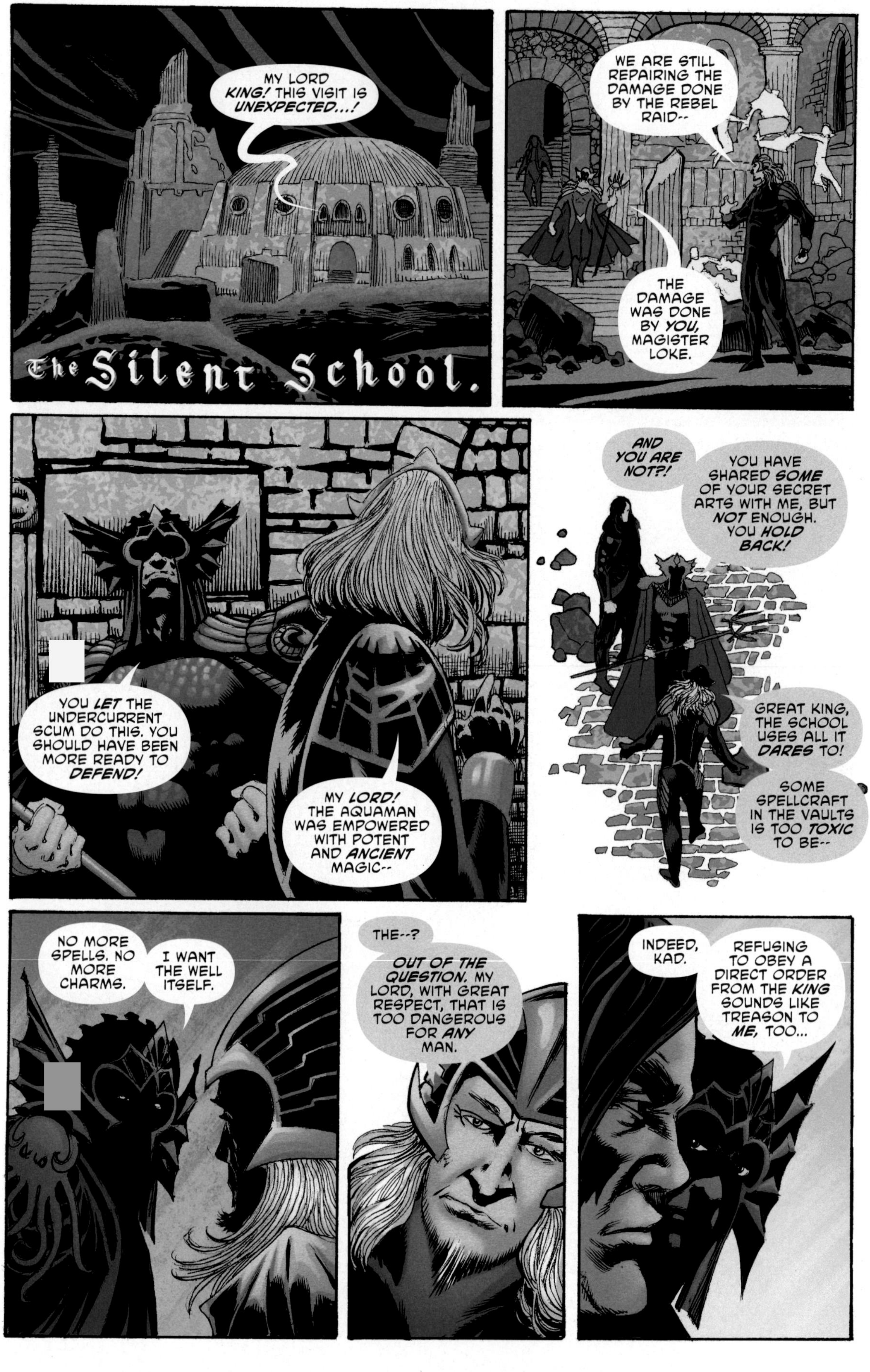
MY LORD KING! THIS VISIT IS UNEXPECTED...!
The Silent School.
WE ARE STILL REPAIRING THE DAMAGE DONE BY THE REBEL RAID--
THE DAMAGE WAS DONE BY YOU, MAGISTER LOKE.
YOU LET THE UNDERCURRENT SCUM DO THIS. YOU SHOULD HAVE BEEN MORE READY TO DEFEND!
MY LORD! THE AQUAMAN WAS EMPOWERED WITH POTENT AND ANCIENT MAGIC--
AND YOU ARE NOT?!
YOU HAVE SHARED SOME OF YOUR SECRET ARTS WITH ME, BUT NOT ENOUGH. YOU HOLD BACK!
GREAT KING, THE SCHOOL USES ALL IT DARES TO!
SOME SPELLCRAFT IN THE VAULTS IS TOO TOXIC TO BE--
NO MORE SPELLS. NO MORE CHARMS.
I WANT THE WELL ITSELF.
THE--?
OUT OF THE QUESTION. MY LORD, WITH GREAT RESPECT, THAT IS TOO DANGEROUS FOR ANY MAN.
INDEED, KAD.
REFUSING TO OBEY A DIRECT ORDER FROM THE KING SOUNDS LIKE TREASON TO ME, TOO...

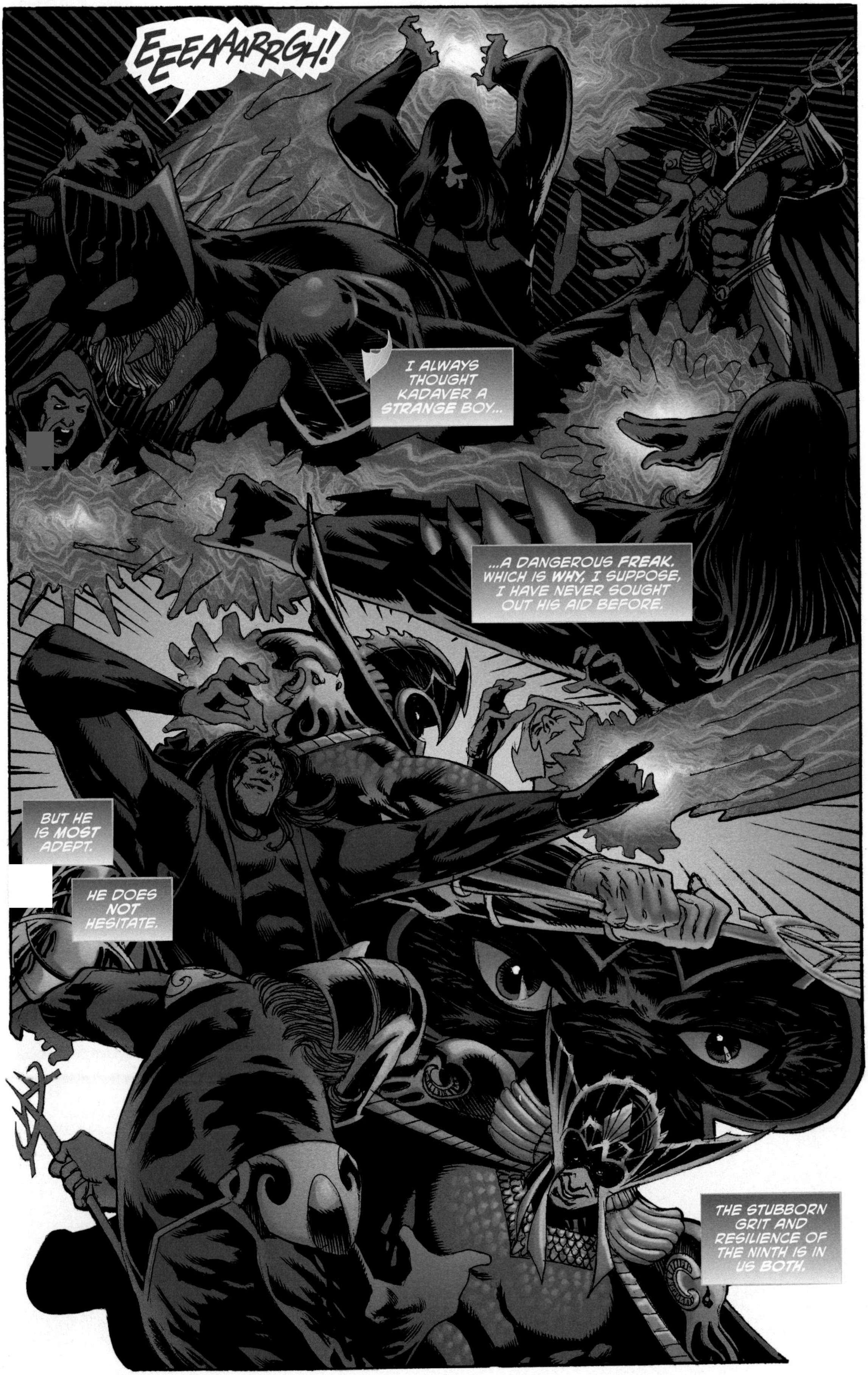
EEEAAARRGH!
I ALWAYS THOUGHT KADAVER A STRANGE BOY...
...A DANGEROUS FREAK. WHICH IS WHY, I SUPPOSE, I HAVE NEVER SOUGHT OUT HIS AID BEFORE.
BUT HE IS MOST ADEPT.
HE DOES NOT HESITATE.
THE STUBBORN GRIT AND RESILIENCE OF THE NINTH IS IN US BOTH.

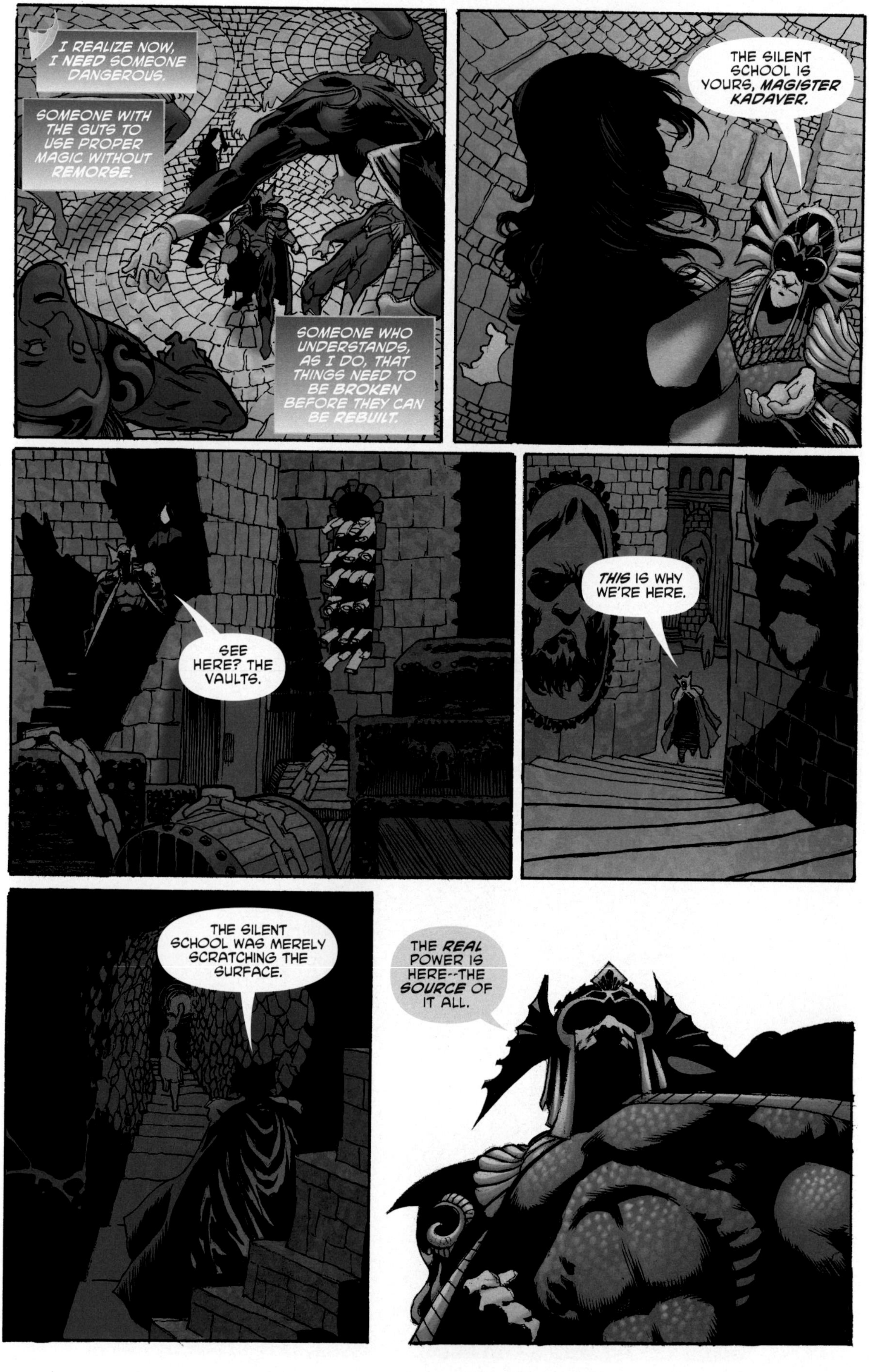
I REALIZE NOW, I NEED SOMEONE DANGEROUS.
SOMEONE WITH THE GUTS TO USE PROPER MAGIC WITHOUT REMORSE.
SOMEONE WHO UNDERSTANDS, AS I DO, THAT THINGS NEED TO BE BROKEN BEFORE THEY CAN BE REBUILT.
THE SILENT SCHOOL IS YOURS, MAGISTER KADAVER.
SEE HERE? THE VAULTS.
THIS IS WHY WE'RE HERE.
THE SILENT SCHOOL WAS MERELY SCRATCHING THE SURFACE.
THE REAL POWER IS HERE--THE SOURCE OF IT ALL.

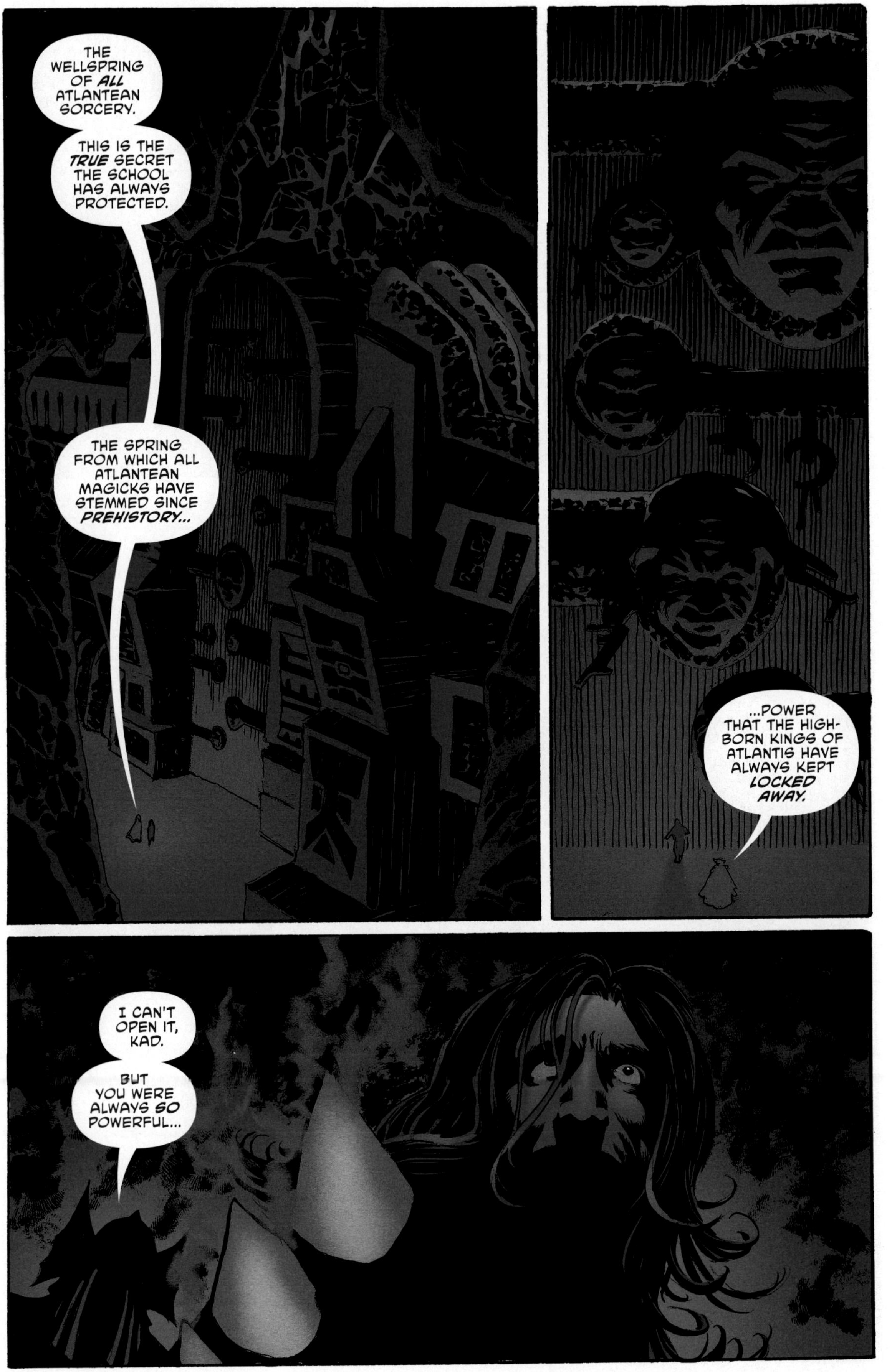
THE WELLSPRING OF ALL ATLANTEAN SORCERY.
THIS IS THE TRUE SECRET THE SCHOOL HAS ALWAYS PROTECTED.
THE SPRING FROM WHICH ALL ATLANTEAN MAGICKS HAVE STEMMED SINCE PREHISTORY...
...POWER THAT THE HIGH-BORN KINGS OF ATLANTIS HAVE ALWAYS KEPT LOCKED AWAY.
I CAN'T OPEN IT, KAD.
BUT YOU WERE ALWAYS SO POWERFUL...

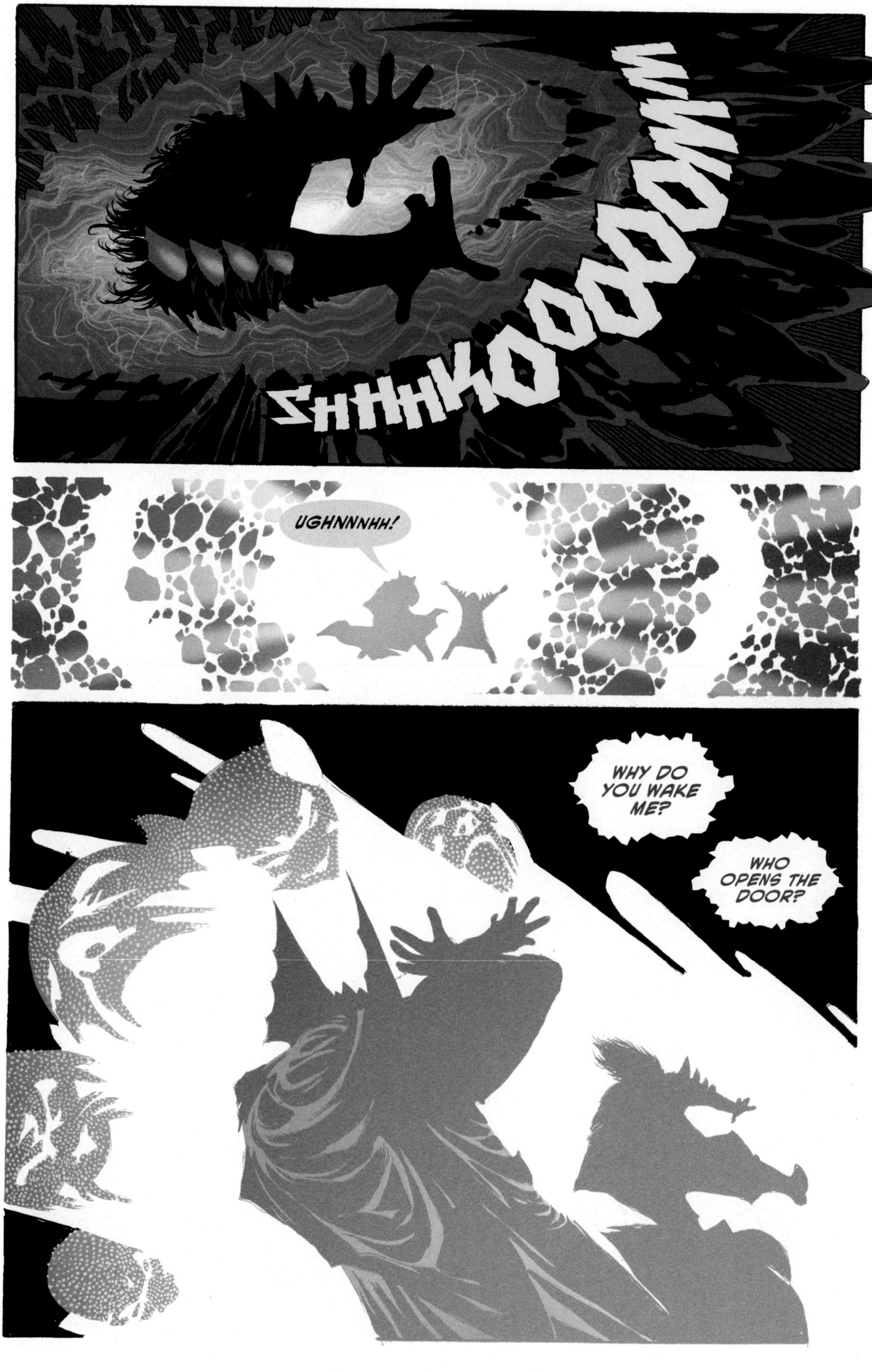
SHHHKOOOOOOWW
UGHNNNHH!
WHY DO YOU WAKE ME?
WHO OPENS THE DOOR?

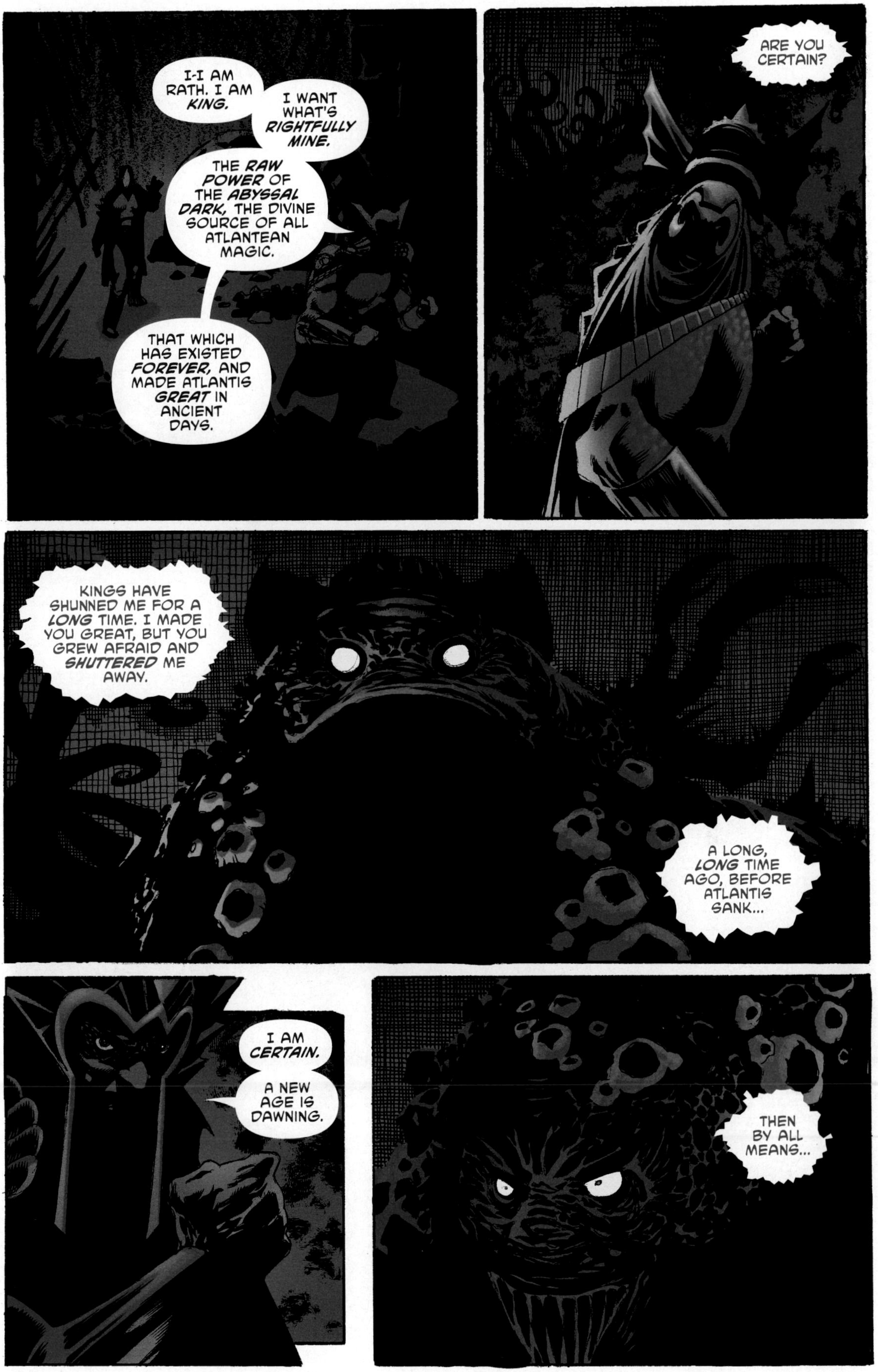

I-I AM RATH. I AM KING.
I WANT WHAT'S RIGHTFULLY MINE.
THE RAW POWER OF THE ABYSSAL DARK, THE DIVINE SOURCE OF ALL ATLANTEAN MAGIC.
THAT WHICH HAS EXISTED FOREVER, AND MADE ATLANTIS GREAT IN ANCIENT DAYS.
ARE YOU CERTAIN?
KINGS HAVE SHUNNED ME FOR A LONG TIME. I MADE YOU GREAT, BUT YOU GREW AFRAID AND SHUTTERED ME AWAY.
A LONG, LONG TIME AGO, BEFORE ATLANTIS SANK...
I AM CERTAIN.
A NEW AGE IS DAWNING.
THEN BY ALL MEANS...

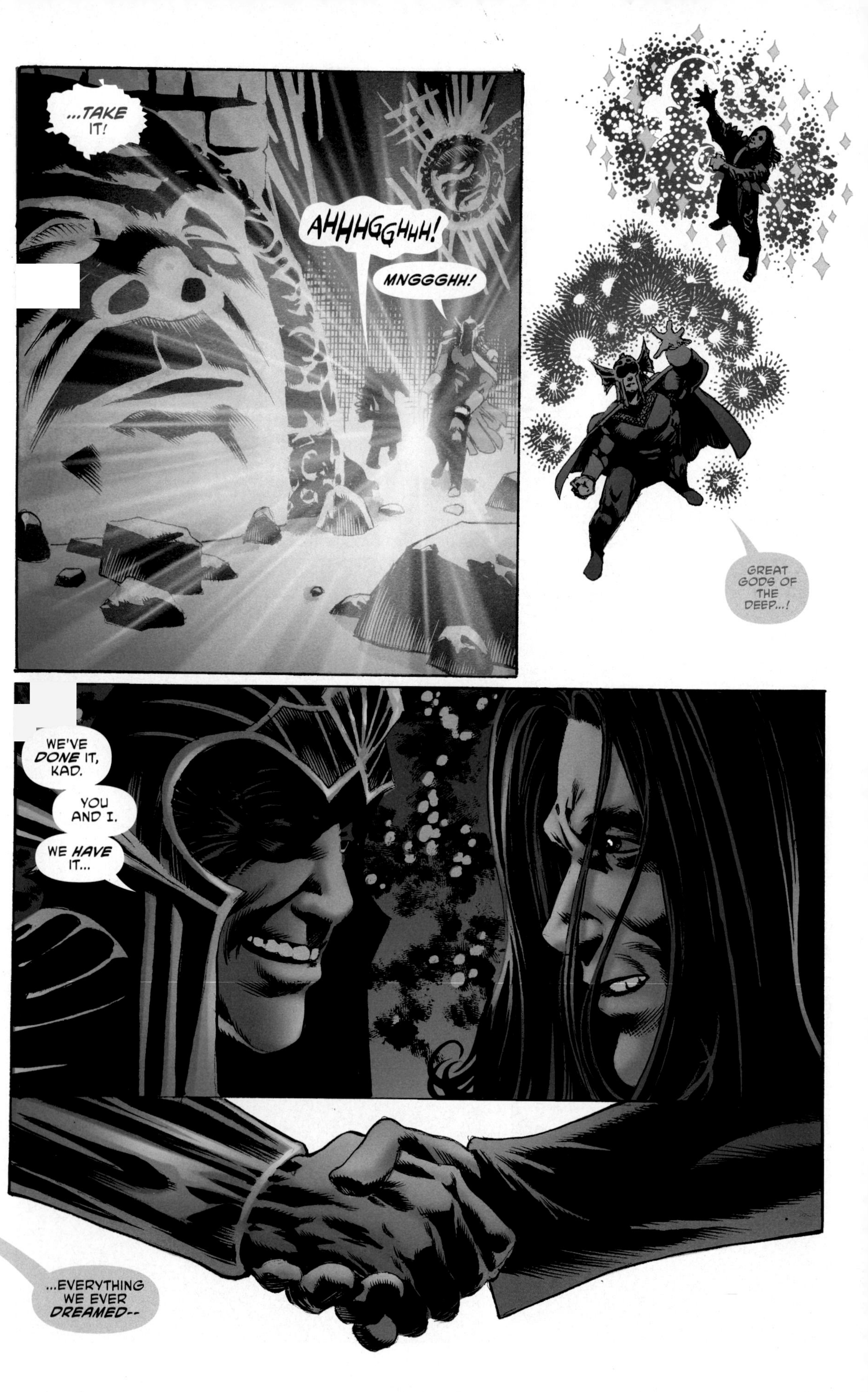
...TAKE IT!
AHHHGGHHH!
MNGGGHH!
GREAT GODS OF THE DEEP...!
WE'VE DONE IT, KAD.
YOU AND I.
WE HAVE IT...
...EVERYTHING WE EVER DREAMED--

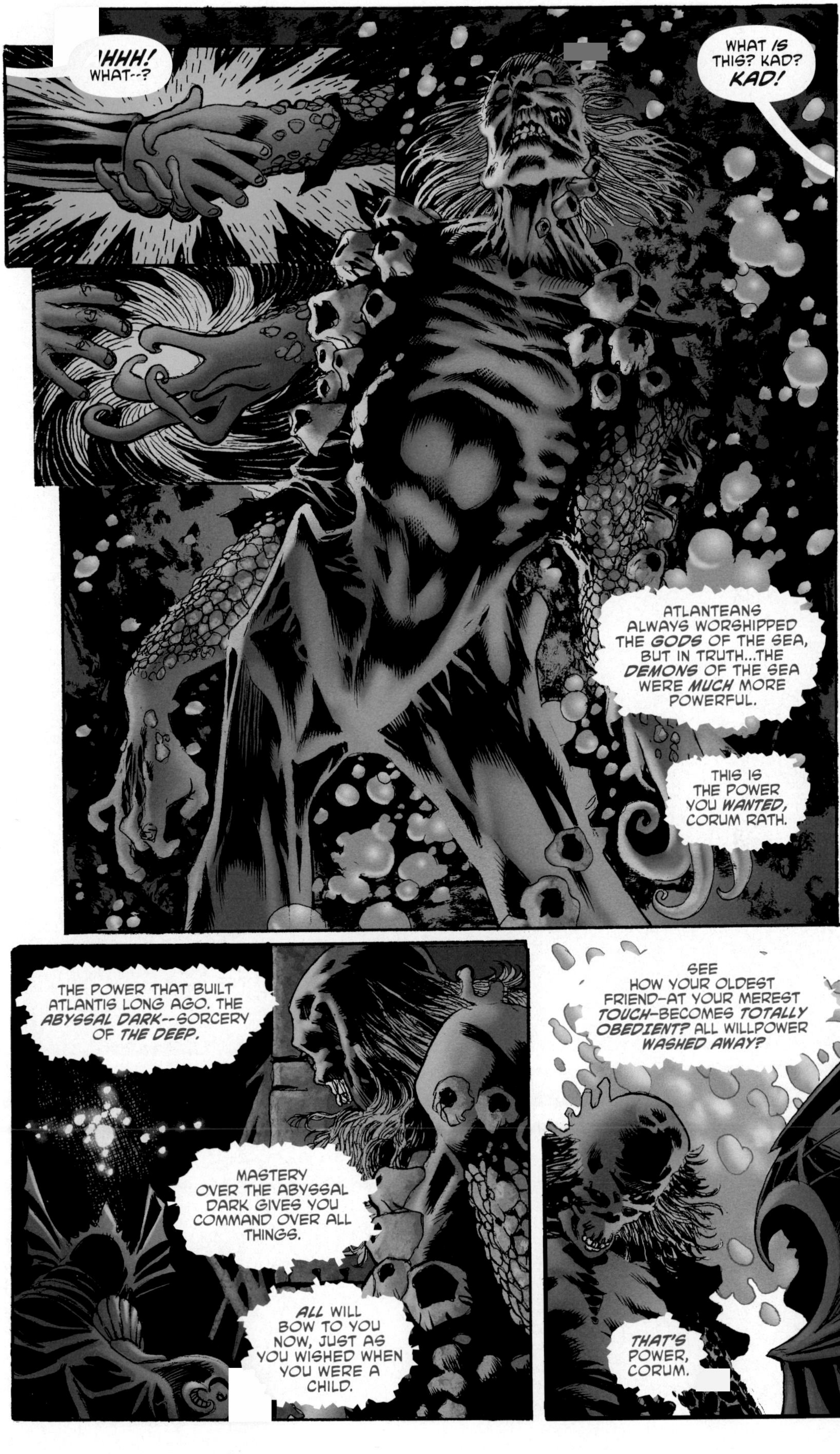
HHH! WHAT--?
WHAT *IS* THIS? KAD? ***KAD!***
ATLANTEANS ALWAYS WORSHIPPED THE *GODS* OF THE SEA, BUT IN TRUTH...THE *DEMONS* OF THE SEA WERE *MUCH* MORE POWERFUL.
THIS IS THE POWER YOU *WANTED*, CORUM RATH.
THE POWER THAT BUILT ATLANTIS LONG AGO. THE *ABYSSAL DARK*--SORCERY OF *THE DEEP*.
MASTERY OVER THE ABYSSAL DARK GIVES YOU COMMAND OVER ALL THINGS.
ALL WILL BOW TO YOU NOW, JUST AS YOU WISHED WHEN YOU WERE A CHILD.
SEE HOW YOUR OLDEST FRIEND--AT YOUR MEREST *TOUCH*--BECOMES *TOTALLY OBEDIENT*? ALL WILLPOWER *WASHED AWAY*?
THAT'S POWER, CORUM.

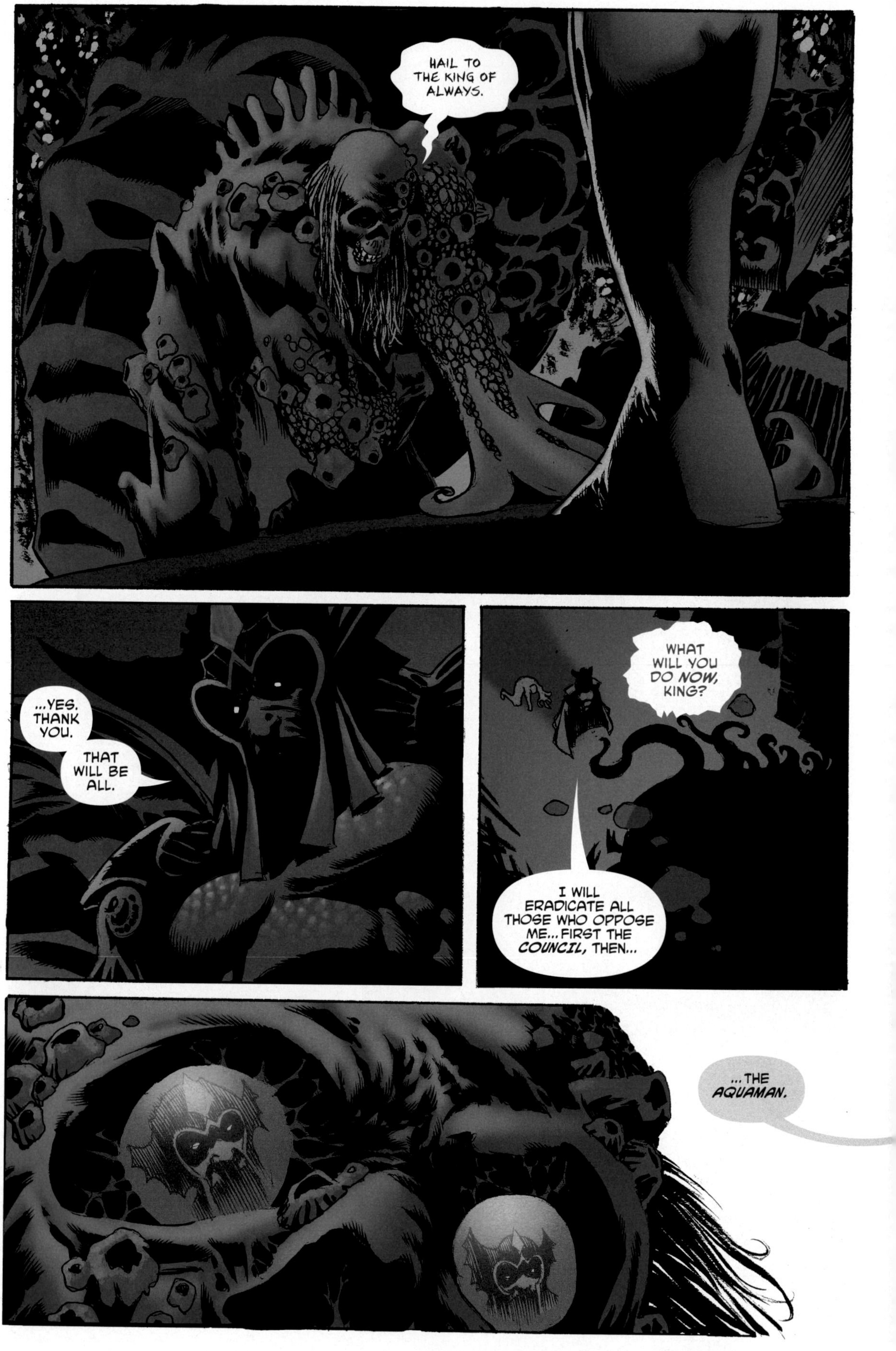
HAIL TO THE KING OF ALWAYS.
...YES. THANK YOU.
THAT WILL BE ALL.
WHAT WILL YOU DO NOW, KING?
I WILL ERADICATE ALL THOSE WHO OPPOSE ME...FIRST THE COUNCIL, THEN...
...THE AQUAMAN.

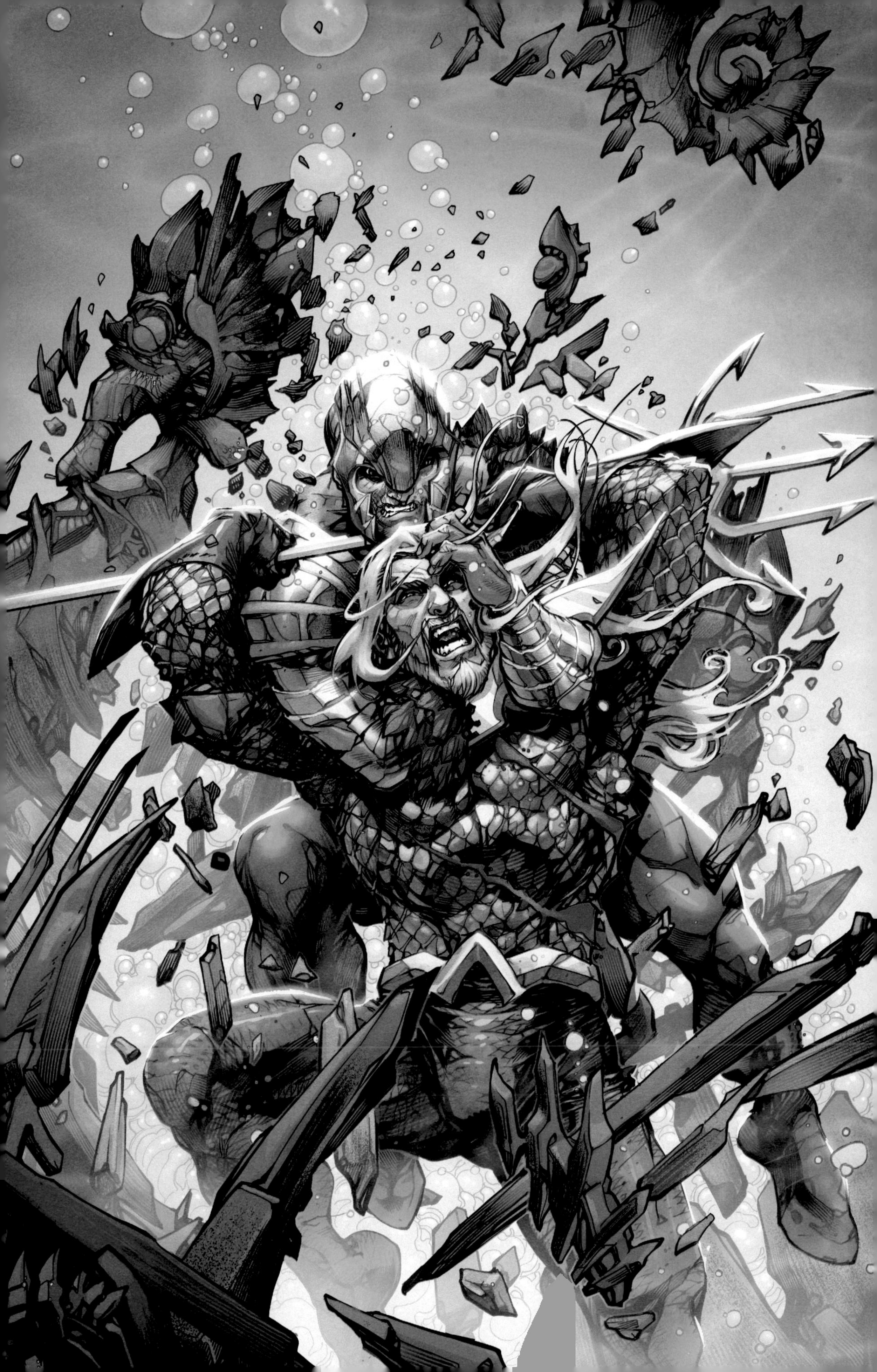

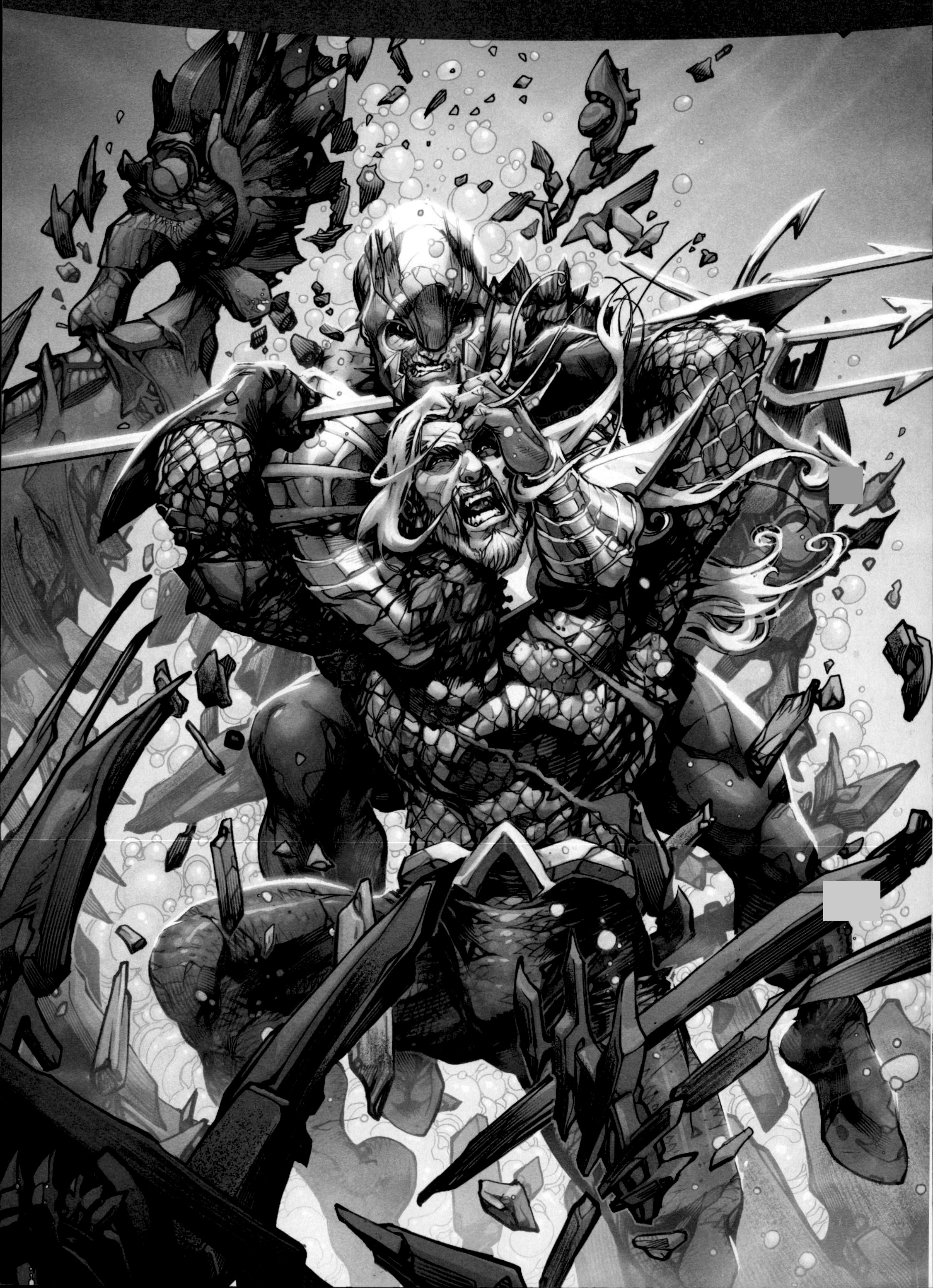

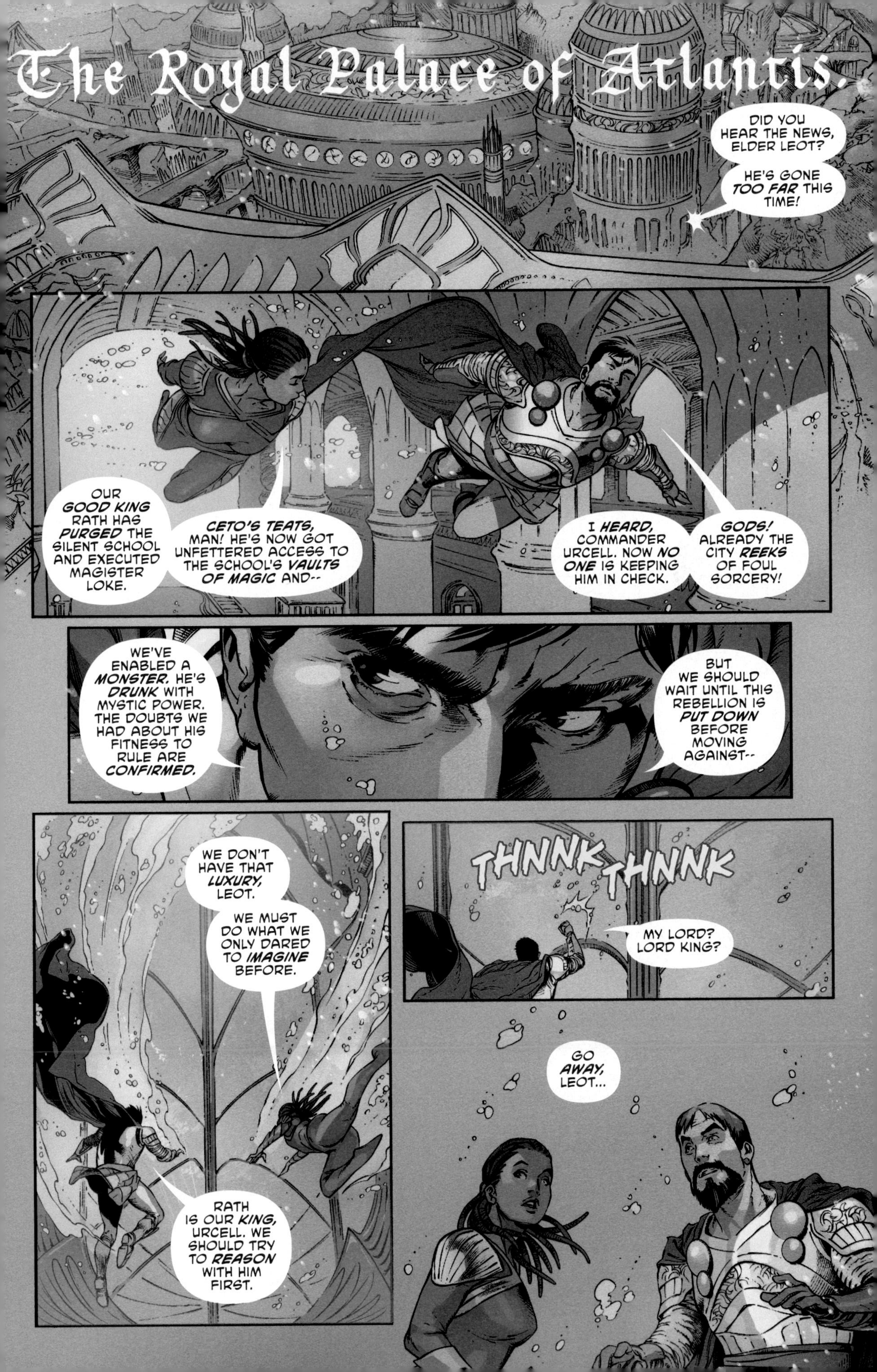
The Royal Palace of Atlantis.
DID YOU HEAR THE NEWS, ELDER LEOT?
HE'S GONE TOO FAR THIS TIME!
OUR GOOD KING RATH HAS PURGED THE SILENT SCHOOL AND EXECUTED MAGISTER LOKE.
CETO'S TEATS, MAN! HE'S NOW GOT UNFETTERED ACCESS TO THE SCHOOL'S VAULTS OF MAGIC AND--
I HEARD, COMMANDER URCELL. NOW NO ONE IS KEEPING HIM IN CHECK.
GODS! ALREADY THE CITY REEKS OF FOUL SORCERY!
WE'VE ENABLED A MONSTER. HE'S DRUNK WITH MYSTIC POWER. THE DOUBTS WE HAD ABOUT HIS FITNESS TO RULE ARE CONFIRMED.
BUT WE SHOULD WAIT UNTIL THIS REBELLION IS PUT DOWN BEFORE MOVING AGAINST--
WE DON'T HAVE THAT LUXURY, LEOT.
WE MUST DO WHAT WE ONLY DARED TO IMAGINE BEFORE.
RATH IS OUR KING, URCELL. WE SHOULD TRY TO REASON WITH HIM FIRST.
THNNK THNNK
MY LORD? LORD KING?
GO AWAY, LEOT...

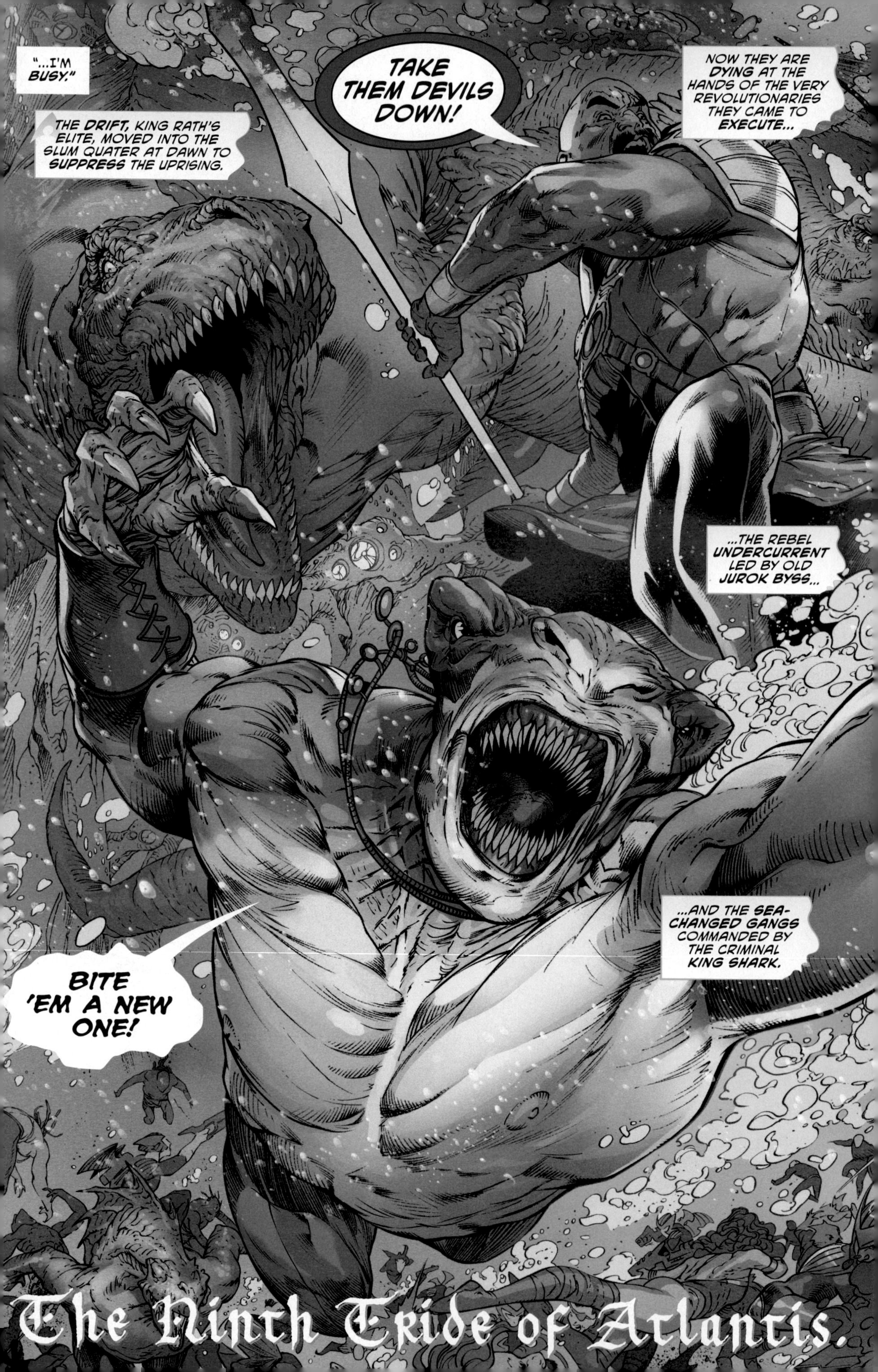
"...I'M BUSY."
THE DRIFT, KING RATH'S ELITE, MOVED INTO THE SLUM QUATER AT DAWN TO SUPPRESS THE UPRISING.
TAKE THEM DEVILS DOWN!
NOW THEY ARE DYING AT THE HANDS OF THE VERY REVOLUTIONARIES THEY CAME TO EXECUTE...
...THE REBEL UNDERCURRENT LED BY OLD JUROK BYSS...
...AND THE SEA-CHANGED GANGS COMMANDED BY THE CRIMINAL KING SHARK.
BITE 'EM A NEW ONE!
The Ninth Tride of Atlantis.

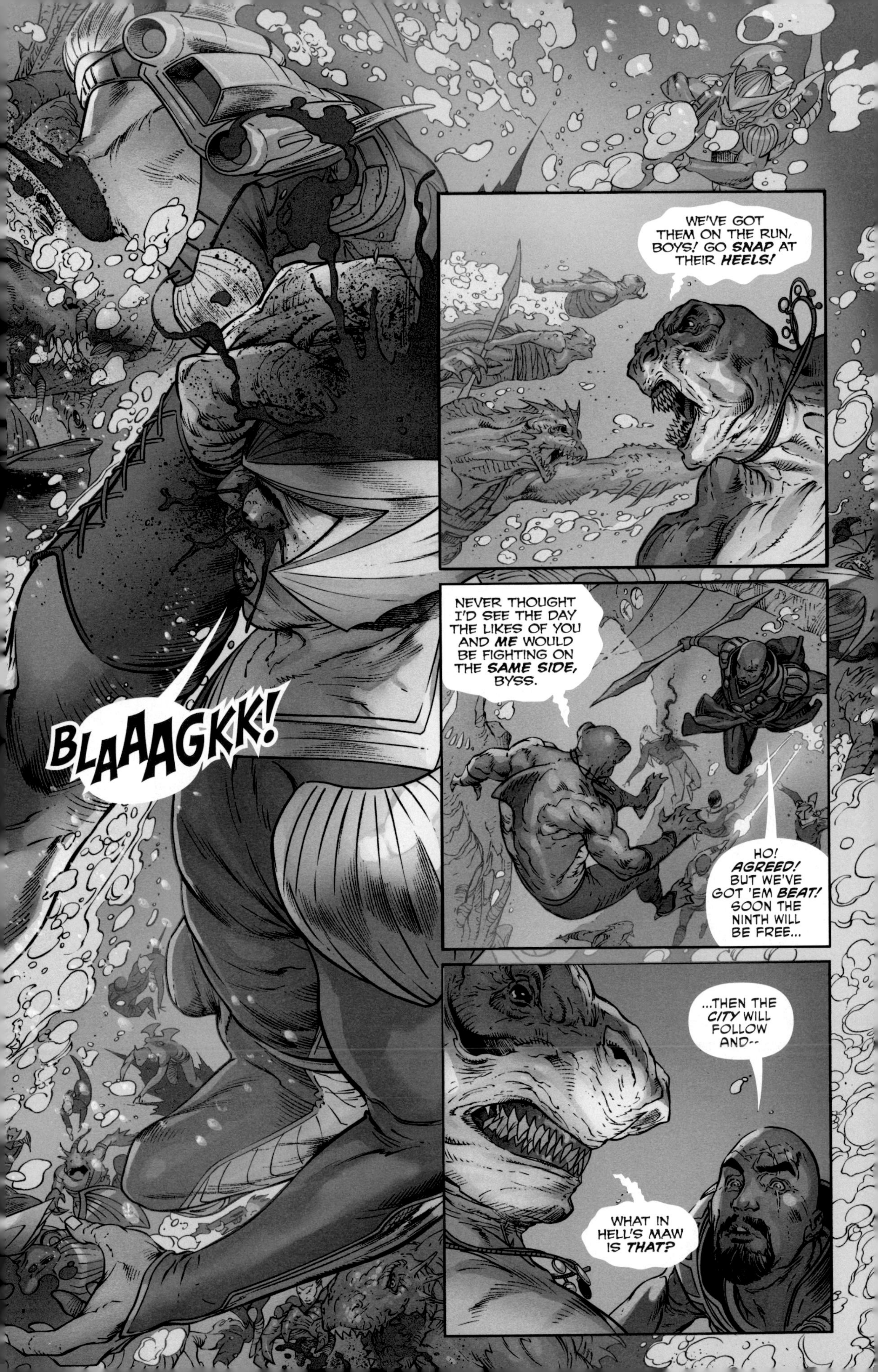
BLAAAGKK!
WE'VE GOT THEM ON THE RUN, BOYS! GO SNAP AT THEIR HEELS!
NEVER THOUGHT I'D SEE THE DAY THE LIKES OF YOU AND ME WOULD BE FIGHTING ON THE SAME SIDE, BYSS.
HO! AGREED! BUT WE'VE GOT 'EM BEAT! SOON THE NINTH WILL BE FREE...
...THEN THE CITY WILL FOLLOW AND--
WHAT IN HELL'S MAW IS THAT?

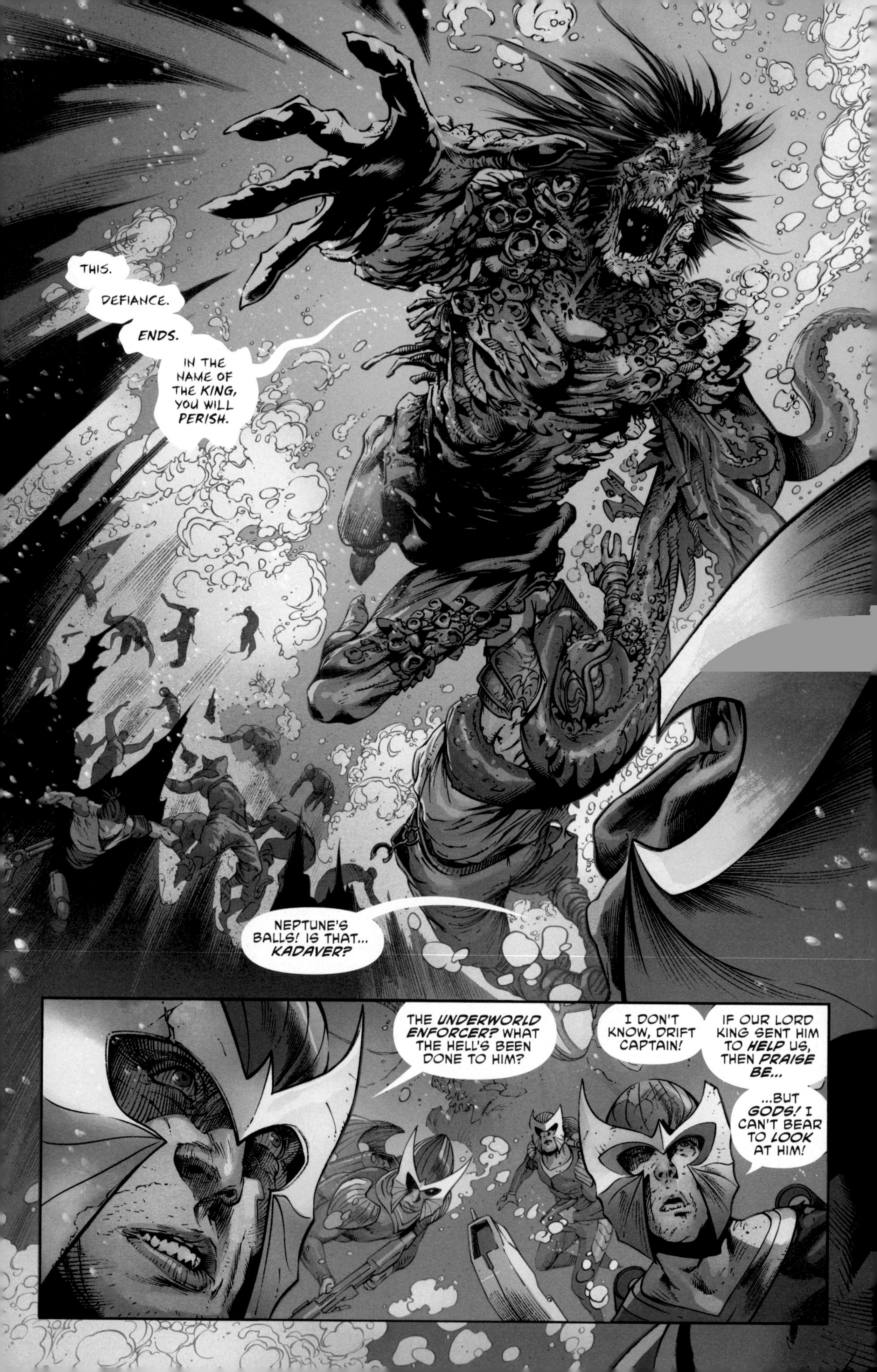

THIS.
DEFIANCE.
ENDS.
IN THE NAME OF THE KING, YOU WILL PERISH.
NEPTUNE'S BALLS! IS THAT... KADAVER?
THE UNDERWORLD ENFORCER? WHAT THE HELL'S BEEN DONE TO HIM?
I DON'T KNOW, DRIFT CAPTAIN!
IF OUR LORD KING SENT HIM TO HELP US, THEN PRAISE BE...
...BUT GODS! I CAN'T BEAR TO LOOK AT HIM!

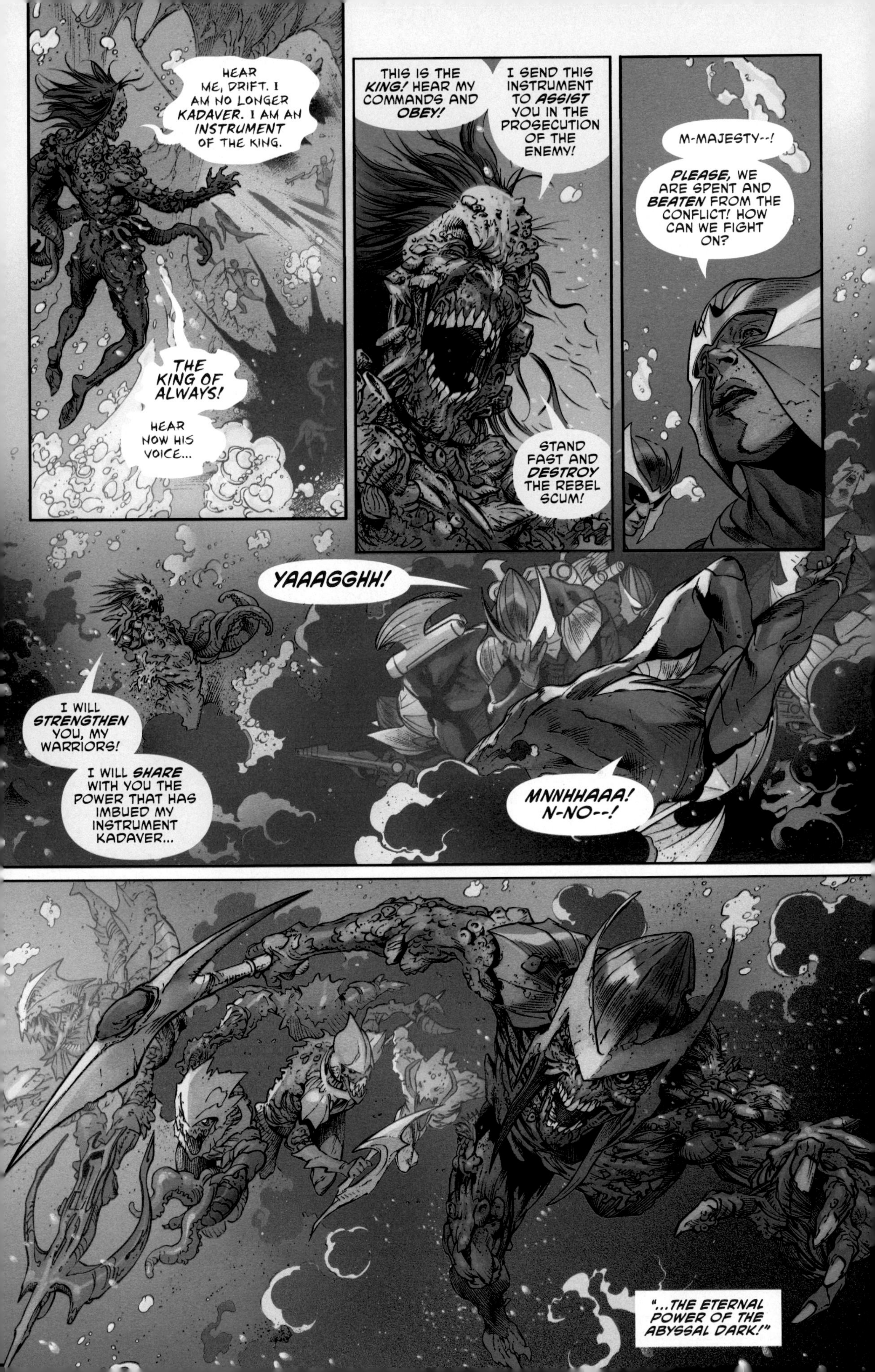
HEAR ME, DRIFT. I AM NO LONGER KADAVER. I AM AN INSTRUMENT OF THE KING.
THE KING OF ALWAYS!
HEAR NOW HIS VOICE...
THIS IS THE KING! HEAR MY COMMANDS AND OBEY!
I SEND THIS INSTRUMENT TO ASSIST YOU IN THE PROSECUTION OF THE ENEMY!
STAND FAST AND DESTROY THE REBEL SCUM!
M-MAJESTY--!
PLEASE, WE ARE SPENT AND BEATEN FROM THE CONFLICT! HOW CAN WE FIGHT ON?
YAAAGGHH!
I WILL STRENGTHEN YOU, MY WARRIORS!
I WILL SHARE WITH YOU THE POWER THAT HAS IMBUED MY INSTRUMENT KADAVER...
MNNHHAAA! N-NO--!
"...THE ETERNAL POWER OF THE ABYSSAL DARK!"

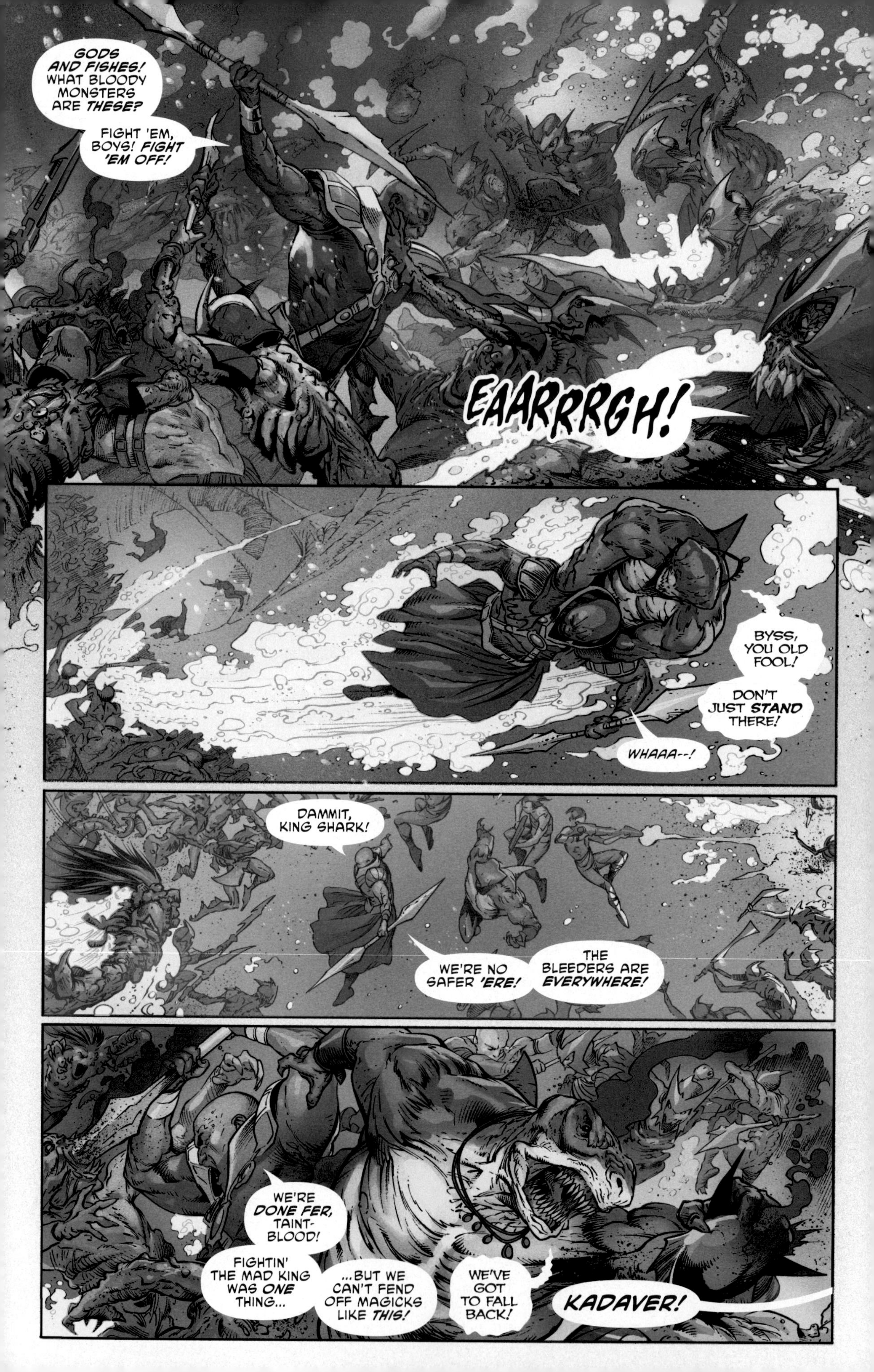
GODS AND FISHES! WHAT BLOODY MONSTERS ARE THESE?
FIGHT 'EM, BOYS! FIGHT 'EM OFF!
EAARRRGH!
BYSS, YOU OLD FOOL!
DON'T JUST STAND THERE!
WHAAA--!
DAMMIT, KING SHARK!
WE'RE NO SAFER 'ERE!
THE BLEEDERS ARE EVERYWHERE!
WE'RE DONE FER, TAINT-BLOOD!
FIGHTIN' THE MAD KING WAS ONE THING...
...BUT WE CAN'T FEND OFF MAGICKS LIKE THIS!
WE'VE GOT TO FALL BACK!
KADAVER!

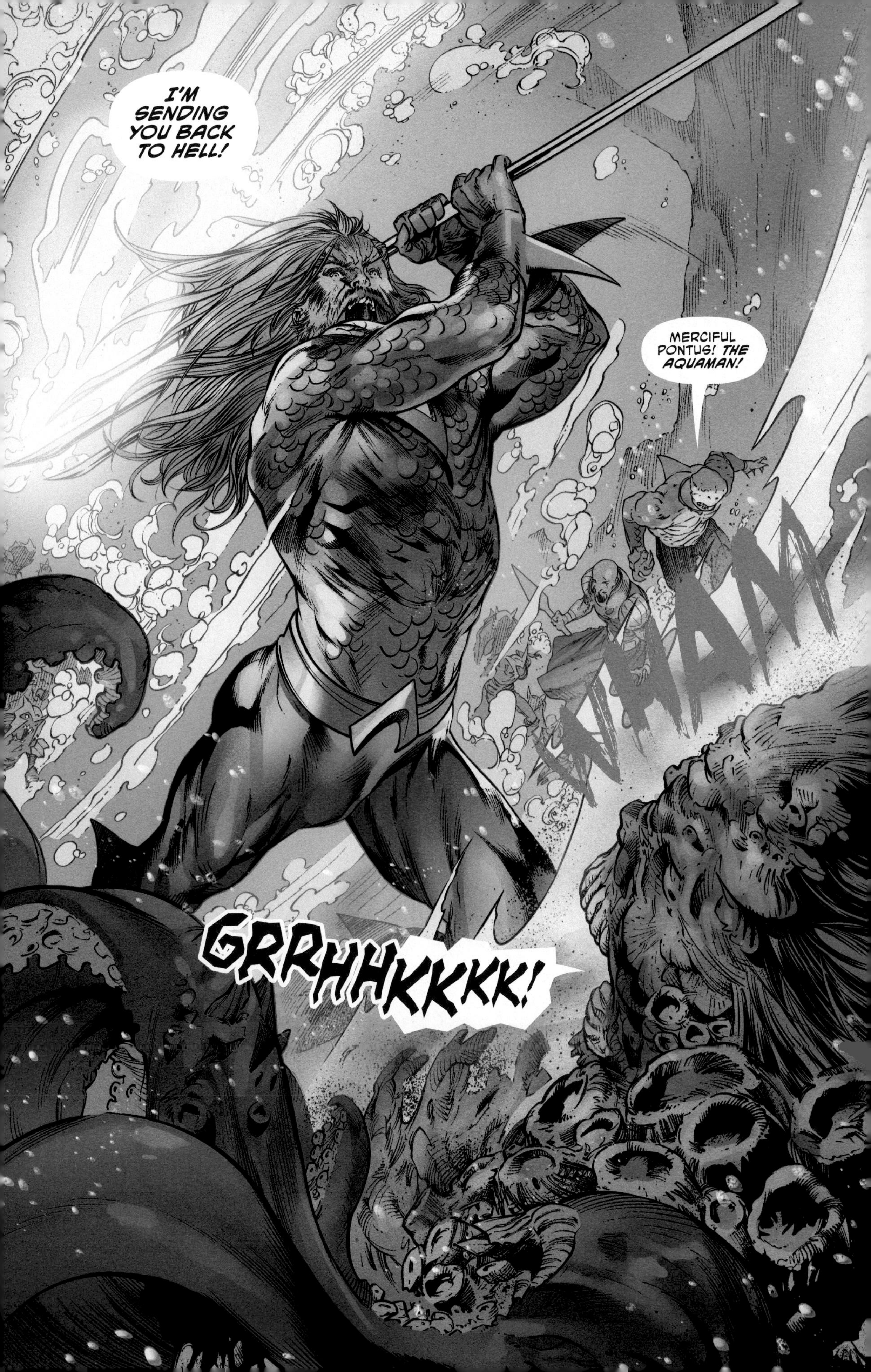
I'M SENDING YOU BACK TO HELL!
MERCIFUL PONTUS! THE AQUAMAN!
GRRHHKKKK!

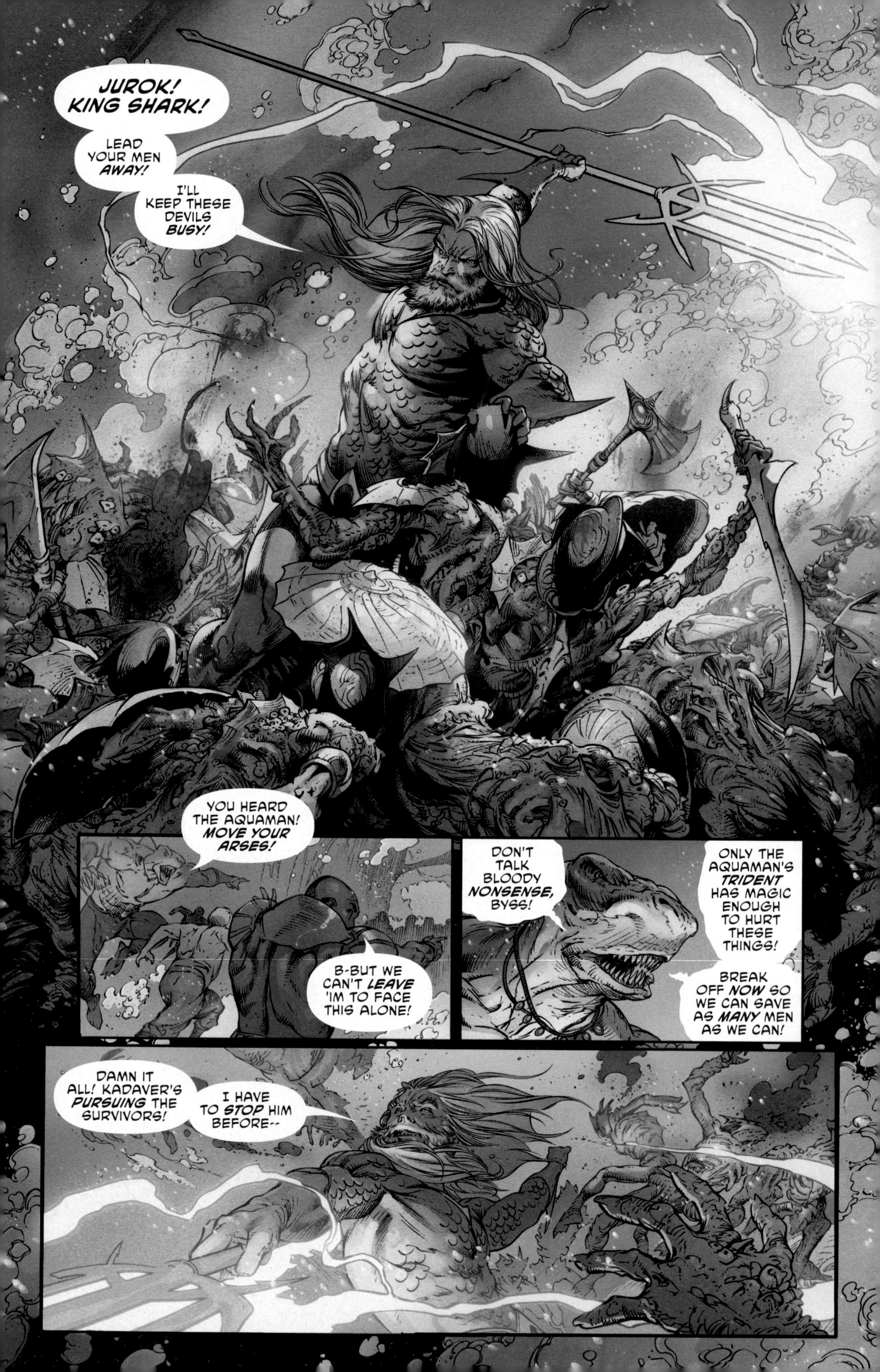
JUROK! KING SHARK!
LEAD YOUR MEN AWAY!
I'LL KEEP THESE DEVILS BUSY!
YOU HEARD THE AQUAMAN! MOVE YOUR ARSES!
B-BUT WE CAN'T LEAVE 'IM TO FACE THIS ALONE!
DON'T TALK BLOODY NONSENSE, BYSS!
ONLY THE AQUAMAN'S TRIDENT HAS MAGIC ENOUGH TO HURT THESE THINGS!
BREAK OFF NOW SO WE CAN SAVE AS MANY MEN AS WE CAN!
DAMN IT ALL! KADAVER'S PURSUING THE SURVIVORS!
I HAVE TO STOP HIM BEFORE--

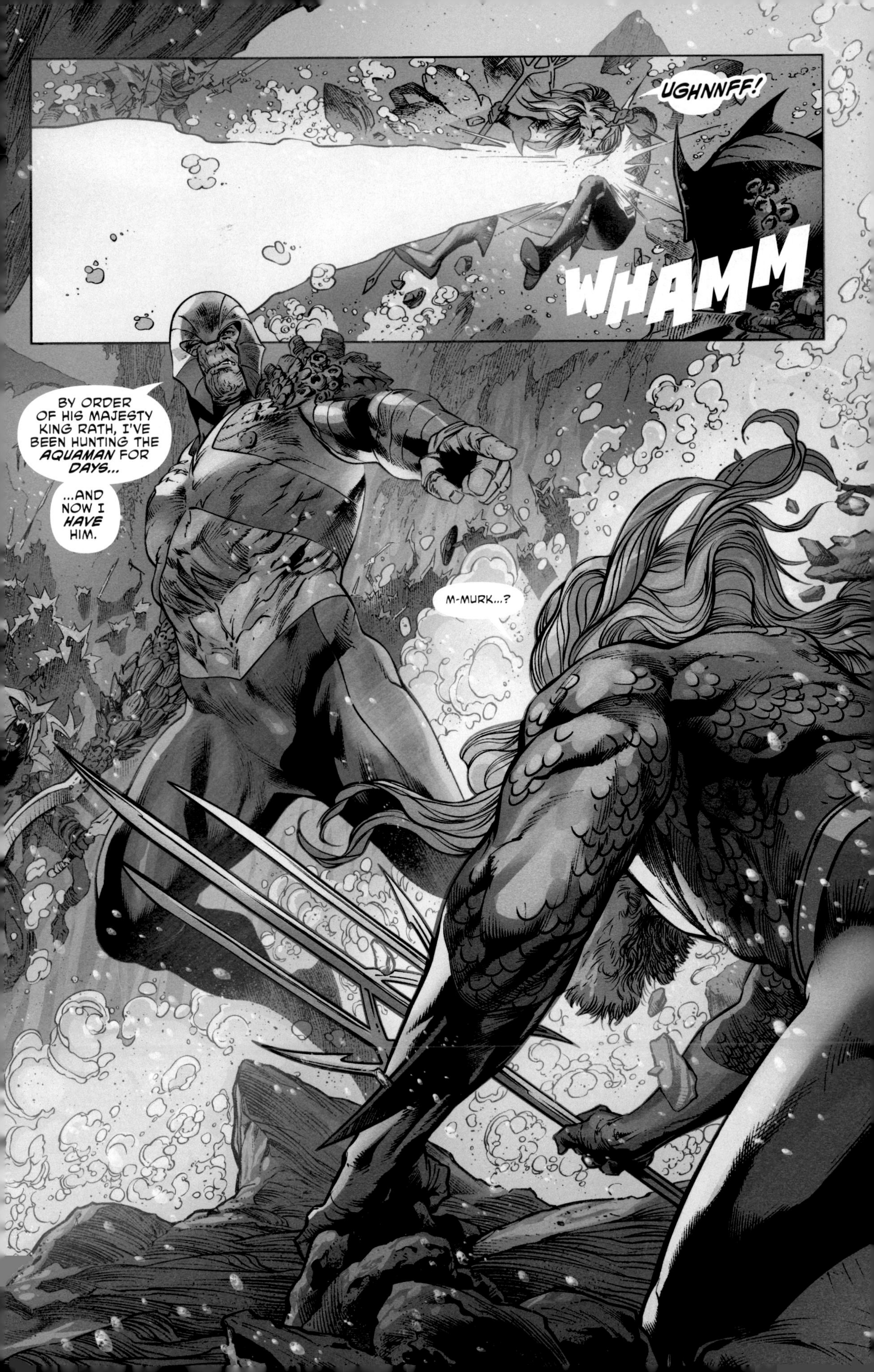
UGHNNFF!
WHAMM
BY ORDER OF HIS MAJESTY KING RATH, I'VE BEEN HUNTING THE AQUAMAN FOR DAYS...
...AND NOW I HAVE HIM.
M-MURK...?

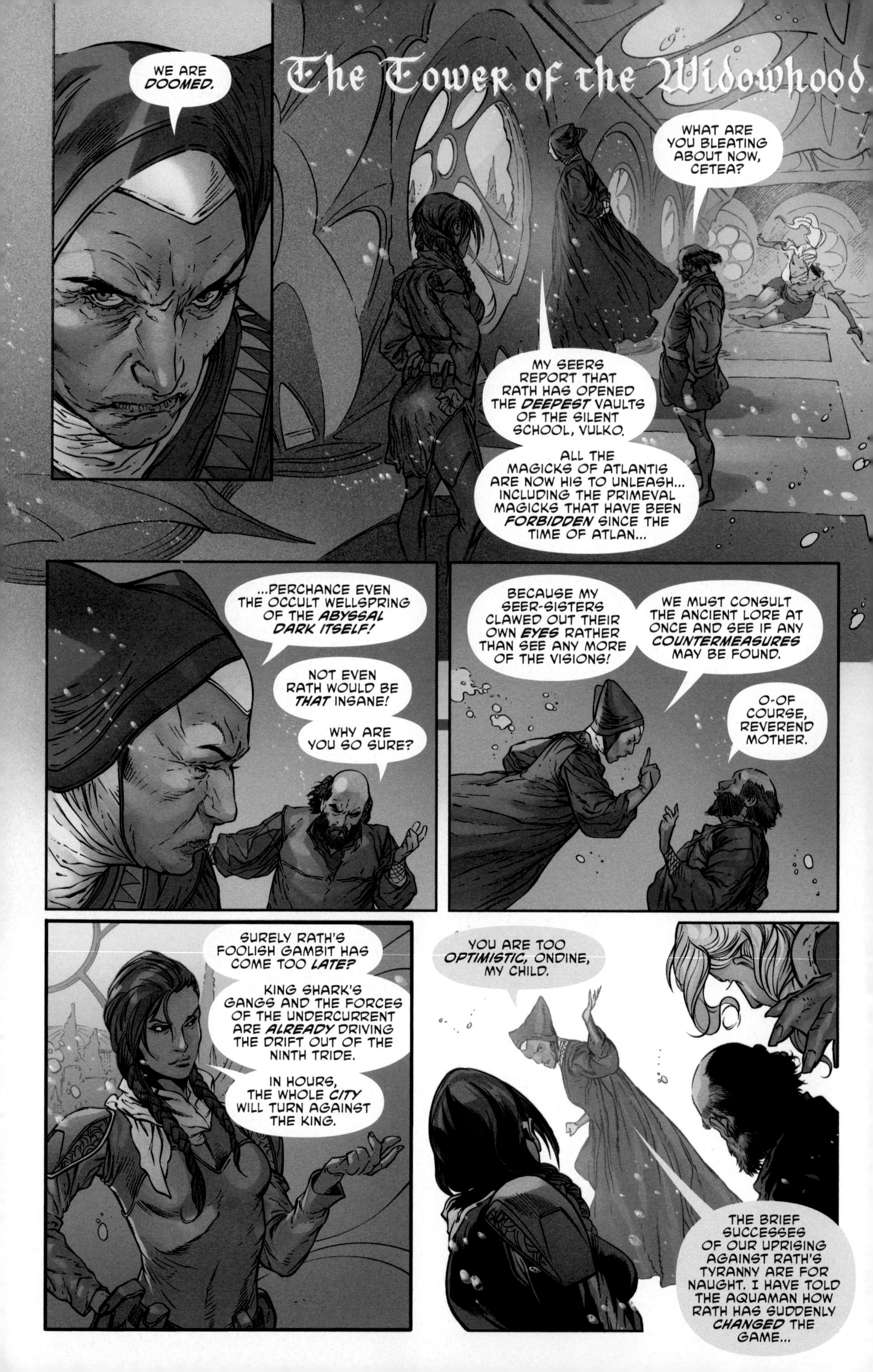
WE ARE DOOMED.
The Tower of the Widowhood.
WHAT ARE YOU BLEATING ABOUT NOW, CETEA?
MY SEERS REPORT THAT RATH HAS OPENED THE DEEPEST VAULTS OF THE SILENT SCHOOL, VULKO.
ALL THE MAGICKS OF ATLANTIS ARE NOW HIS TO UNLEASH... INCLUDING THE PRIMEVAL MAGICKS THAT HAVE BEEN FORBIDDEN SINCE THE TIME OF ATLAN...
...PERCHANCE EVEN THE OCCULT WELLSPRING OF THE ABYSSAL DARK ITSELF!
NOT EVEN RATH WOULD BE THAT INSANE!
WHY ARE YOU SO SURE?
BECAUSE MY SEER-SISTERS CLAWED OUT THEIR OWN EYES RATHER THAN SEE ANY MORE OF THE VISIONS!
WE MUST CONSULT THE ANCIENT LORE AT ONCE AND SEE IF ANY COUNTERMEASURES MAY BE FOUND.
O-OF COURSE, REVEREND MOTHER.
SURELY RATH'S FOOLISH GAMBIT HAS COME TOO LATE?
KING SHARK'S GANGS AND THE FORCES OF THE UNDERCURRENT ARE ALREADY DRIVING THE DRIFT OUT OF THE NINTH TRIDE.
IN HOURS, THE WHOLE CITY WILL TURN AGAINST THE KING.
YOU ARE TOO OPTIMISTIC, ONDINE, MY CHILD.
THE BRIEF SUCCESSES OF OUR UPRISING AGAINST RATH'S TYRANNY ARE FOR NAUGHT. I HAVE TOLD THE AQUAMAN HOW RATH HAS SUDDENLY CHANGED THE GAME...

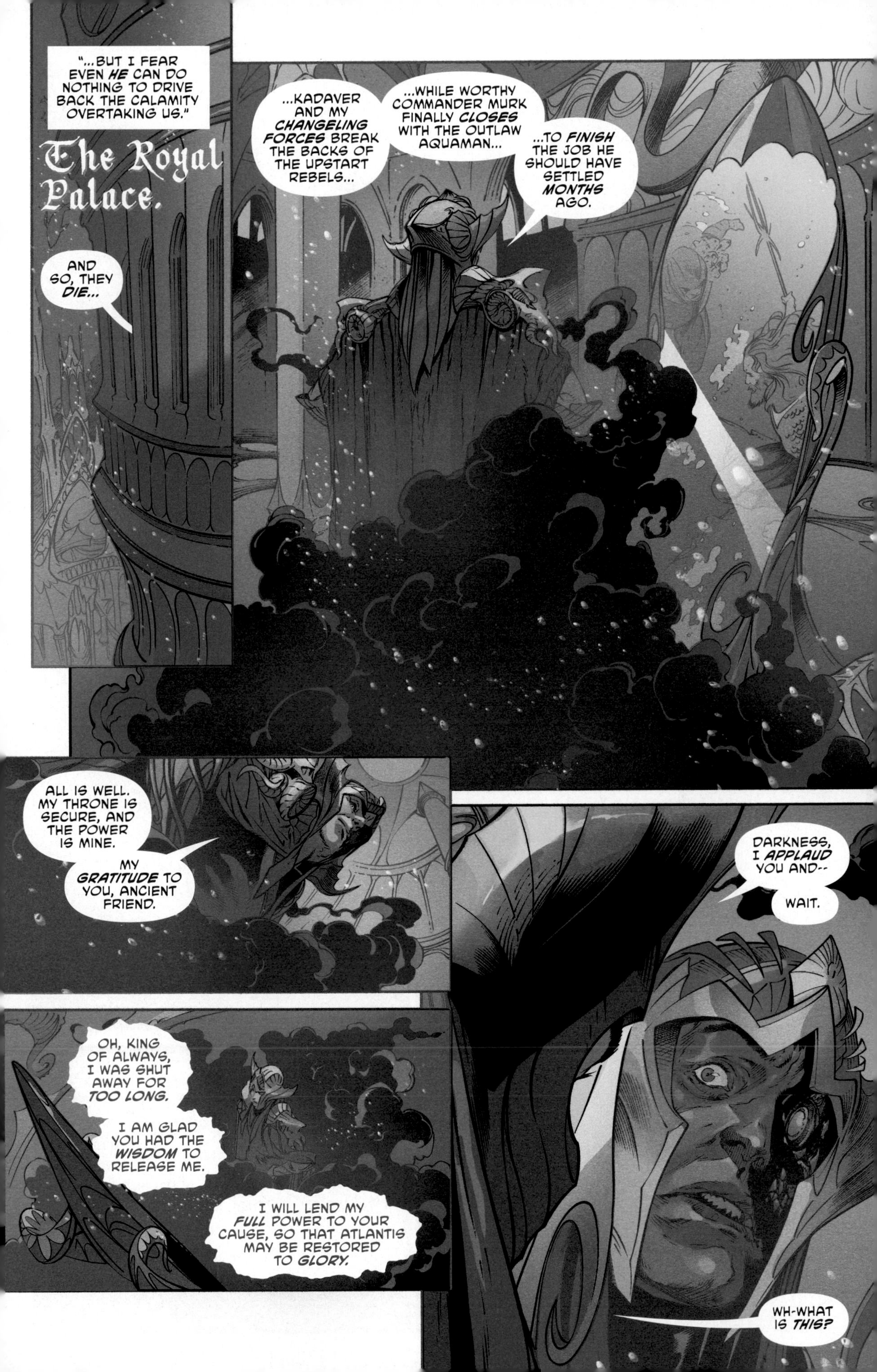
"...BUT I FEAR EVEN HE CAN DO NOTHING TO DRIVE BACK THE CALAMITY OVERTAKING US."
The Royal Palace.
AND SO, THEY DIE...
...KADAVER AND MY CHANGELING FORCES BREAK THE BACKS OF THE UPSTART REBELS...
...WHILE WORTHY COMMANDER MURK FINALLY CLOSES WITH THE OUTLAW AQUAMAN...
...TO FINISH THE JOB HE SHOULD HAVE SETTLED MONTHS AGO.
ALL IS WELL. MY THRONE IS SECURE, AND THE POWER IS MINE.
MY GRATITUDE TO YOU, ANCIENT FRIEND.
OH, KING OF ALWAYS, I WAS SHUT AWAY FOR TOO LONG.
I AM GLAD YOU HAD THE WISDOM TO RELEASE ME.
I WILL LEND MY FULL POWER TO YOUR CAUSE, SO THAT ATLANTIS MAY BE RESTORED TO GLORY.
DARKNESS, I APPLAUD YOU AND--
WAIT.
WH-WHAT IS THIS?

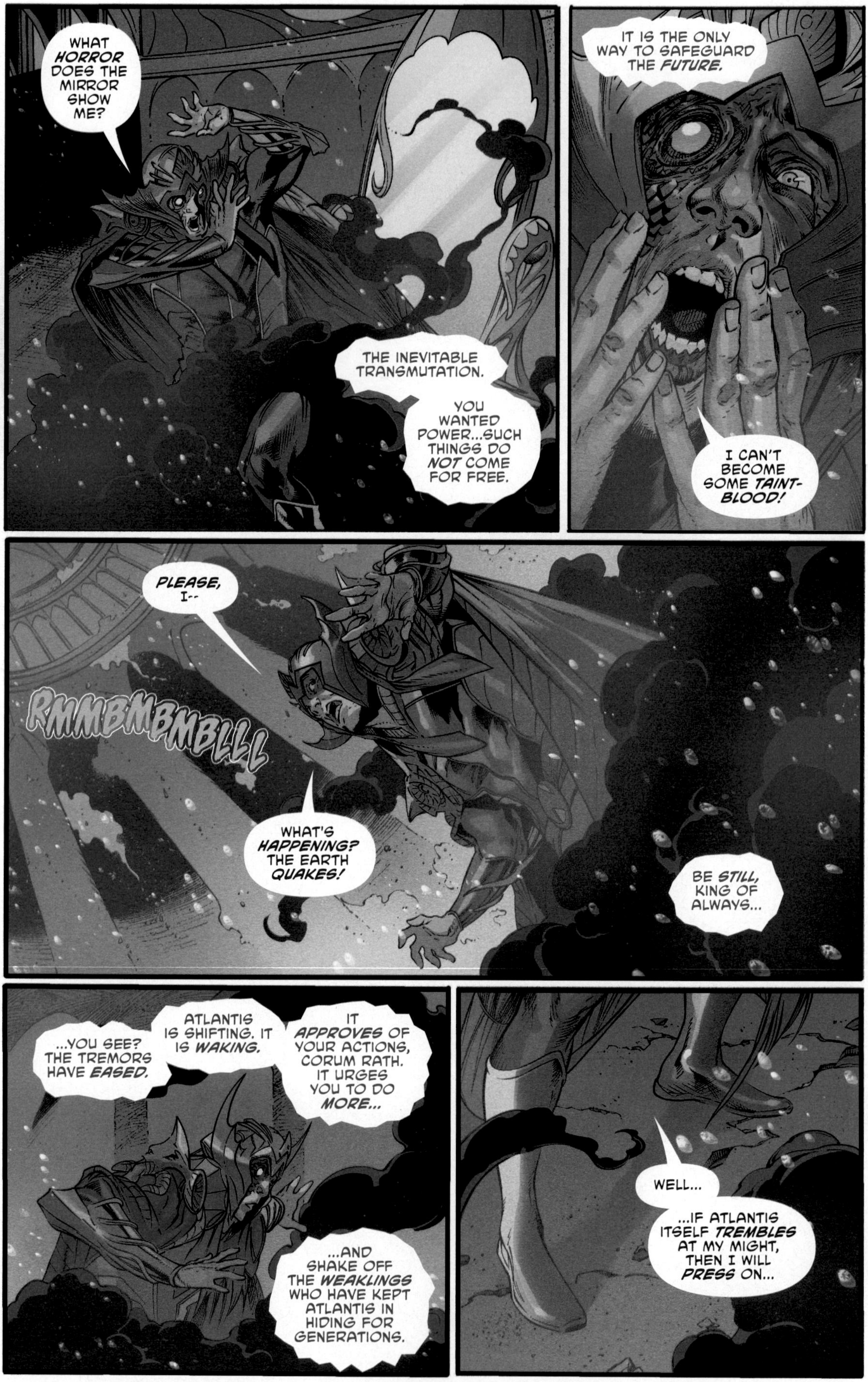
WHAT *HORROR* DOES THE MIRROR SHOW ME?
THE INEVITABLE TRANSMUTATION.
YOU WANTED POWER...SUCH THINGS DO *NOT* COME FOR FREE.
IT IS THE ONLY WAY TO SAFEGUARD THE *FUTURE.*
I CAN'T BECOME SOME *TAINT-BLOOD!*
PLEASE, I--
RMMBMBMBLLL
WHAT'S *HAPPENING?* THE EARTH *QUAKES!*
BE *STILL,* KING OF ALWAYS...
...YOU SEE? THE TREMORS HAVE *EASED.*
ATLANTIS IS SHIFTING. IT IS *WAKING.*
IT *APPROVES* OF YOUR ACTIONS, CORUM RATH. IT URGES YOU TO DO *MORE...*
...AND SHAKE OFF THE *WEAKLINGS* WHO HAVE KEPT ATLANTIS IN HIDING FOR GENERATIONS.
WELL...
...IF ATLANTIS ITSELF *TREMBLES* AT MY MIGHT, THEN I WILL *PRESS* ON...

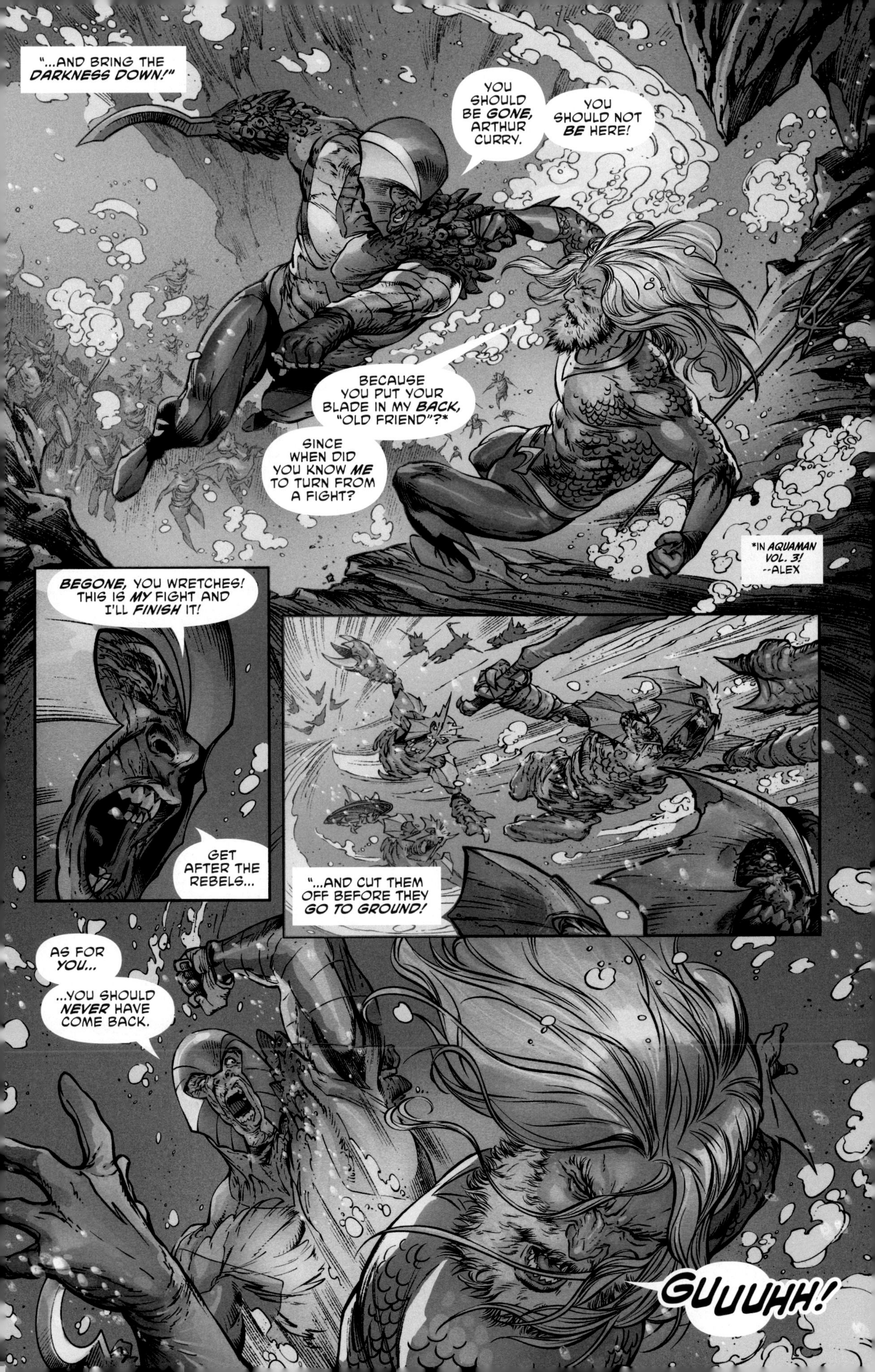
"...AND BRING THE *DARKNESS DOWN!*"
YOU SHOULD BE ***GONE,*** ARTHUR CURRY.
YOU SHOULD NOT ***BE*** HERE!
BECAUSE YOU PUT YOUR BLADE IN MY *BACK,* "OLD FRIEND"?*
SINCE WHEN DID YOU KNOW ***ME*** TO TURN FROM A FIGHT?
*IN *AQUAMAN VOL. 3!* --ALEX
BEGONE, YOU WRETCHES! THIS IS ***MY*** FIGHT AND I'LL ***FINISH*** IT!
GET AFTER THE REBELS...
"...AND CUT THEM OFF BEFORE THEY ***GO TO GROUND!***
AS FOR ***YOU...***
...YOU SHOULD ***NEVER*** HAVE COME BACK.
GUUUHH!

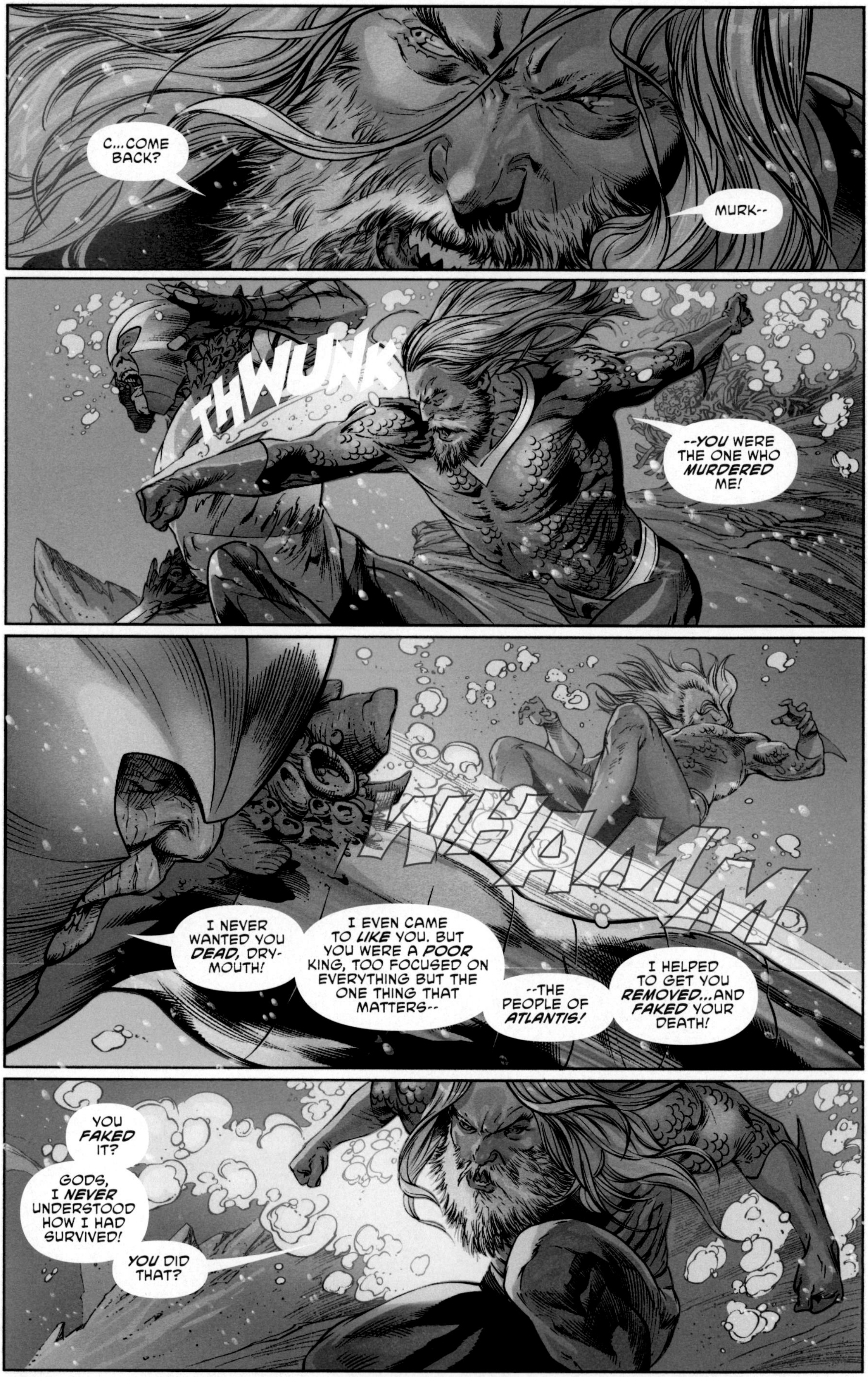
C...COME BACK?
MURK--
THWUNK
--*YOU* WERE THE ONE WHO *MURDERED* ME!
WHAAAM
I NEVER WANTED YOU *DEAD*, DRY-MOUTH!
I EVEN CAME TO *LIKE* YOU. BUT YOU WERE A *POOR* KING, TOO FOCUSED ON EVERYTHING BUT THE ONE THING THAT MATTERS--
--THE PEOPLE OF *ATLANTIS!*
I HELPED TO GET YOU *REMOVED*...AND *FAKED* YOUR DEATH!
YOU *FAKED* IT?
GODS, I *NEVER* UNDERSTOOD HOW I HAD SURVIVED!
YOU DID THAT?

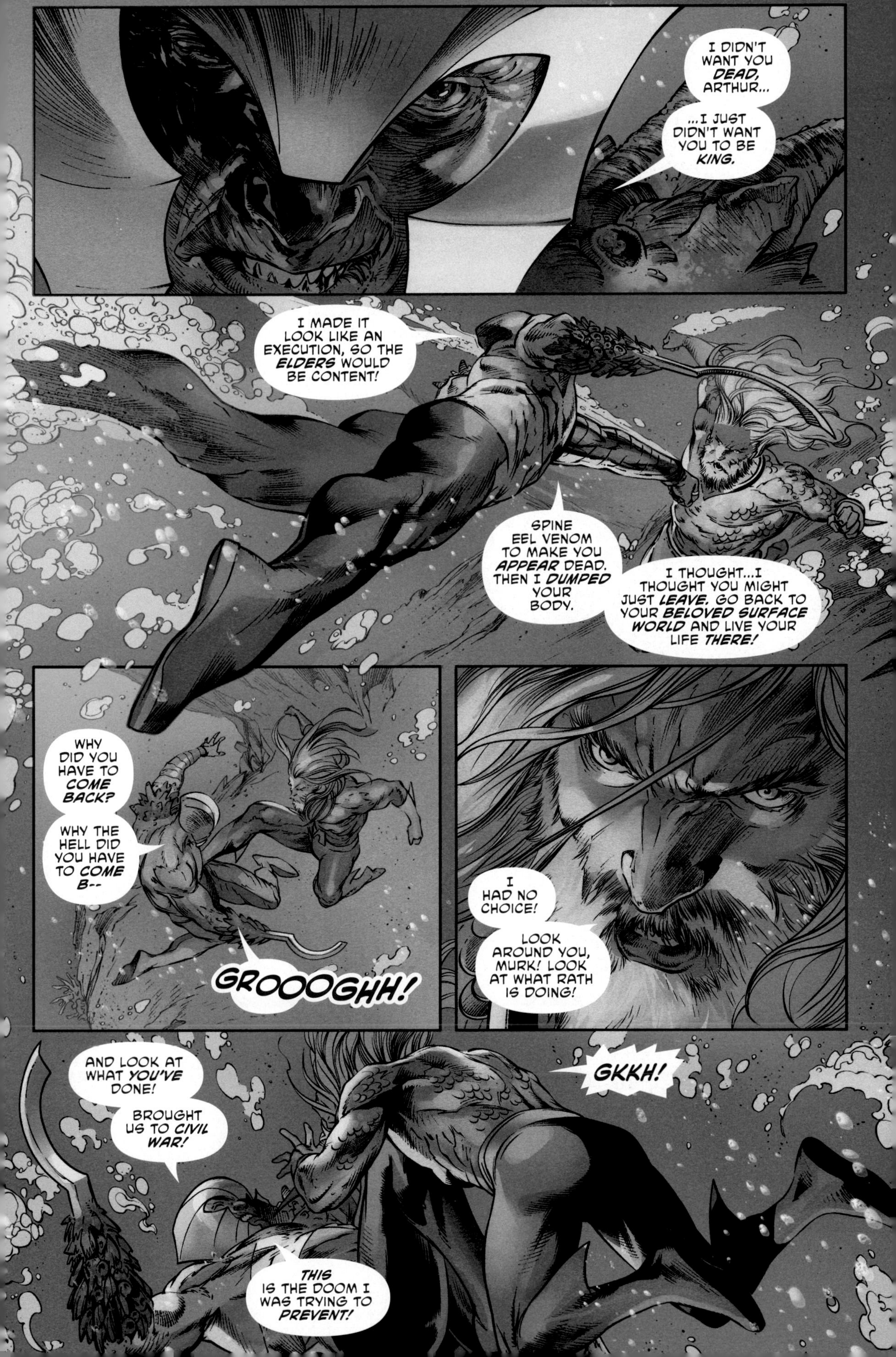

I DIDN'T WANT YOU DEAD, ARTHUR...
...I JUST DIDN'T WANT YOU TO BE KING.
I MADE IT LOOK LIKE AN EXECUTION, SO THE ELDERS WOULD BE CONTENT!
SPINE EEL VENOM TO MAKE YOU APPEAR DEAD. THEN I DUMPED YOUR BODY.
I THOUGHT...I THOUGHT YOU MIGHT JUST LEAVE. GO BACK TO YOUR BELOVED SURFACE WORLD AND LIVE YOUR LIFE THERE!
WHY DID YOU HAVE TO COME BACK?
WHY THE HELL DID YOU HAVE TO COME B--
GROOOGHH!
I HAD NO CHOICE!
LOOK AROUND YOU, MURK! LOOK AT WHAT RATH IS DOING!
AND LOOK AT WHAT YOU'VE DONE!
BROUGHT US TO CIVIL WAR!
GKKH!
THIS IS THE DOOM I WAS TRYING TO PREVENT!

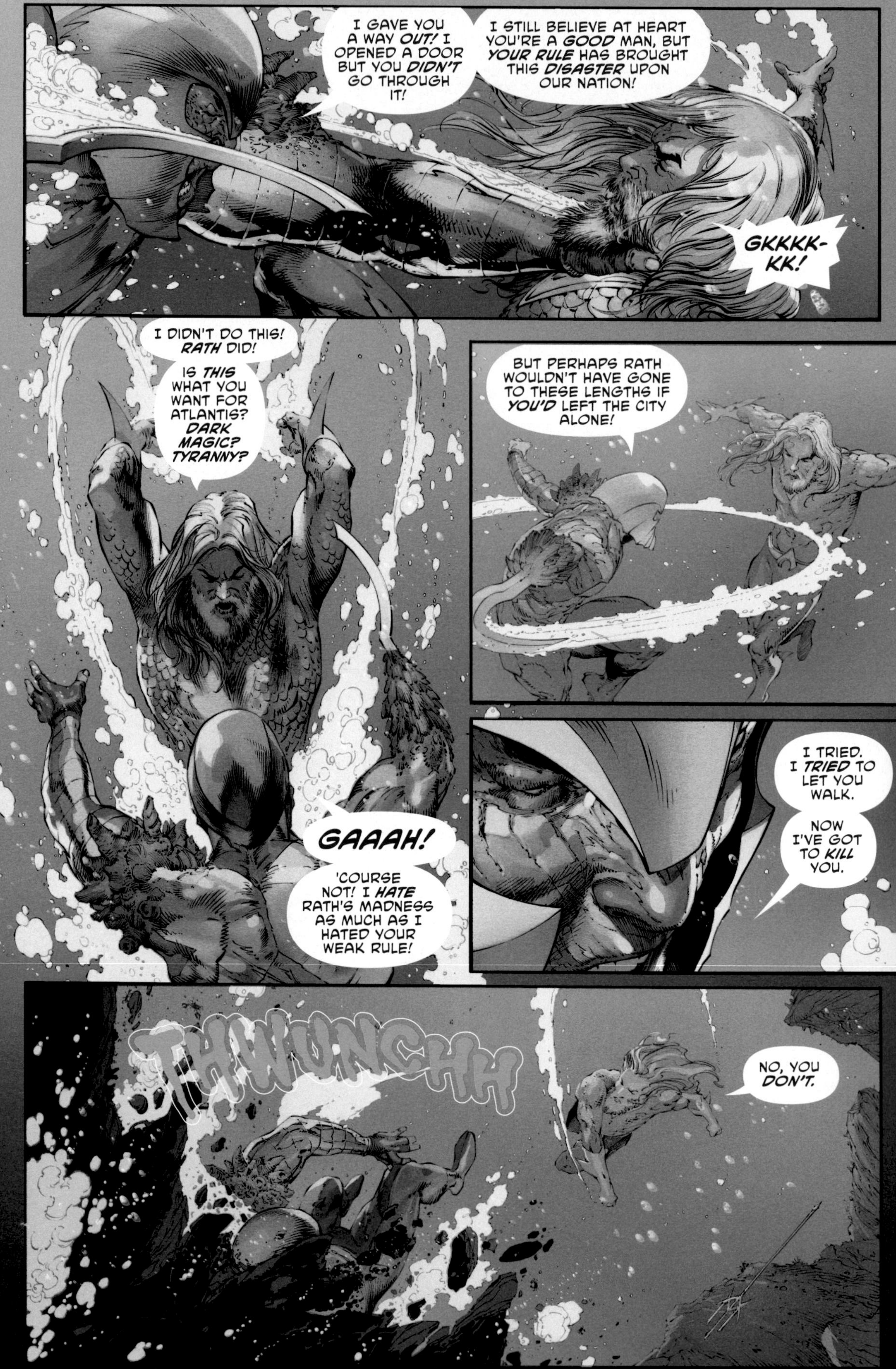
I GAVE YOU A WAY OUT! I OPENED A DOOR BUT YOU DIDN'T GO THROUGH IT!
I STILL BELIEVE AT HEART YOU'RE A GOOD MAN, BUT YOUR RULE HAS BROUGHT THIS DISASTER UPON OUR NATION!
GKKKK-KK!
I DIDN'T DO THIS! RATH DID!
IS THIS WHAT YOU WANT FOR ATLANTIS? DARK MAGIC? TYRANNY?
GAAAH!
'COURSE NOT! I HATE RATH'S MADNESS AS MUCH AS I HATED YOUR WEAK RULE!
BUT PERHAPS RATH WOULDN'T HAVE GONE TO THESE LENGTHS IF YOU'D LEFT THE CITY ALONE!
I TRIED. I TRIED TO LET YOU WALK.
NOW I'VE GOT TO KILL YOU.
THWUNCHH
NO, YOU DON'T.

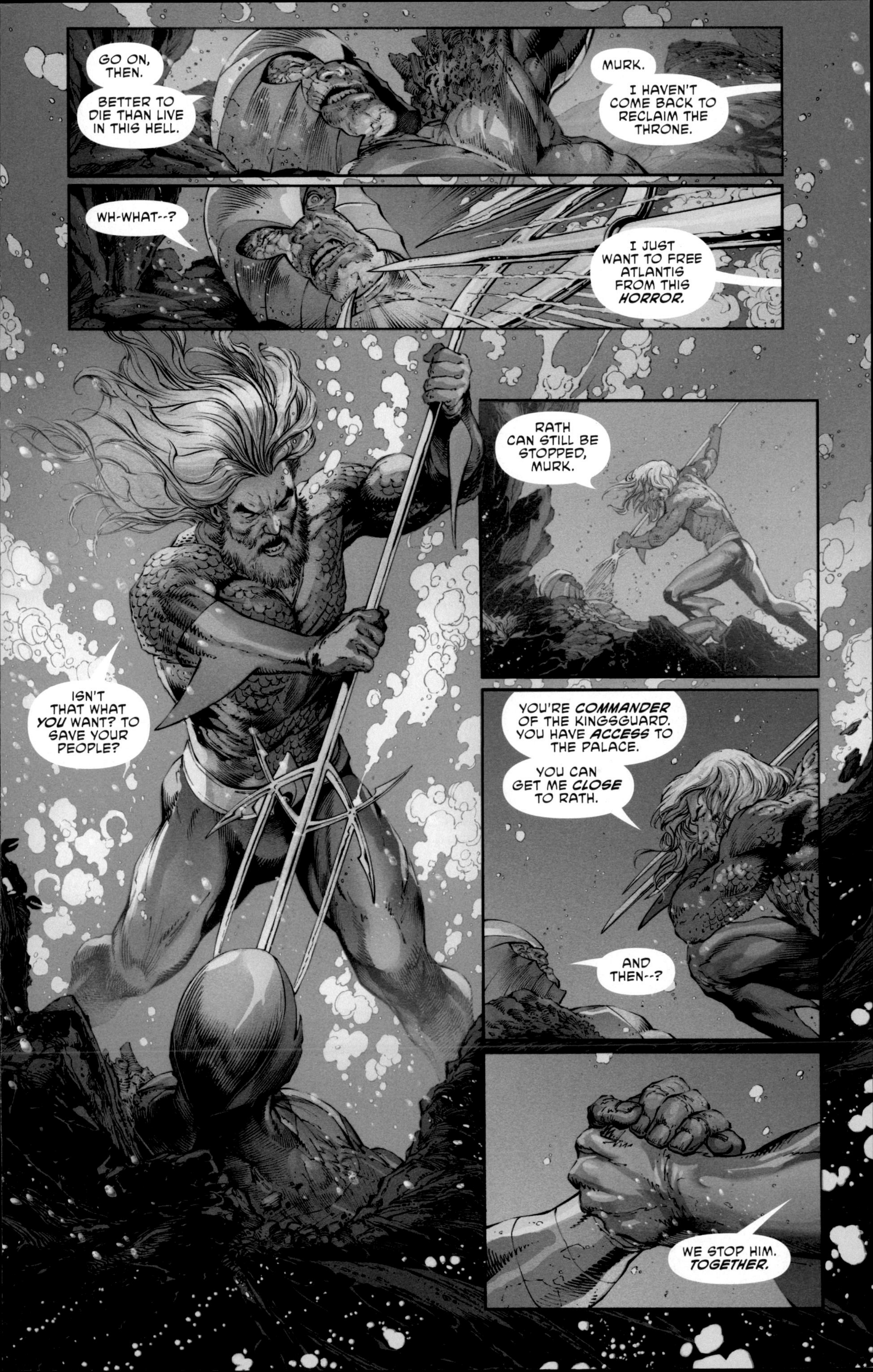
GO ON, THEN.
BETTER TO DIE THAN LIVE IN THIS HELL.
MURK.
I HAVEN'T COME BACK TO RECLAIM THE THRONE.
WH-WHAT--?
I JUST WANT TO FREE ATLANTIS FROM THIS *HORROR.*
RATH CAN STILL BE STOPPED, MURK.
ISN'T THAT WHAT *YOU* WANT? TO SAVE YOUR PEOPLE?
YOU'RE *COMMANDER* OF THE KINGSGUARD. YOU HAVE *ACCESS* TO THE PALACE.
YOU CAN GET ME *CLOSE* TO RATH.
AND THEN--?
WE STOP HIM. *TOGETHER.*

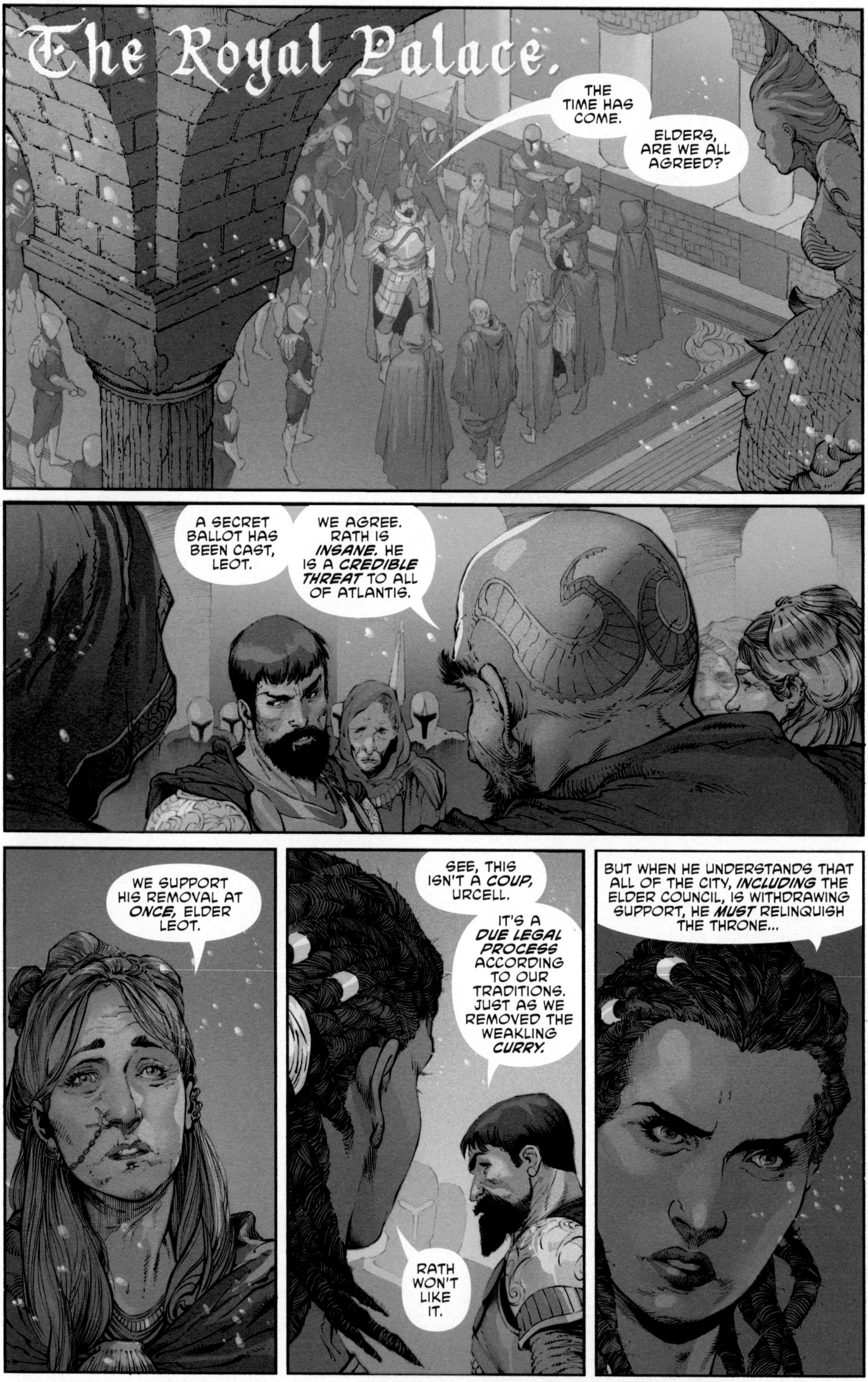
The Royal Palace.
THE TIME HAS COME.
ELDERS, ARE WE ALL AGREED?
A SECRET BALLOT HAS BEEN CAST, LEOT.
WE AGREE. RATH IS INSANE. HE IS A CREDIBLE THREAT TO ALL OF ATLANTIS.
WE SUPPORT HIS REMOVAL AT ONCE, ELDER LEOT.
SEE, THIS ISN'T A COUP, URCELL.
IT'S A DUE LEGAL PROCESS ACCORDING TO OUR TRADITIONS. JUST AS WE REMOVED THE WEAKLING CURRY.
RATH WON'T LIKE IT.
BUT WHEN HE UNDERSTANDS THAT ALL OF THE CITY, INCLUDING THE ELDER COUNCIL, IS WITHDRAWING SUPPORT, HE MUST RELINQUISH THE THRONE...

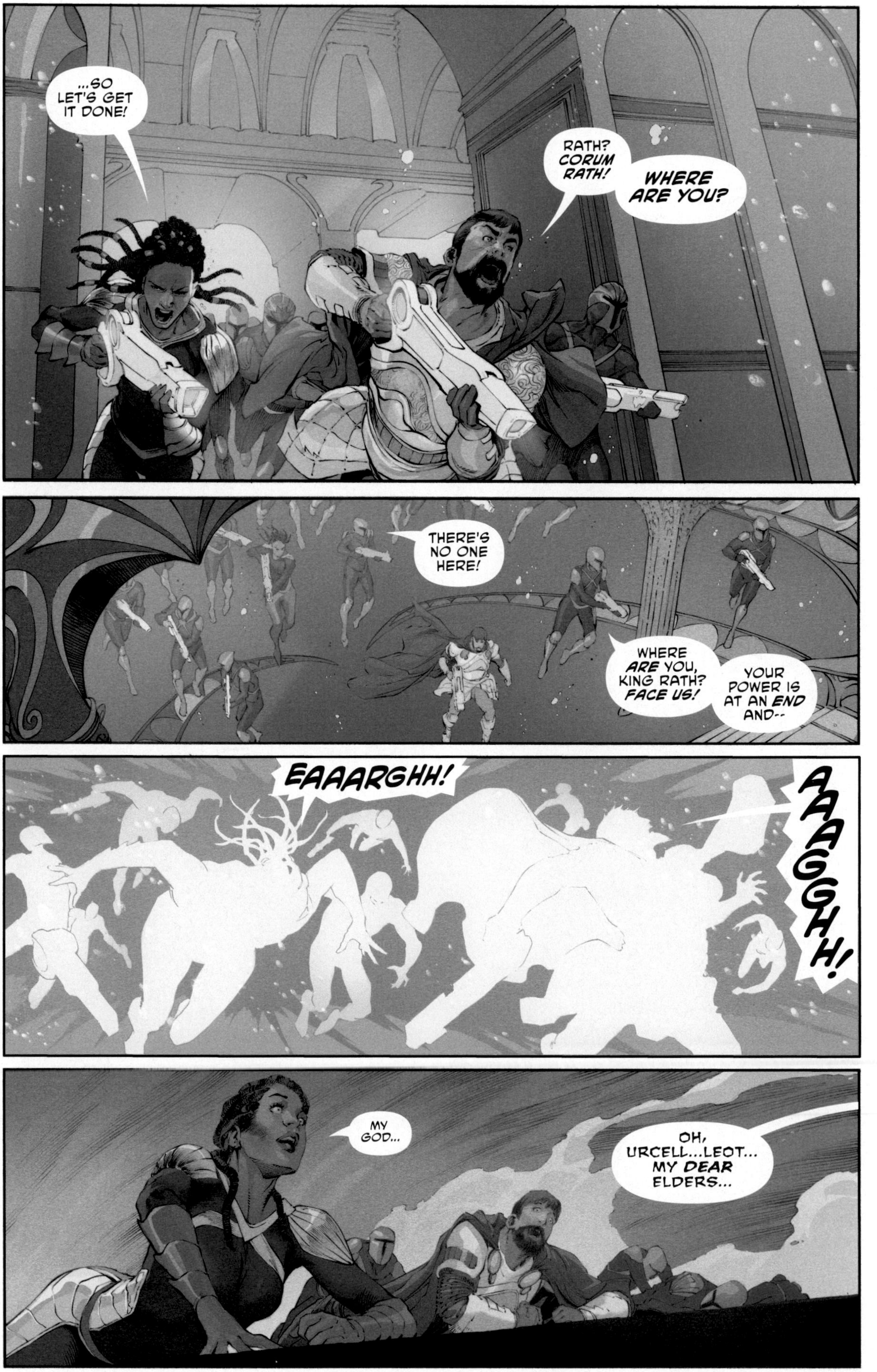
...SO LET'S GET IT DONE!
RATH? CORUM RATH!
WHERE ARE YOU?
THERE'S NO ONE HERE!
WHERE ARE YOU, KING RATH? FACE US!
YOUR POWER IS AT AN END AND--
EAAARGHH!
AAAGGHH!
MY GOD...
OH, URCELL...LEOT... MY DEAR ELDERS...

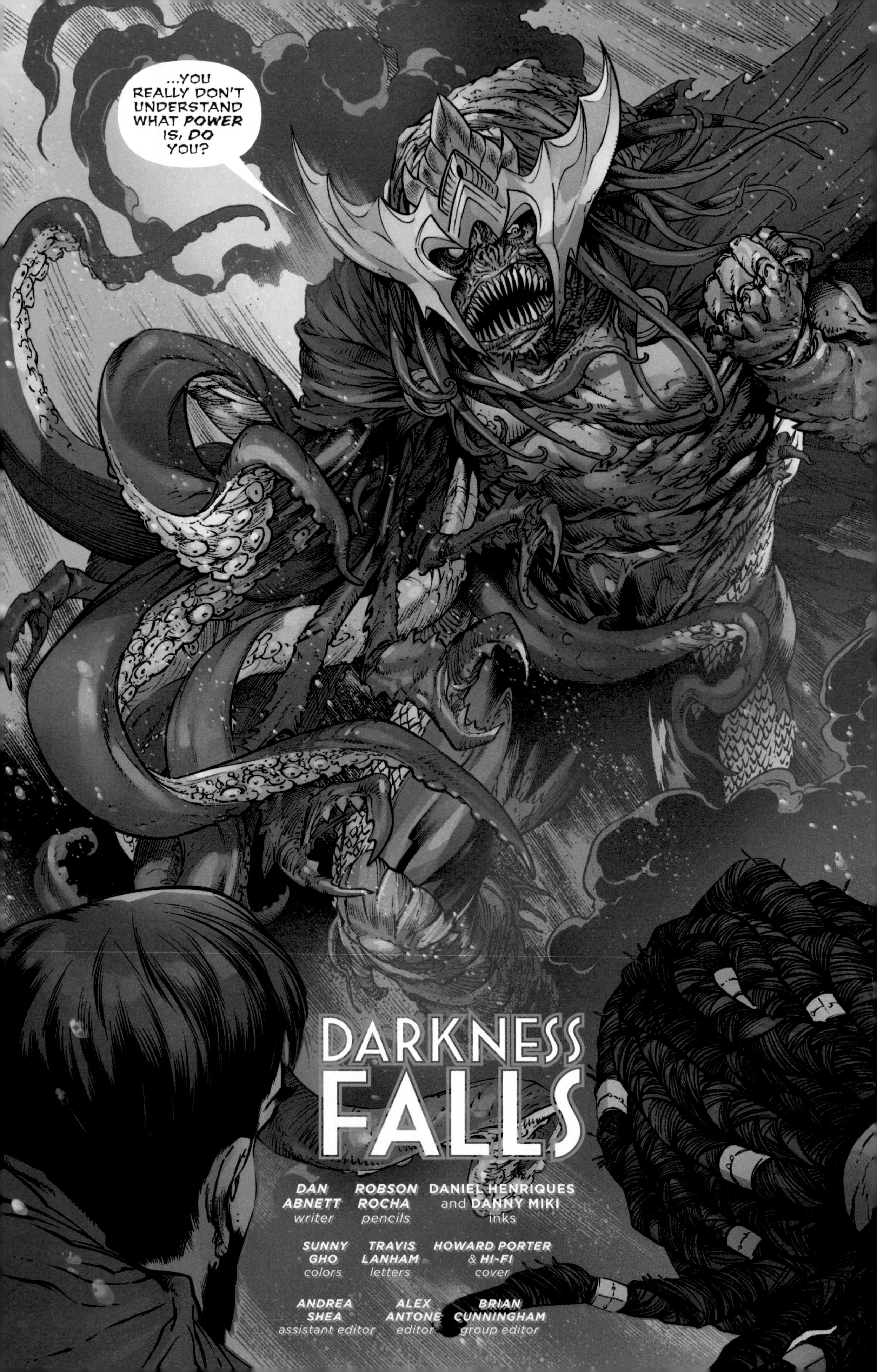

...YOU REALLY DON'T UNDERSTAND WHAT POWER IS, DO YOU?
DARKNESS FALLS
DAN ABNETT writer
ROBSON ROCHA pencils
DANIEL HENRIQUES and DANNY MIKI inks
SUNNY GHO colors
TRAVIS LANHAM letters
HOWARD PORTER & HI-FI cover
ANDREA SHEA assistant editor
ALEX ANTONE editor
BRIAN CUNNINGHAM group editor

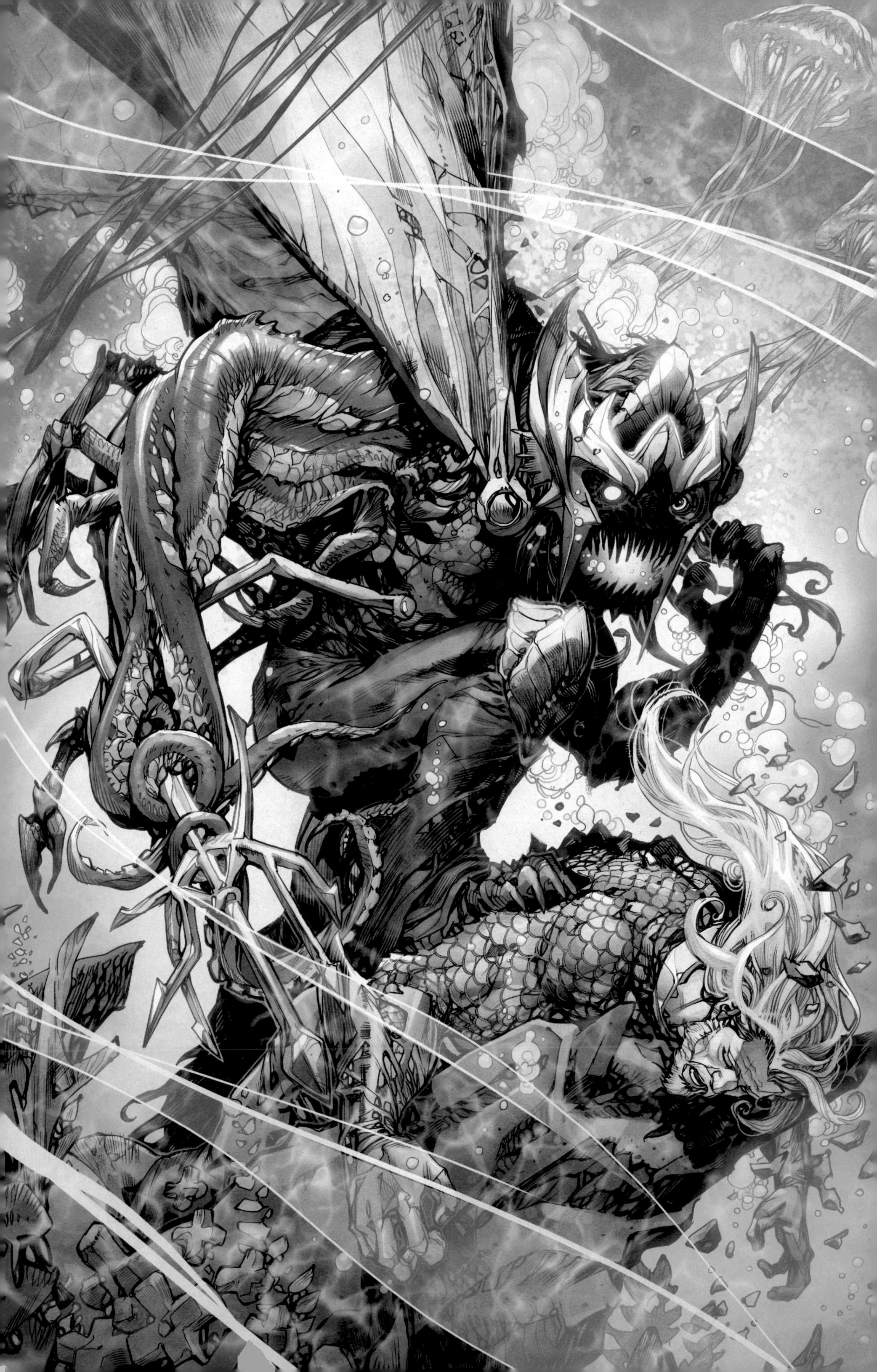

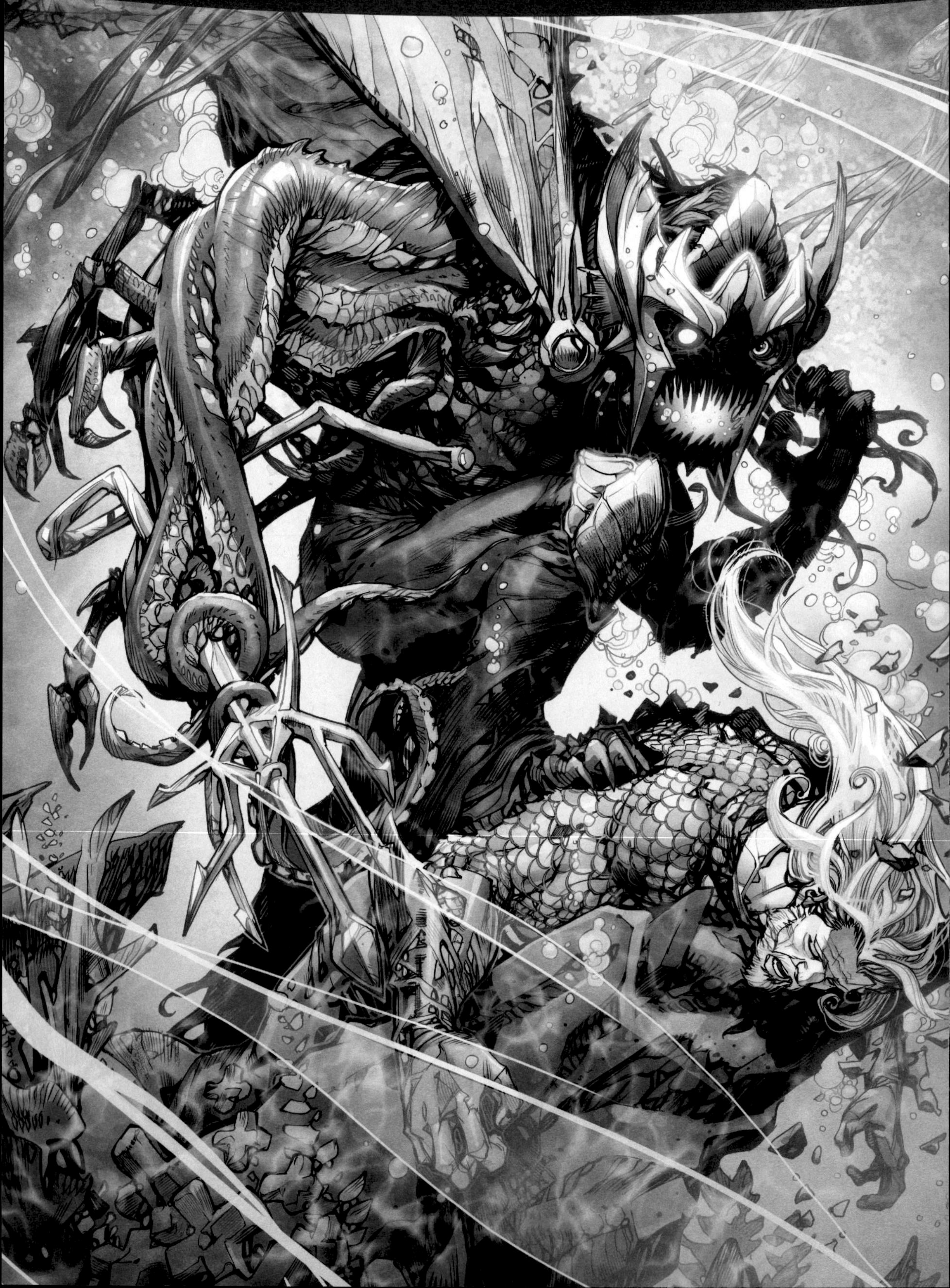

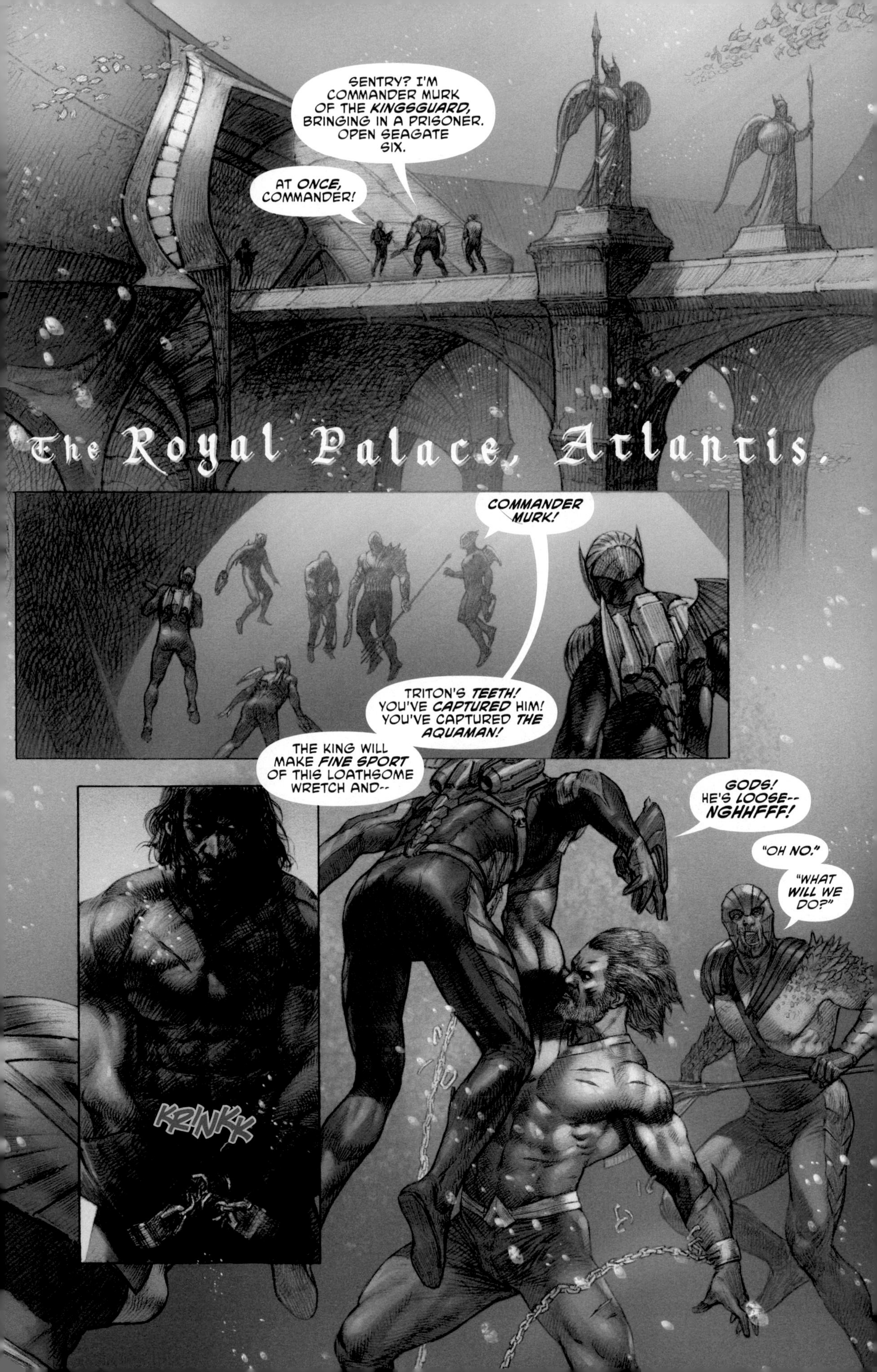
SENTRY? I'M COMMANDER MURK OF THE KINGSGUARD, BRINGING IN A PRISONER. OPEN SEAGATE SIX.
AT ONCE, COMMANDER!
The Royal Palace, Atlantis.
COMMANDER MURK!
TRITON'S TEETH! YOU'VE CAPTURED HIM! YOU'VE CAPTURED THE AQUAMAN!
THE KING WILL MAKE FINE SPORT OF THIS LOATHSOME WRETCH AND--
KRINKK
GODS! HE'S LOOSE--NGHHFFF!
"OH NO."
"WHAT WILL WE DO?"

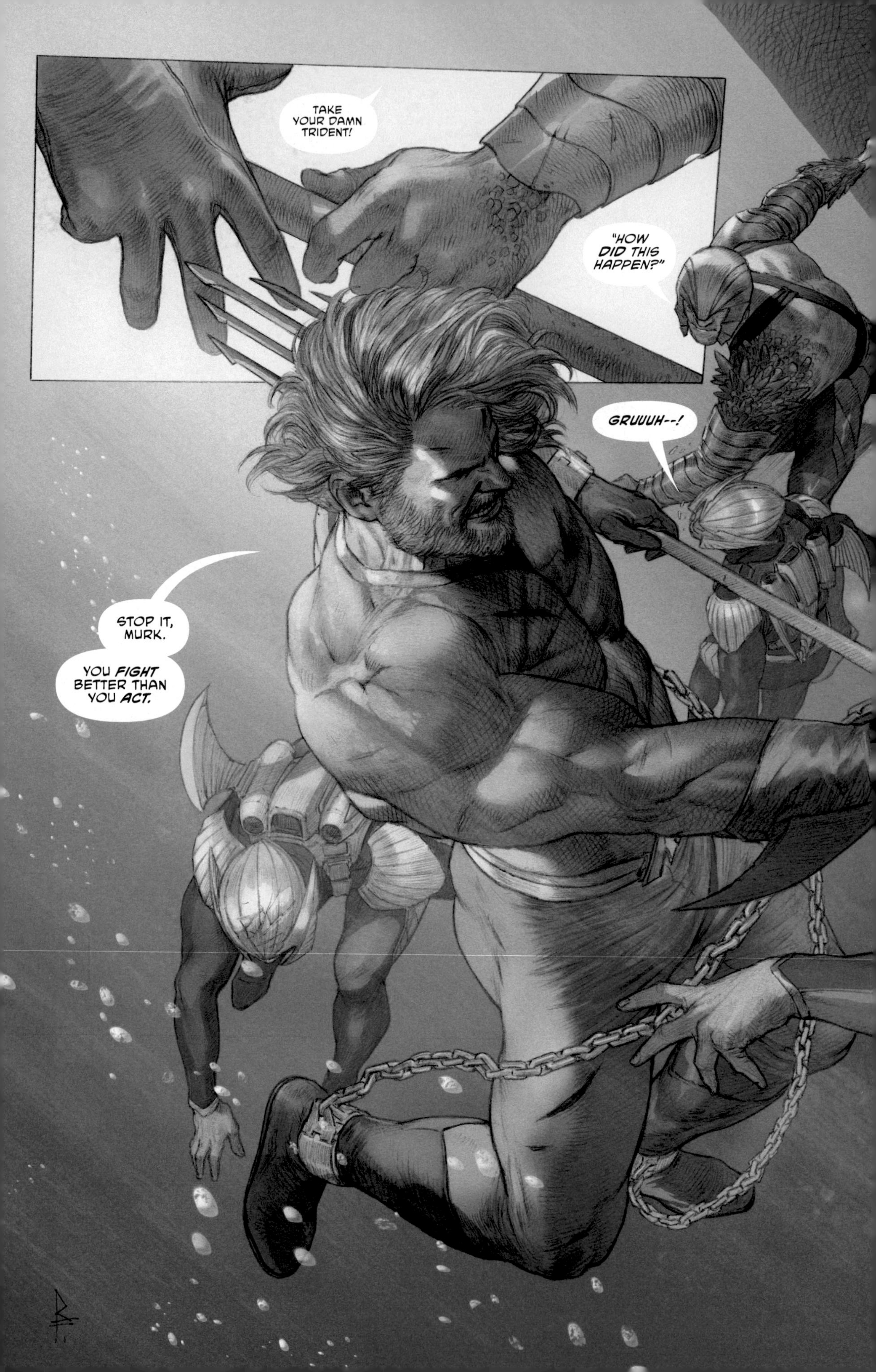
TAKE YOUR DAMN TRIDENT!
"HOW DID THIS HAPPEN?"
GRUUUH--!
STOP IT, MURK.
YOU FIGHT BETTER THAN YOU ACT.

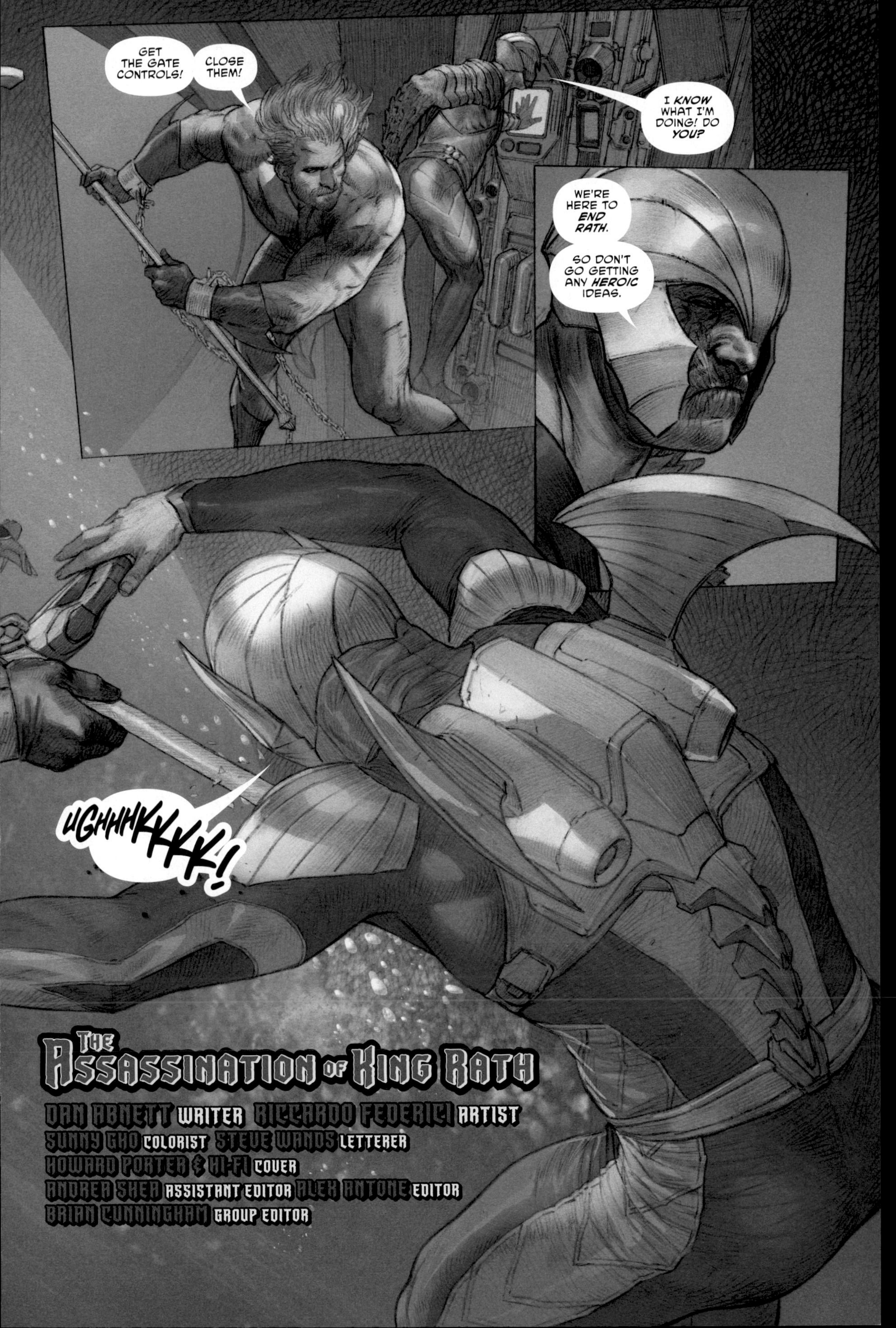
GET THE GATE CONTROLS!
CLOSE THEM!
I KNOW WHAT I'M DOING! DO YOU?
WE'RE HERE TO END RATH.
SO DON'T GO GETTING ANY HEROIC IDEAS.
UGHHHKKKK!
THE ASSASSINATION OF KING RATH
DAN ABNETT WRITER RICCARDO FEDERICI ARTIST
SUNNY GHO COLORIST STEVE WANDS LETTERER
HOWARD PORTER & HI-FI COVER
ANDREA SHEA ASSISTANT EDITOR ALEX ANTONE EDITOR
BRIAN CUNNINGHAM GROUP EDITOR

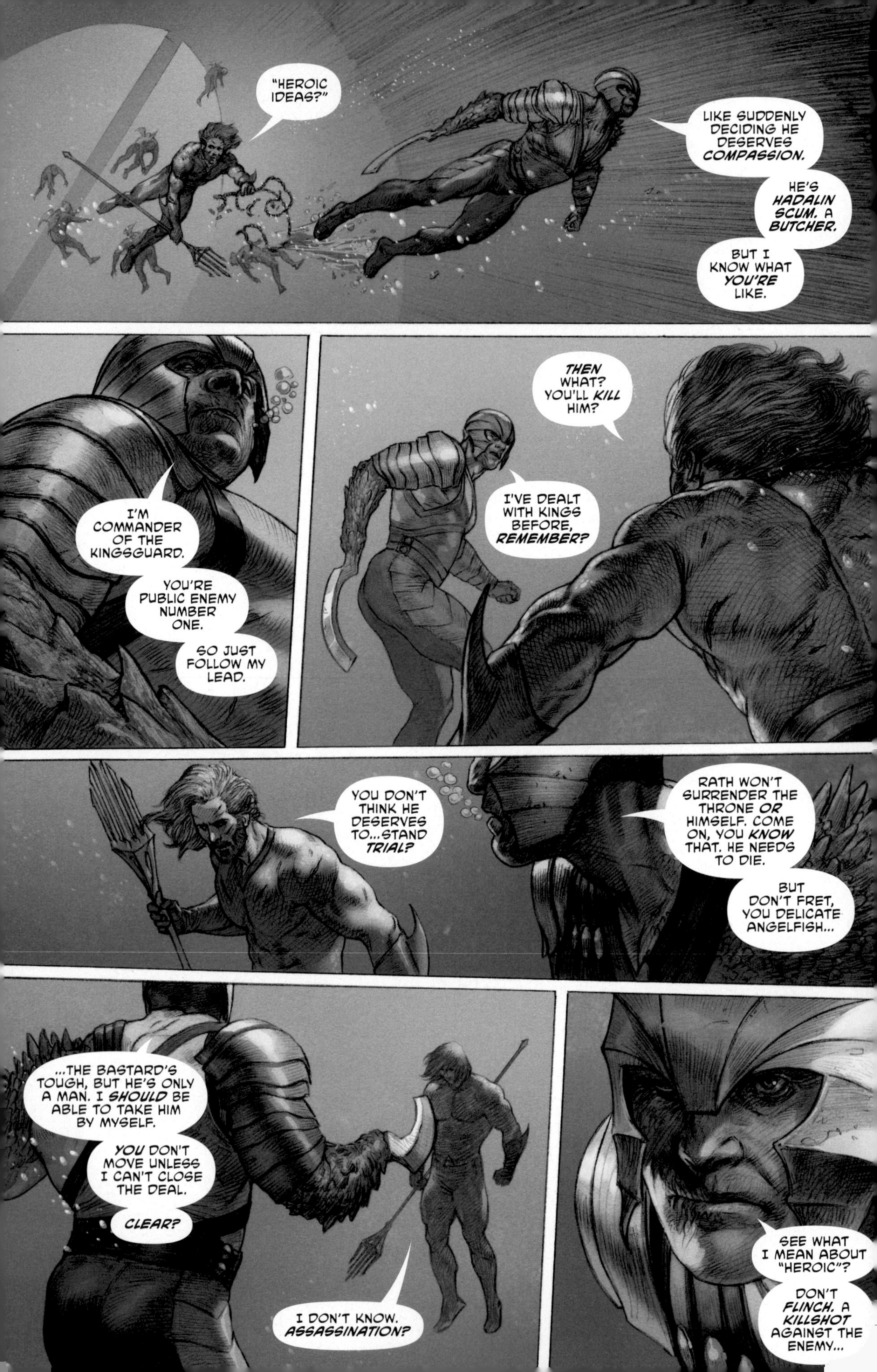
"HEROIC IDEAS?"
LIKE SUDDENLY DECIDING HE DESERVES COMPASSION.
HE'S HADALIN SCUM. A BUTCHER.
BUT I KNOW WHAT YOU'RE LIKE.
I'M COMMANDER OF THE KINGSGUARD.
YOU'RE PUBLIC ENEMY NUMBER ONE.
SO JUST FOLLOW MY LEAD.
THEN WHAT? YOU'LL KILL HIM?
I'VE DEALT WITH KINGS BEFORE, REMEMBER?
YOU DON'T THINK HE DESERVES TO...STAND TRIAL?
RATH WON'T SURRENDER THE THRONE OR HIMSELF. COME ON, YOU KNOW THAT. HE NEEDS TO DIE.
BUT DON'T FRET, YOU DELICATE ANGELFISH...
...THE BASTARD'S TOUGH, BUT HE'S ONLY A MAN. I SHOULD BE ABLE TO TAKE HIM BY MYSELF.
YOU DON'T MOVE UNLESS I CAN'T CLOSE THE DEAL.
CLEAR?
I DON'T KNOW. ASSASSINATION?
SEE WHAT I MEAN ABOUT "HEROIC"?
DON'T FLINCH. A KILLSHOT AGAINST THE ENEMY...

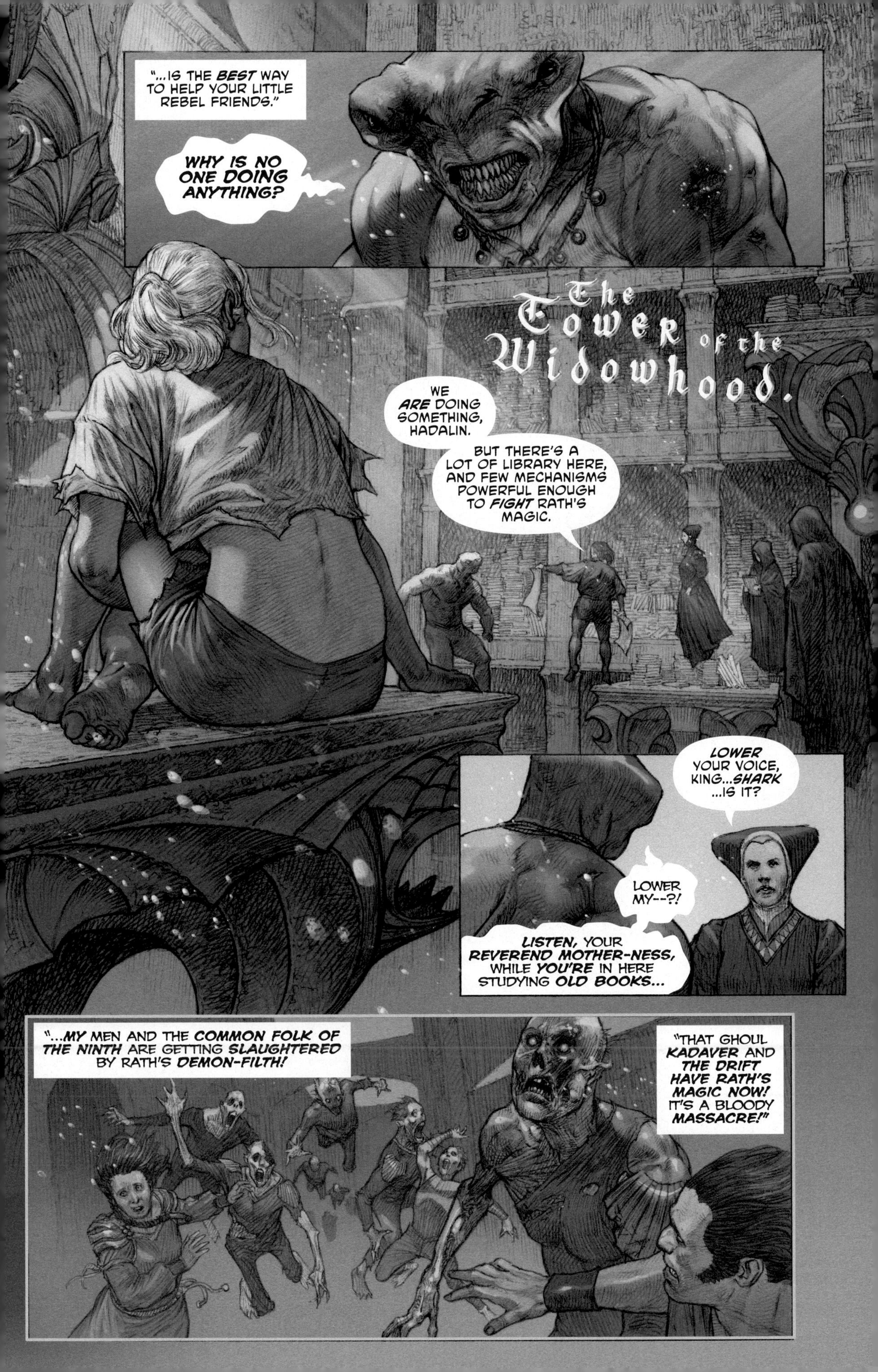

"...IS THE BEST WAY TO HELP YOUR LITTLE REBEL FRIENDS."
WHY IS NO ONE DOING ANYTHING?
The Tower of the Widowhood.
WE ARE DOING SOMETHING, HADALIN.
BUT THERE'S A LOT OF LIBRARY HERE, AND FEW MECHANISMS POWERFUL ENOUGH TO FIGHT RATH'S MAGIC.
LOWER YOUR VOICE, KING...SHARK ...IS IT?
LOWER MY--?!
LISTEN, YOUR REVEREND MOTHER-NESS, WHILE YOU'RE IN HERE STUDYING OLD BOOKS...
"...MY MEN AND THE COMMON FOLK OF THE NINTH ARE GETTING SLAUGHTERED BY RATH'S DEMON-FILTH!
"THAT GHOUL KADAVER AND THE DRIFT HAVE RATH'S MAGIC NOW! IT'S A BLOODY MASSACRE!"

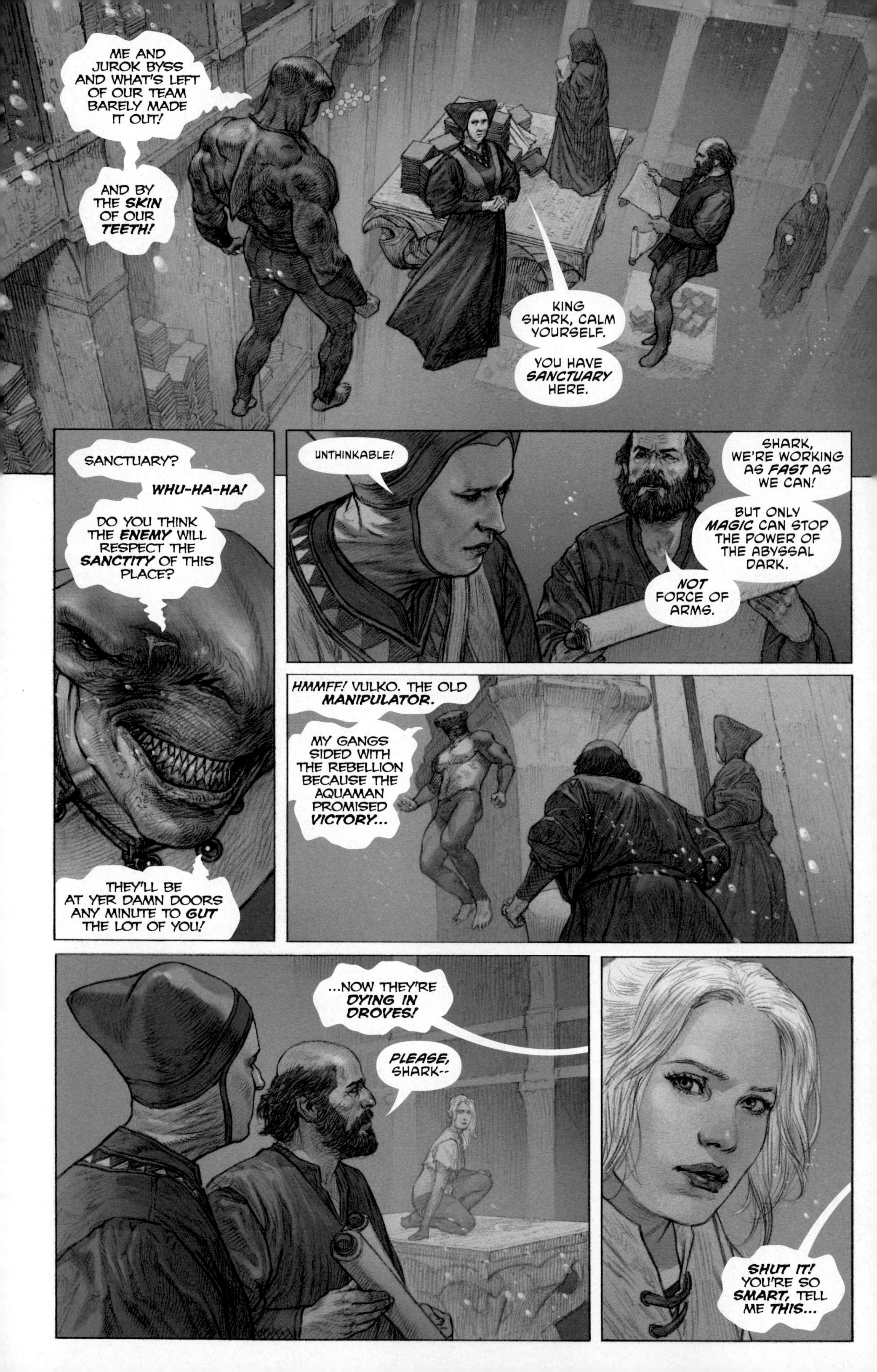

ME AND JUROK BYSS AND WHAT'S LEFT OF OUR TEAM BARELY MADE IT OUT!
AND BY THE SKIN OF OUR TEETH!
KING SHARK, CALM YOURSELF.
YOU HAVE SANCTUARY HERE.
SANCTUARY?
WHU-HA-HA!
DO YOU THINK THE ENEMY WILL RESPECT THE SANCTITY OF THIS PLACE?
THEY'LL BE AT YER DAMN DOORS ANY MINUTE TO GUT THE LOT OF YOU!
UNTHINKABLE!
SHARK, WE'RE WORKING AS FAST AS WE CAN!
BUT ONLY MAGIC CAN STOP THE POWER OF THE ABYSSAL DARK.
NOT FORCE OF ARMS.
HMMFF! VULKO. THE OLD MANIPULATOR.
MY GANGS SIDED WITH THE REBELLION BECAUSE THE AQUAMAN PROMISED VICTORY...
...NOW THEY'RE DYING IN DROVES!
PLEASE, SHARK--
SHUT IT! YOU'RE SO SMART, TELL ME THIS...

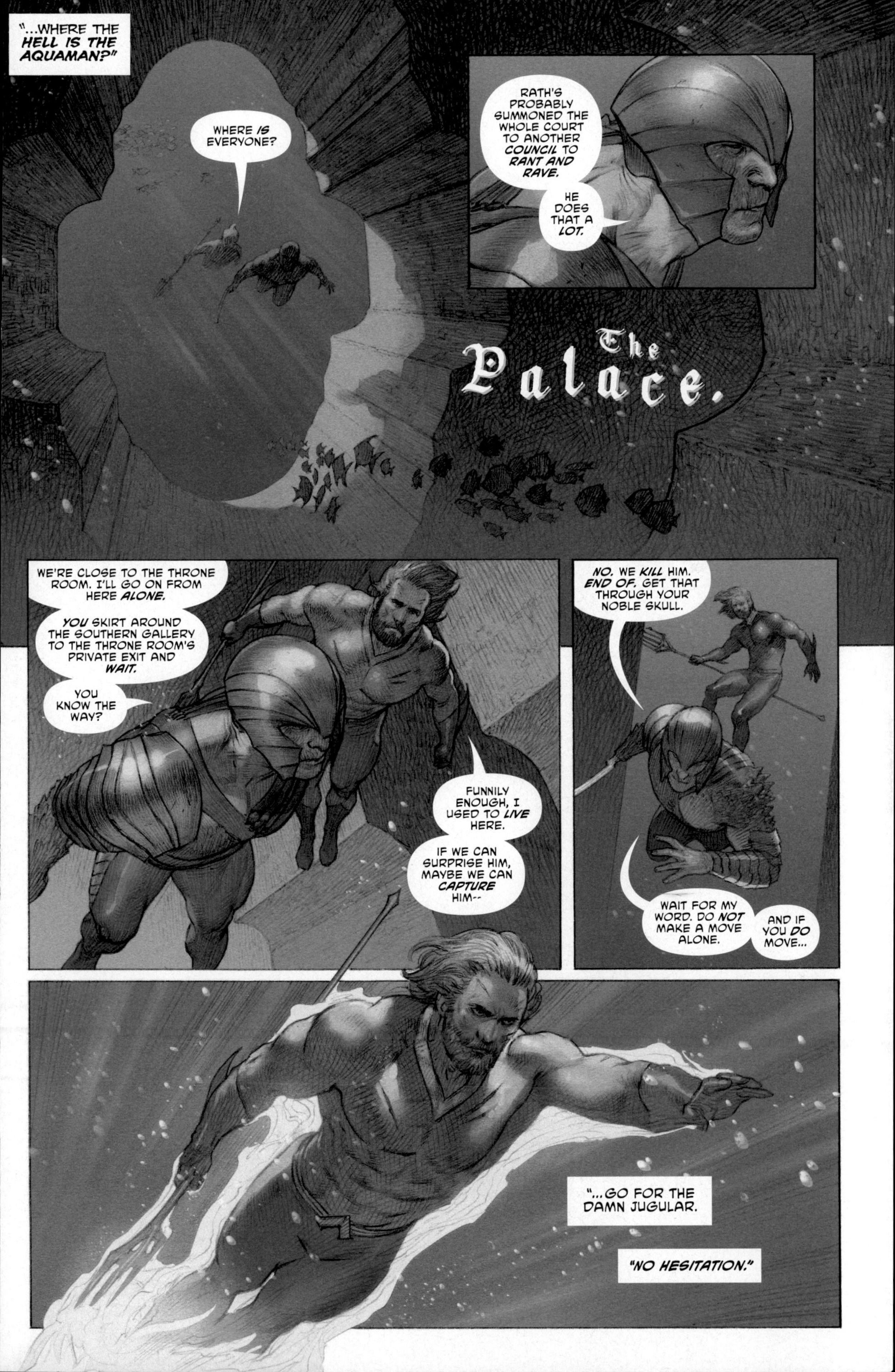
"...WHERE THE *HELL IS THE AQUAMAN?"*
WHERE *IS* EVERYONE?
RATH'S PROBABLY SUMMONED THE WHOLE COURT TO ANOTHER *COUNCIL* TO *RANT AND RAVE.*
HE DOES THAT A *LOT.*
The Palace.
WE'RE CLOSE TO THE THRONE ROOM. I'LL GO ON FROM HERE *ALONE.*
YOU SKIRT AROUND THE SOUTHERN GALLERY TO THE THRONE ROOM'S PRIVATE EXIT AND *WAIT.*
YOU KNOW THE WAY?
FUNNILY ENOUGH, I USED TO *LIVE* HERE.
IF WE CAN SURPRISE HIM, MAYBE WE CAN *CAPTURE* HIM--
NO. WE *KILL* HIM. *END OF.* GET THAT THROUGH YOUR NOBLE SKULL.
WAIT FOR MY WORD. DO *NOT* MAKE A MOVE ALONE.
AND IF YOU *DO* MOVE...
"...GO FOR THE DAMN JUGULAR.
"NO HESITATION."

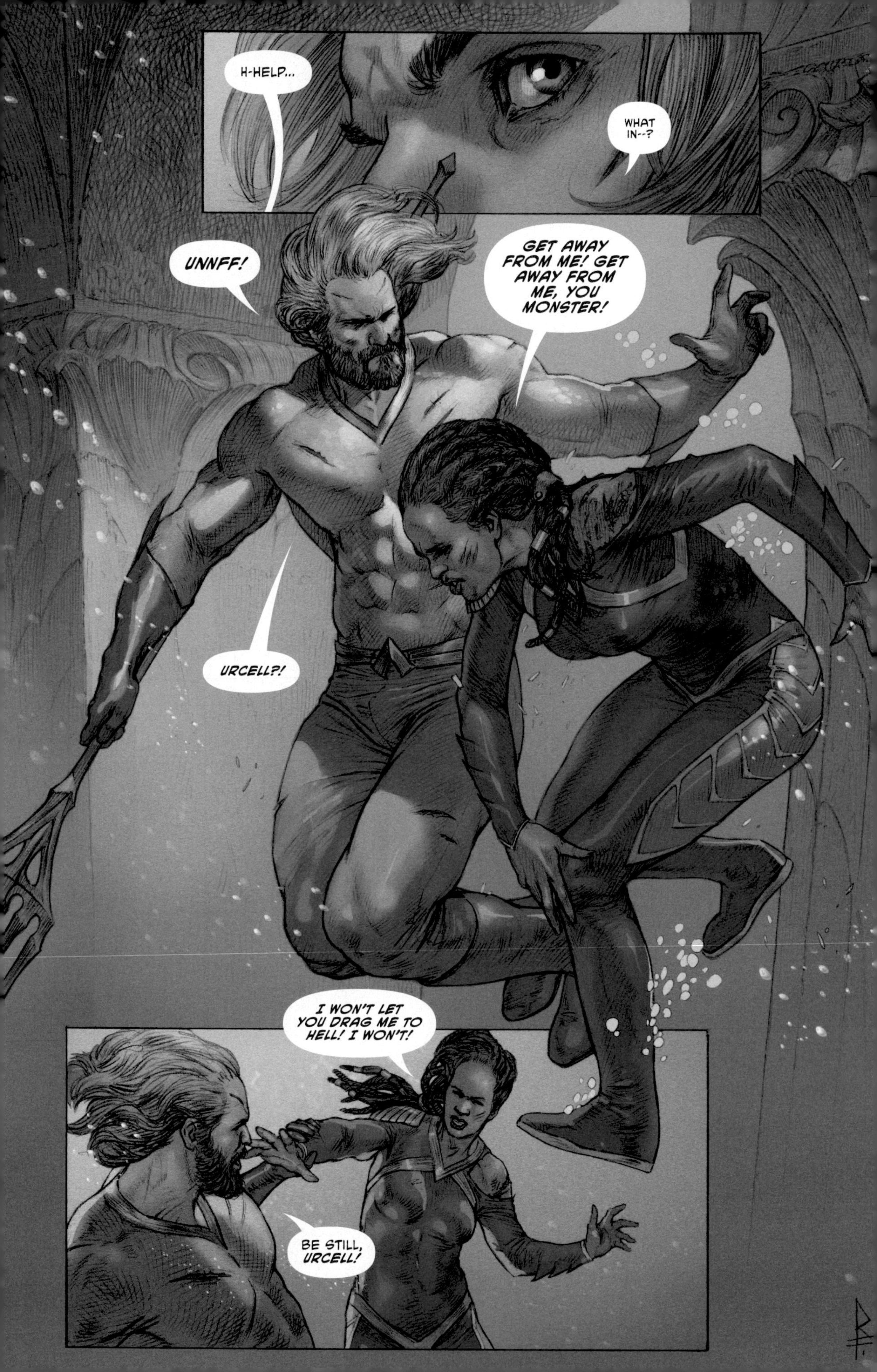
H-HELP...
WHAT IN--?
UNNFF!
GET AWAY FROM ME! GET AWAY FROM ME, YOU MONSTER!
URCELL?!
I WON'T LET YOU DRAG ME TO HELL! I WON'T!
BE STILL, URCELL!

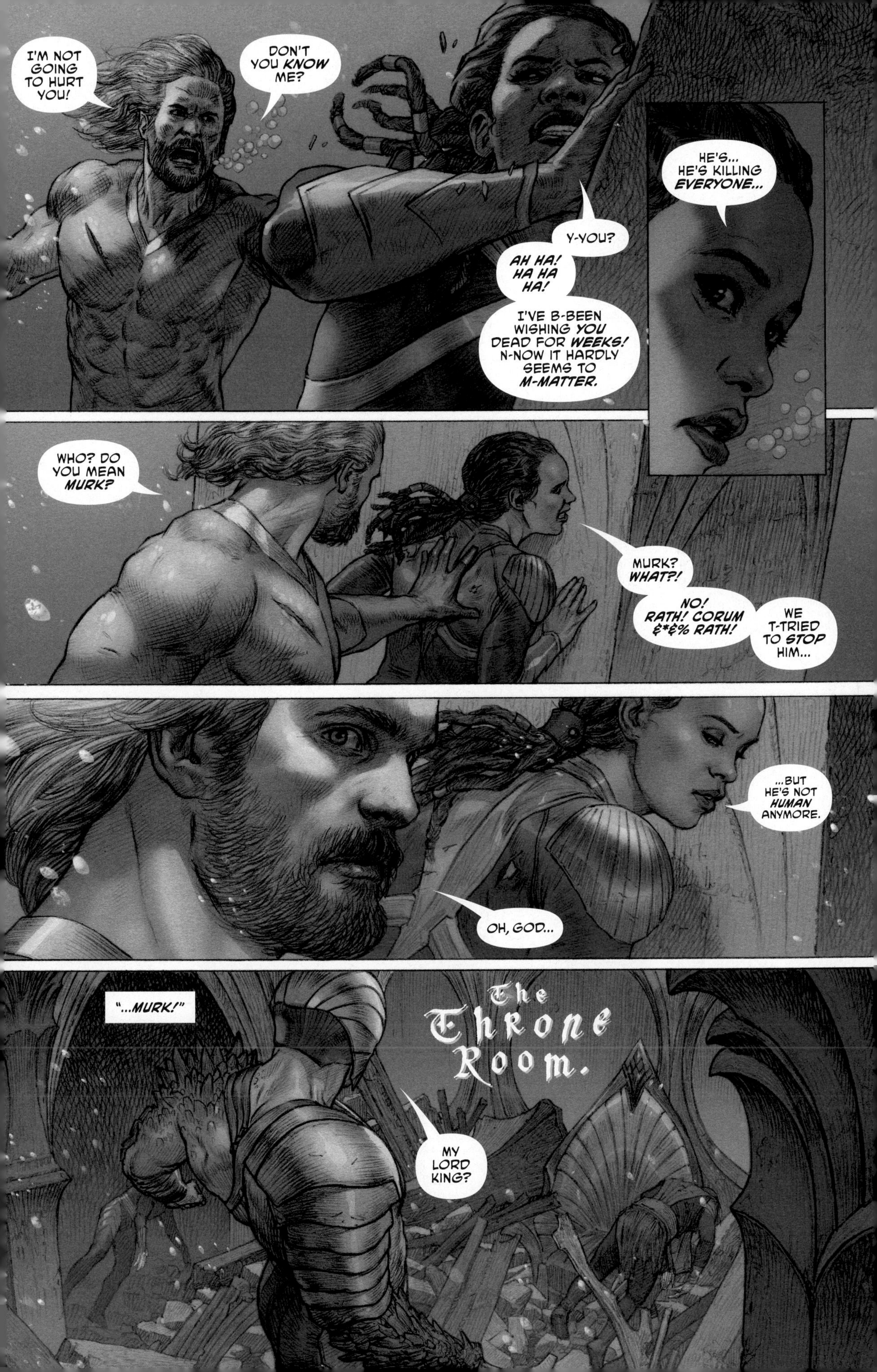

I'M NOT GOING TO HURT YOU!
DON'T YOU *KNOW* ME?
HE'S... HE'S KILLING *EVERYONE*...
Y-YOU?
AH HA! HA HA HA!
I'VE B-BEEN WISHING *YOU* DEAD FOR *WEEKS!* N-NOW IT HARDLY SEEMS TO *M-MATTER.*
WHO? DO YOU MEAN *MURK?*
MURK? *WHAT?!*
NO! RATH! CORUM &&% RATH!*
WE T-TRIED TO *STOP* HIM...
...BUT HE'S NOT *HUMAN* ANYMORE.
OH, GOD...
"...*MURK!*"
The Throne Room.
MY LORD KING?

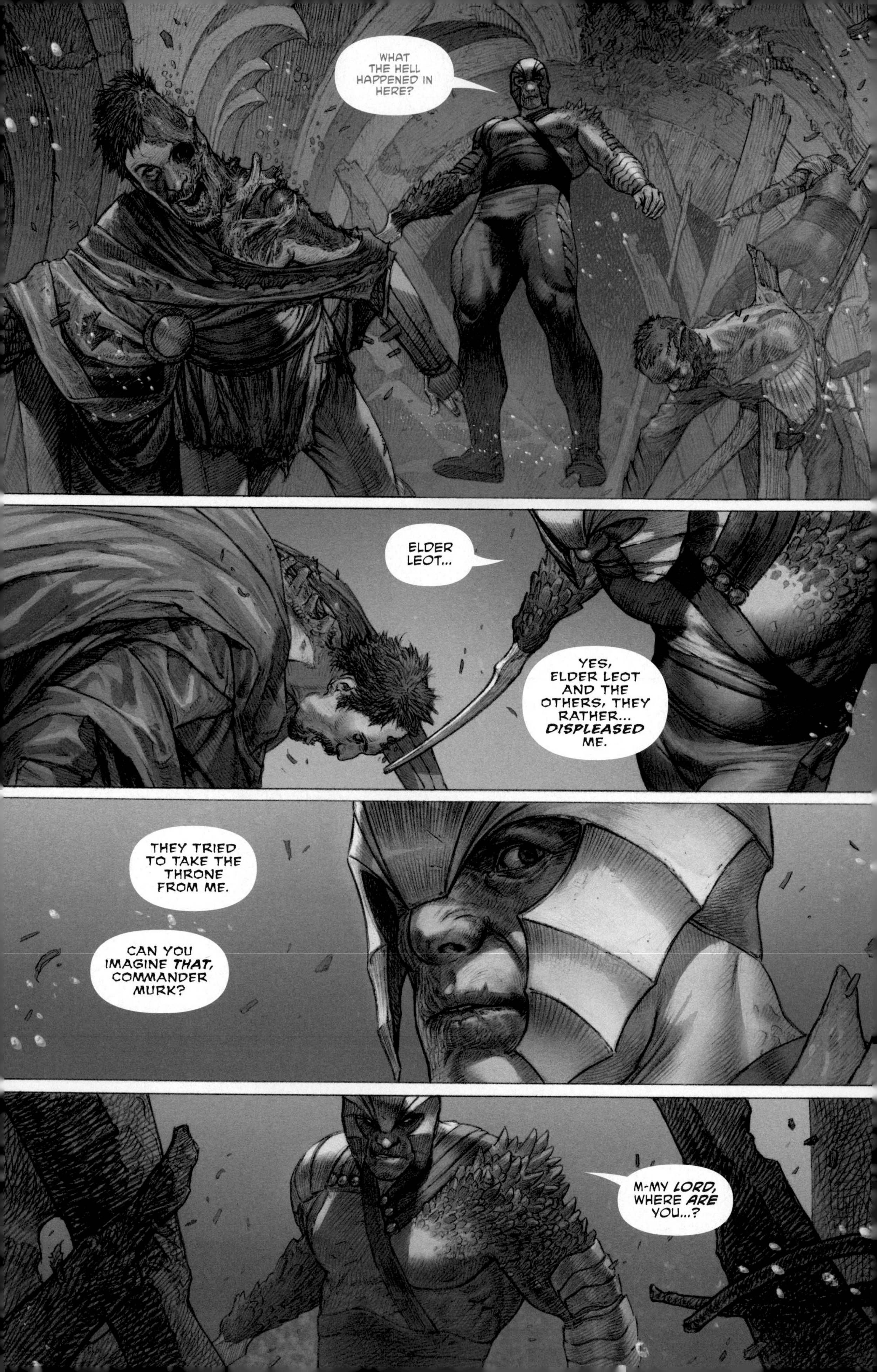
WHAT THE HELL HAPPENED IN HERE?
ELDER LEOT...
YES, ELDER LEOT AND THE OTHERS, THEY RATHER... *DISPLEASED* ME.
THEY TRIED TO TAKE THE THRONE FROM ME.
CAN YOU IMAGINE *THAT,* COMMANDER MURK?
M-MY *LORD,* WHERE *ARE* YOU...?

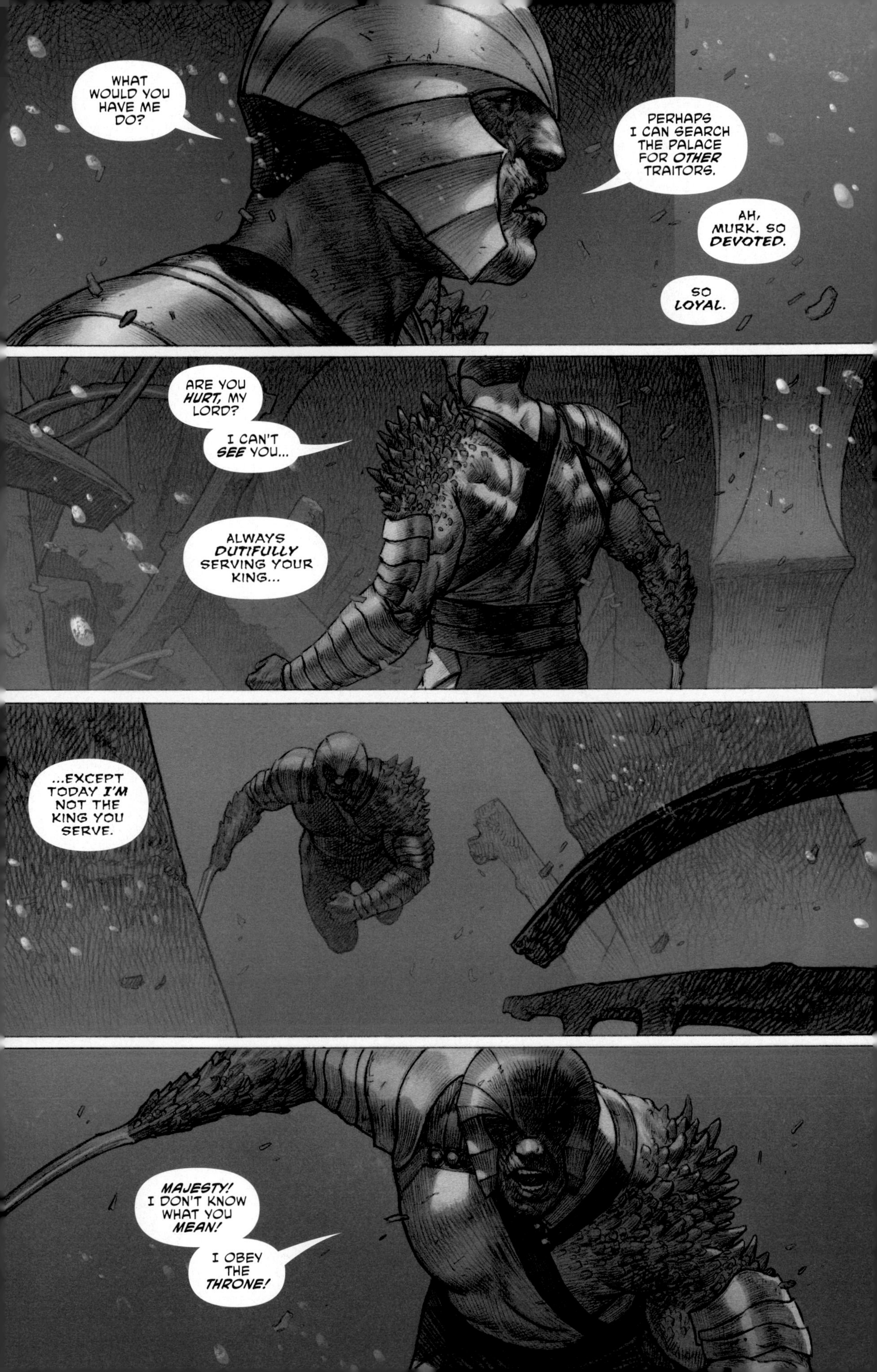
WHAT WOULD YOU HAVE ME DO?
PERHAPS I CAN SEARCH THE PALACE FOR *OTHER* TRAITORS.
AH, MURK. SO *DEVOTED.*
SO *LOYAL.*
ARE YOU *HURT,* MY LORD?
I CAN'T *SEE* YOU...
ALWAYS *DUTIFULLY* SERVING YOUR KING...
...EXCEPT TODAY *I'M* NOT THE KING YOU SERVE.
MAJESTY! I DON'T KNOW WHAT YOU *MEAN!*
I OBEY THE *THRONE!*

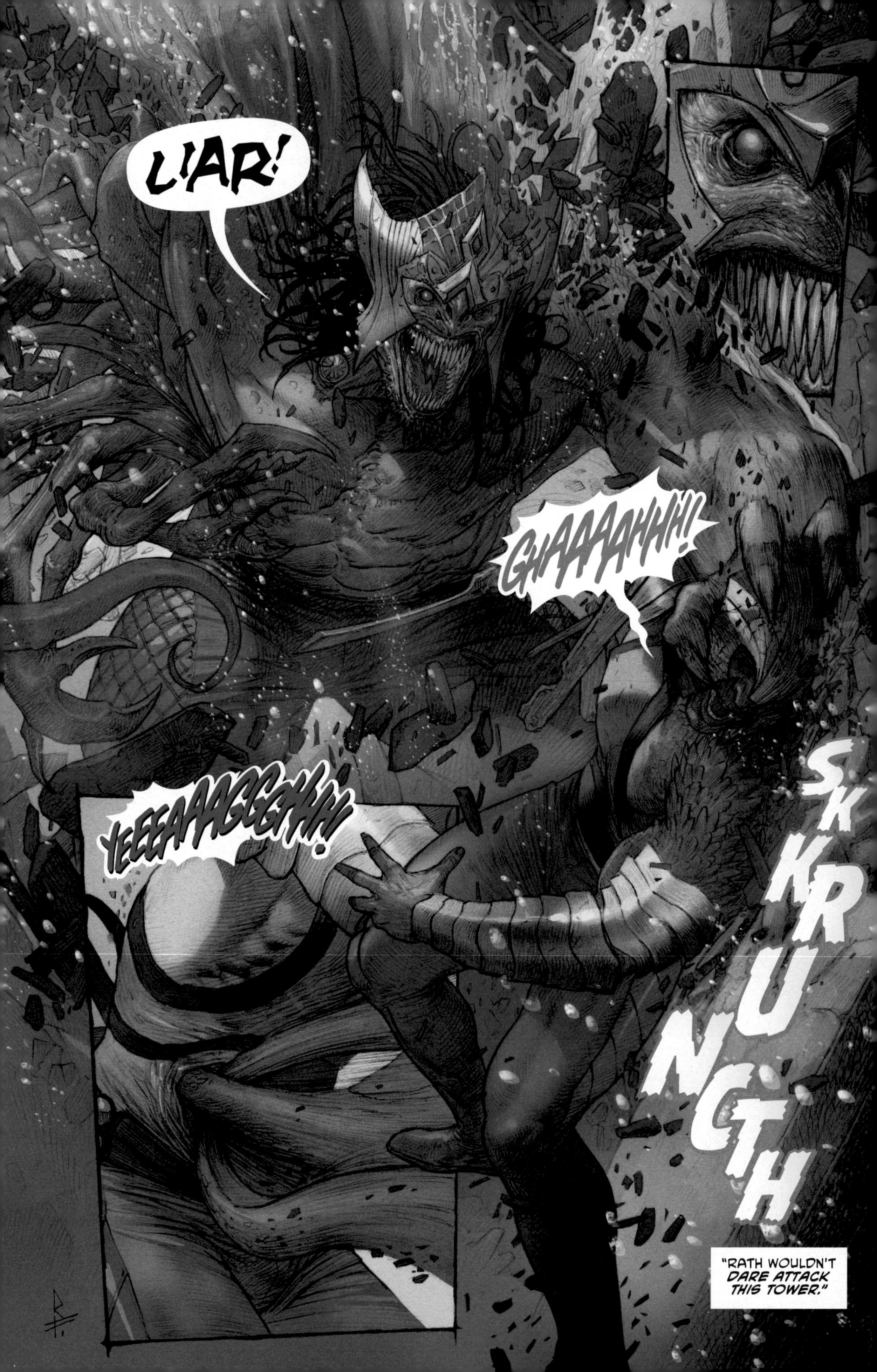

L!AR!
GHAAAAAHHH!
YEEEAAAGGGHHH!
SKKRUNCTH
"RATH WOULDN'T DARE ATTACK THIS TOWER."

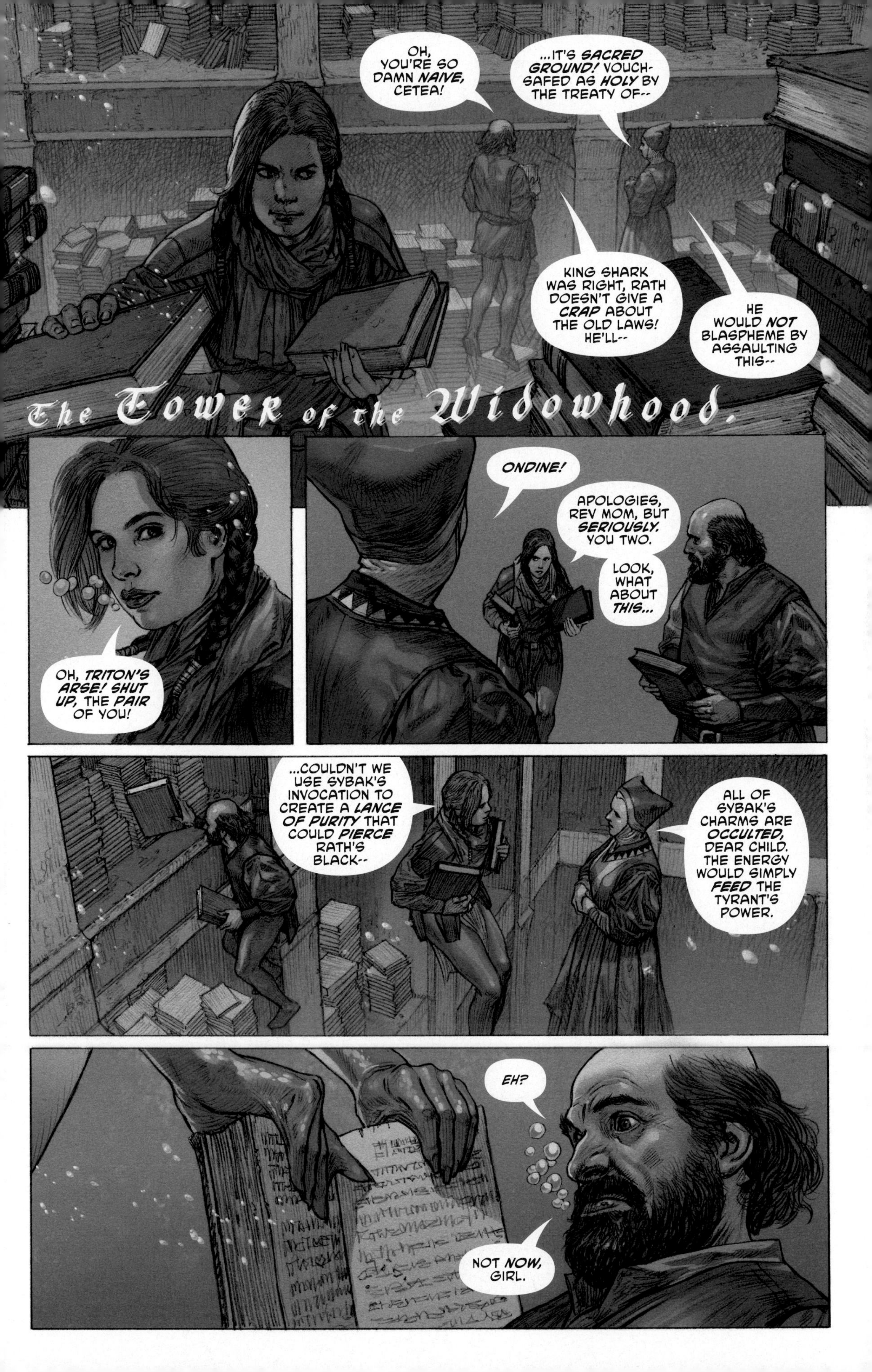
OH, YOU'RE SO DAMN NAIVE, CETEA!
...IT'S SACRED GROUND! VOUCH-SAFED AS HOLY BY THE TREATY OF--
KING SHARK WAS RIGHT, RATH DOESN'T GIVE A CRAP ABOUT THE OLD LAWS! HE'LL--
HE WOULD NOT BLASPHEME BY ASSAULTING THIS--
The Tower of the Widowhood.
OH, TRITON'S ARSE! SHUT UP, THE PAIR OF YOU!
ONDINE!
APOLOGIES, REV MOM, BUT SERIOUSLY. YOU TWO.
LOOK, WHAT ABOUT THIS...
...COULDN'T WE USE SYBAK'S INVOCATION TO CREATE A LANCE OF PURITY THAT COULD PIERCE RATH'S BLACK--
ALL OF SYBAK'S CHARMS ARE OCCULTED, DEAR CHILD. THE ENERGY WOULD SIMPLY FEED THE TYRANT'S POWER.
EH?
NOT NOW, GIRL.

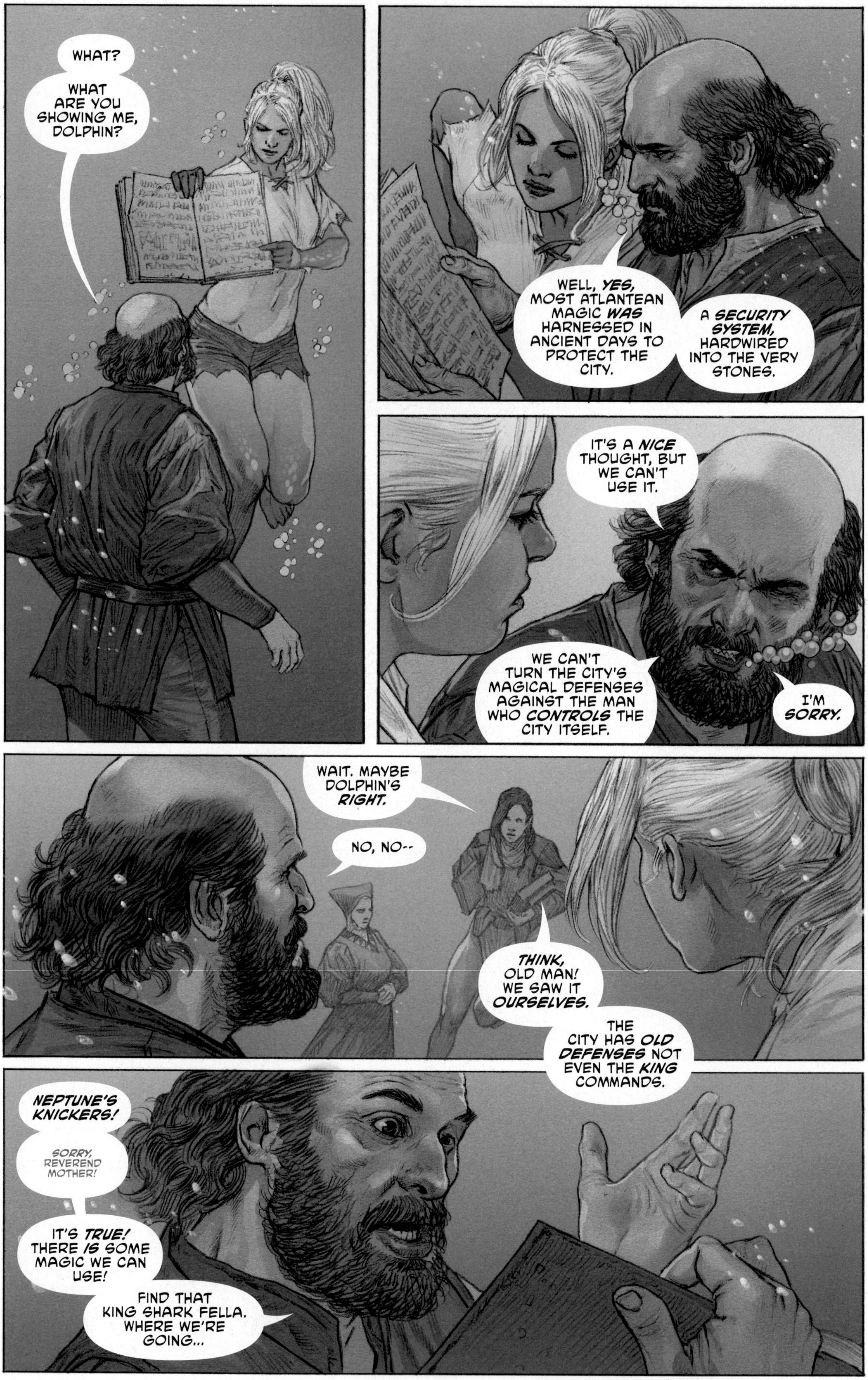
WHAT?
WHAT ARE YOU SHOWING ME, DOLPHIN?
WELL, YES, MOST ATLANTEAN MAGIC WAS HARNESSED IN ANCIENT DAYS TO PROTECT THE CITY.
A SECURITY SYSTEM, HARDWIRED INTO THE VERY STONES.
IT'S A NICE THOUGHT, BUT WE CAN'T USE IT.
WE CAN'T TURN THE CITY'S MAGICAL DEFENSES AGAINST THE MAN WHO CONTROLS THE CITY ITSELF.
I'M SORRY.
WAIT. MAYBE DOLPHIN'S RIGHT.
NO, NO--
THINK, OLD MAN! WE SAW IT OURSELVES.
THE CITY HAS OLD DEFENSES NOT EVEN THE KING COMMANDS.
NEPTUNE'S KNICKERS!
SORRY, REVEREND MOTHER!
IT'S TRUE! THERE IS SOME MAGIC WE CAN USE!
FIND THAT KING SHARK FELLA. WHERE WE'RE GOING...

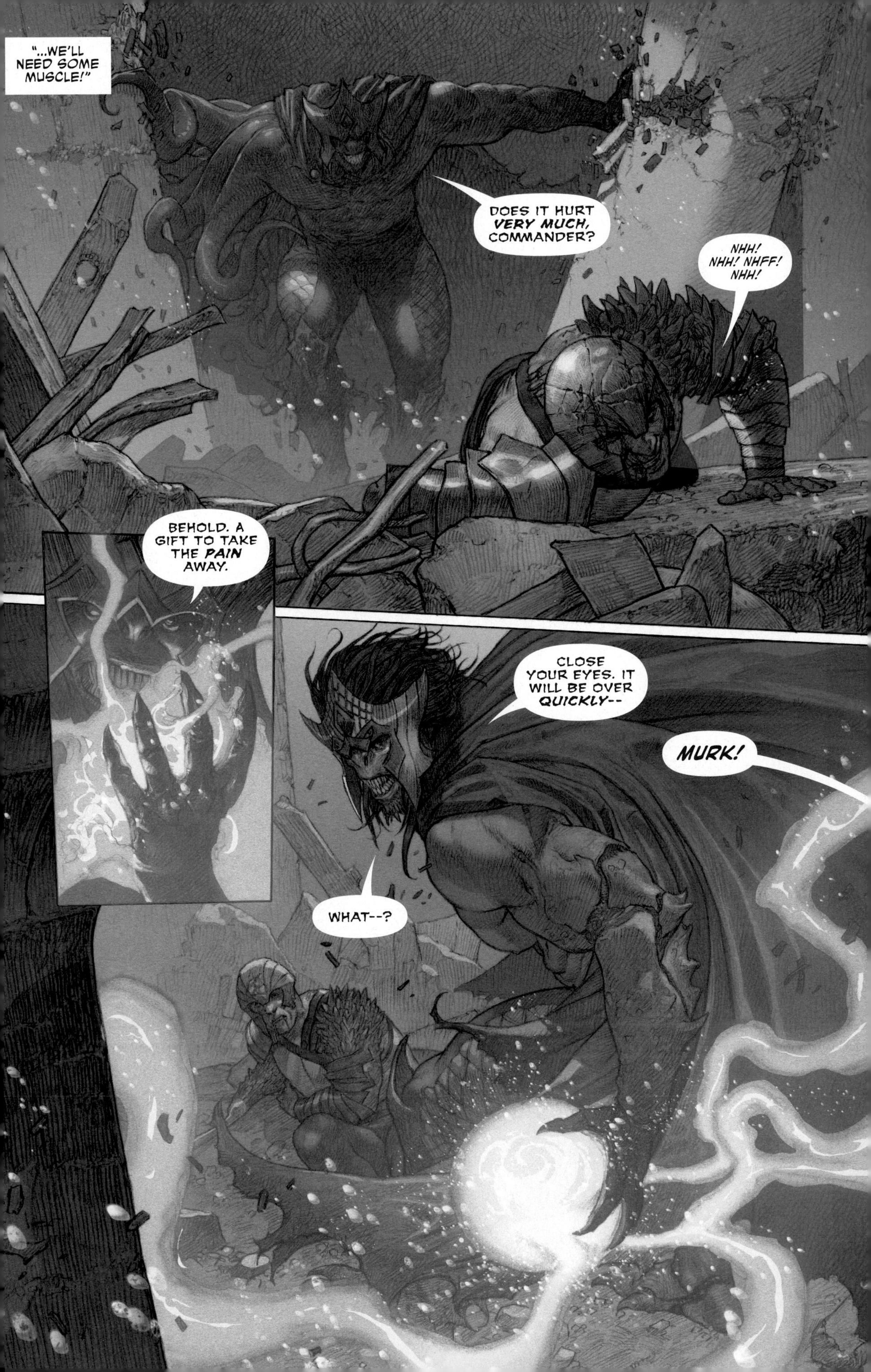
"...WE'LL NEED SOME MUSCLE!"
DOES IT HURT VERY MUCH, COMMANDER?
NHH! NHH! NHFF! NHH!
BEHOLD. A GIFT TO TAKE THE PAIN AWAY.
CLOSE YOUR EYES. IT WILL BE OVER QUICKLY--
MURK!
WHAT--?

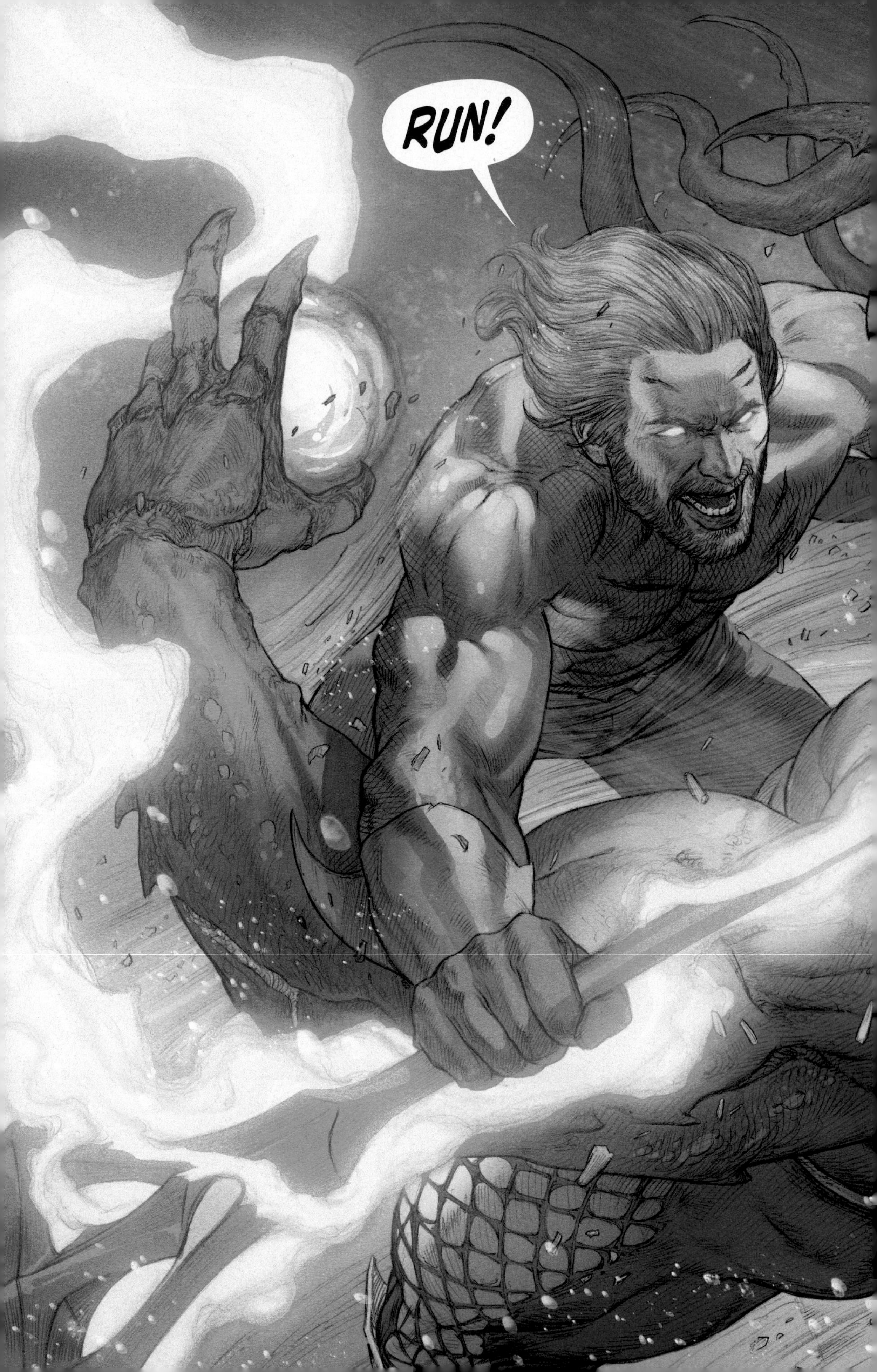
RUN!

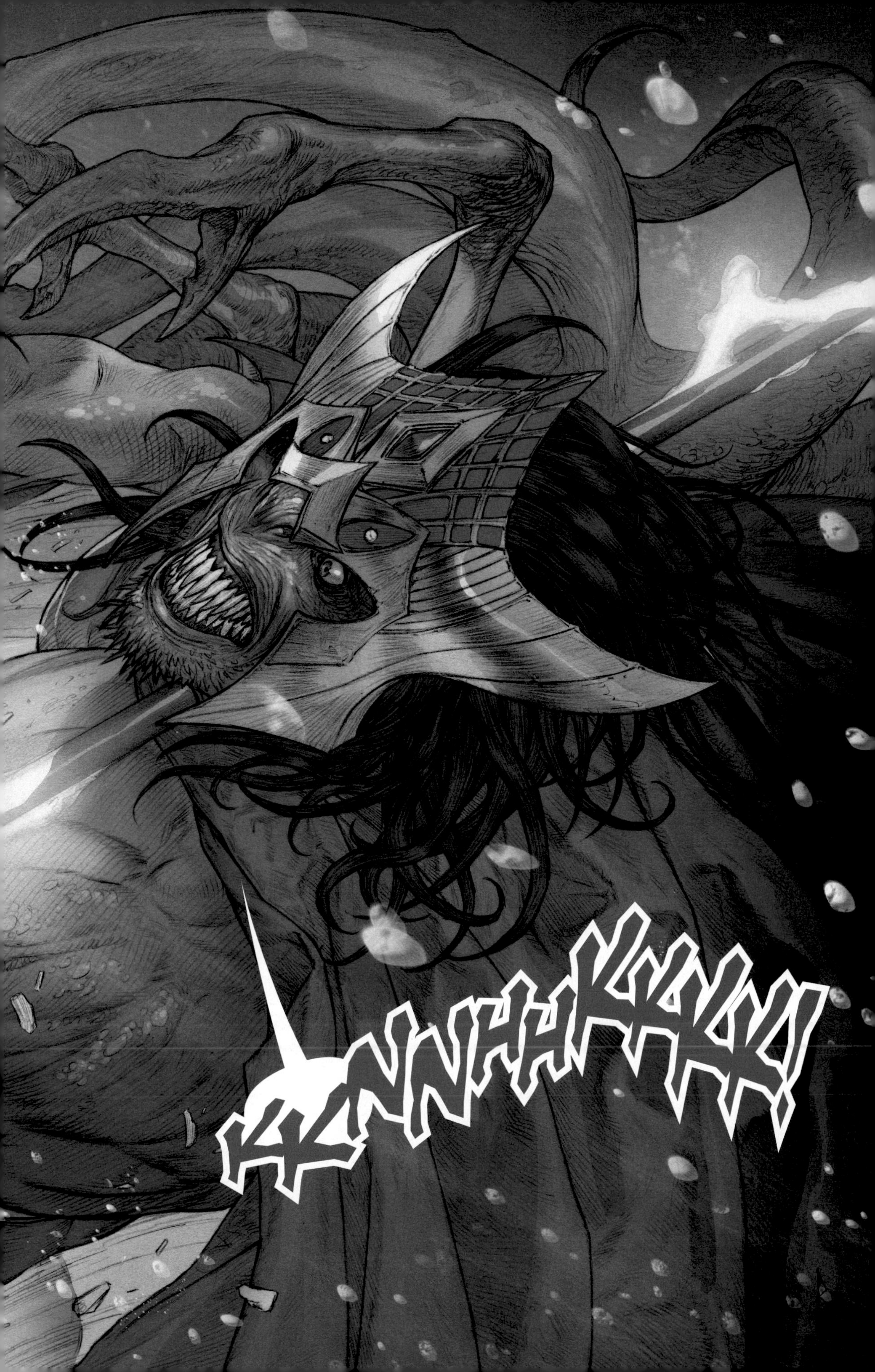
KNNHKKKK!

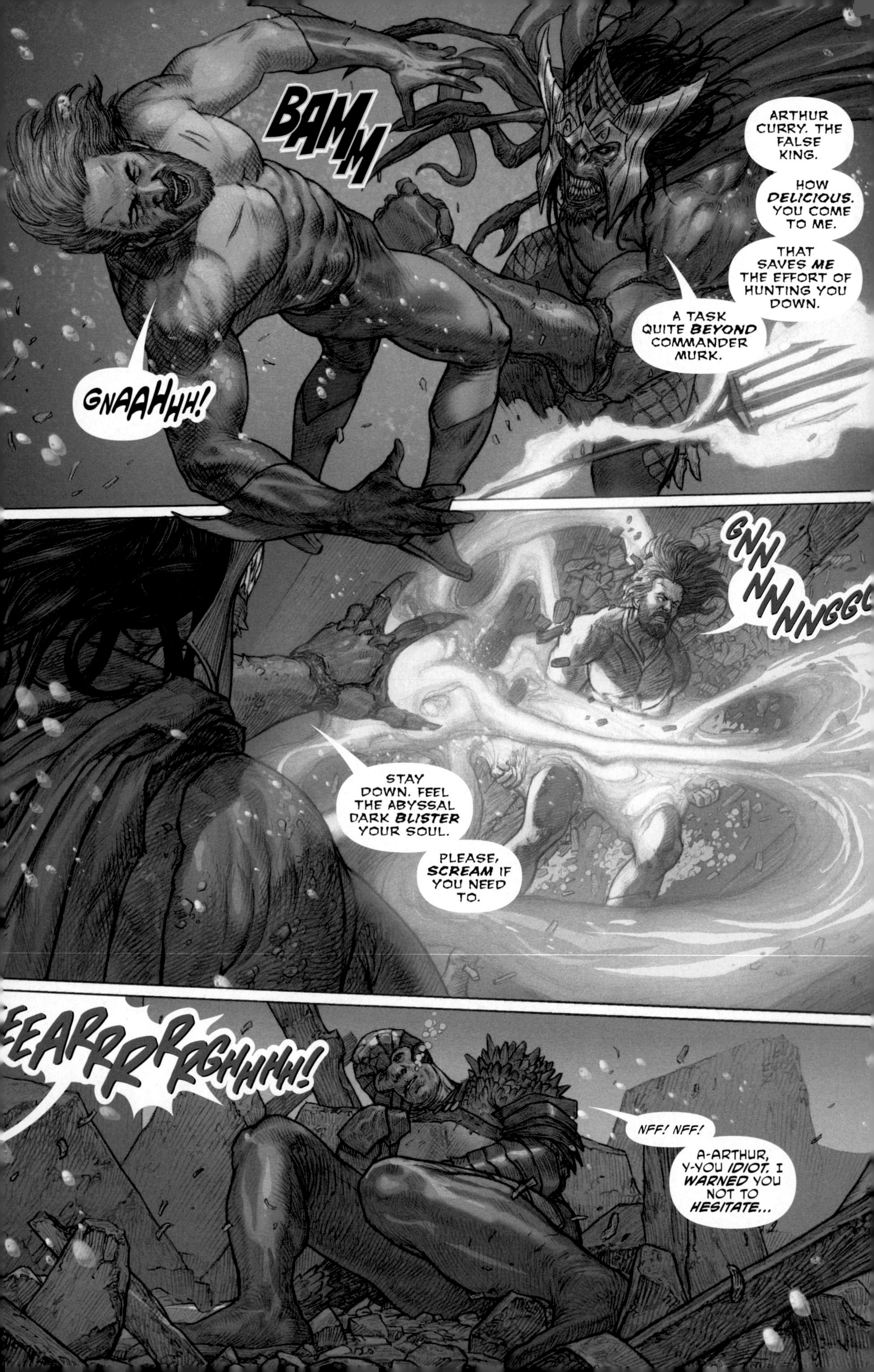
BAMM
ARTHUR CURRY. THE FALSE KING.
HOW DELICIOUS. YOU COME TO ME.
THAT SAVES ME THE EFFORT OF HUNTING YOU DOWN.
A TASK QUITE BEYOND COMMANDER MURK.
GNAAHHH!
GNNNNNGGG
STAY DOWN. FEEL THE ABYSSAL DARK BLISTER YOUR SOUL.
PLEASE, SCREAM IF YOU NEED TO.
EEARRRRGHHHH!
NFF! NFF!
A-ARTHUR, Y-YOU IDIOT. I WARNED YOU NOT TO HESITATE...

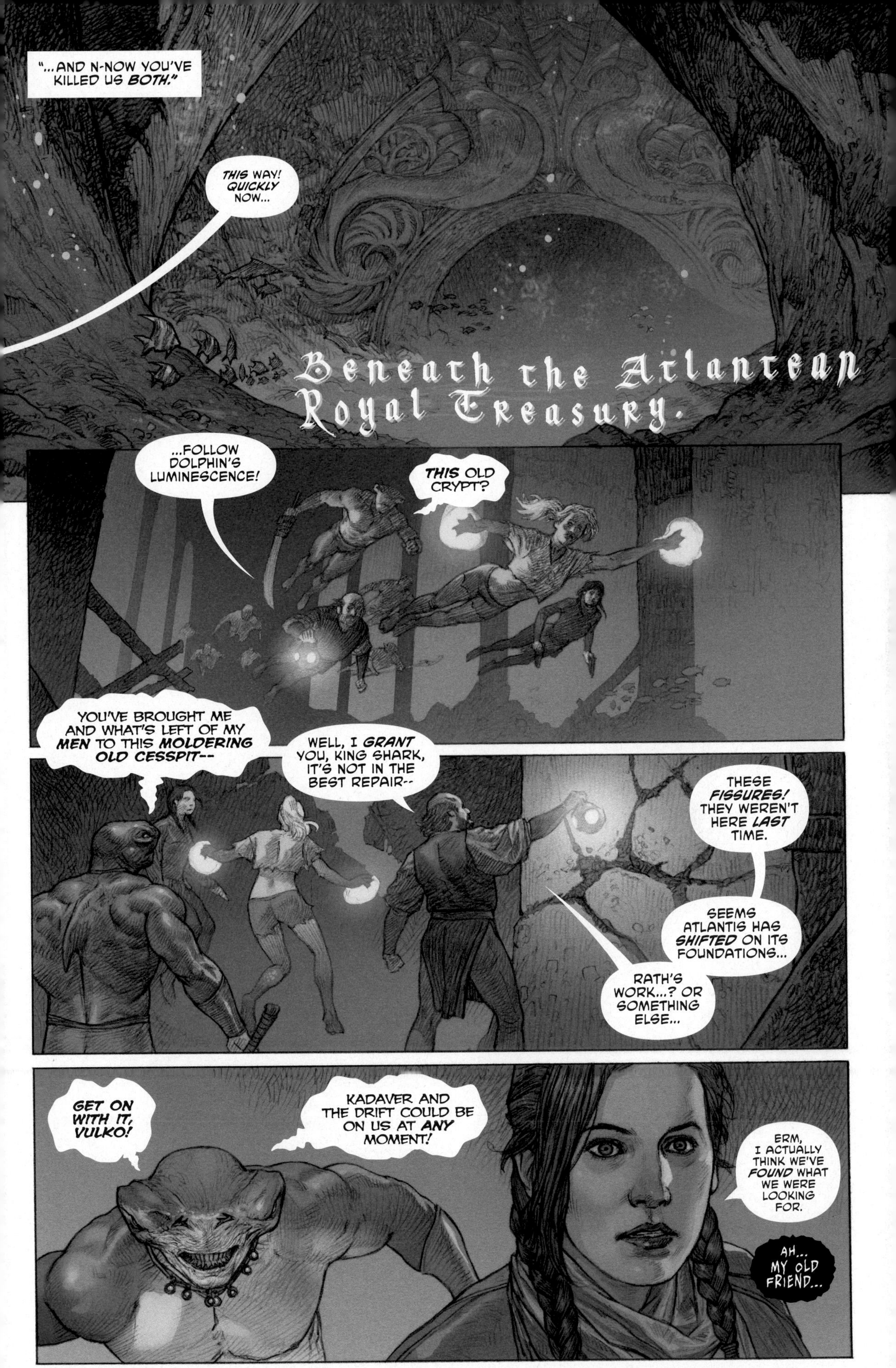
"...AND N-NOW YOU'VE KILLED US BOTH."
THIS WAY! QUICKLY NOW...
Beneath the Atlantean Royal Treasury.
...FOLLOW DOLPHIN'S LUMINESCENCE!
THIS OLD CRYPT?
YOU'VE BROUGHT ME AND WHAT'S LEFT OF MY MEN TO THIS MOLDERING OLD CESSPIT--
WELL, I GRANT YOU, KING SHARK, IT'S NOT IN THE BEST REPAIR--
THESE FISSURES! THEY WEREN'T HERE LAST TIME.
SEEMS ATLANTIS HAS SHIFTED ON ITS FOUNDATIONS...
RATH'S WORK...? OR SOMETHING ELSE...
GET ON WITH IT, VULKO!
KADAVER AND THE DRIFT COULD BE ON US AT ANY MOMENT!
ERM, I ACTUALLY THINK WE'VE FOUND WHAT WE WERE LOOKING FOR.
AH... MY OLD FRIEND...

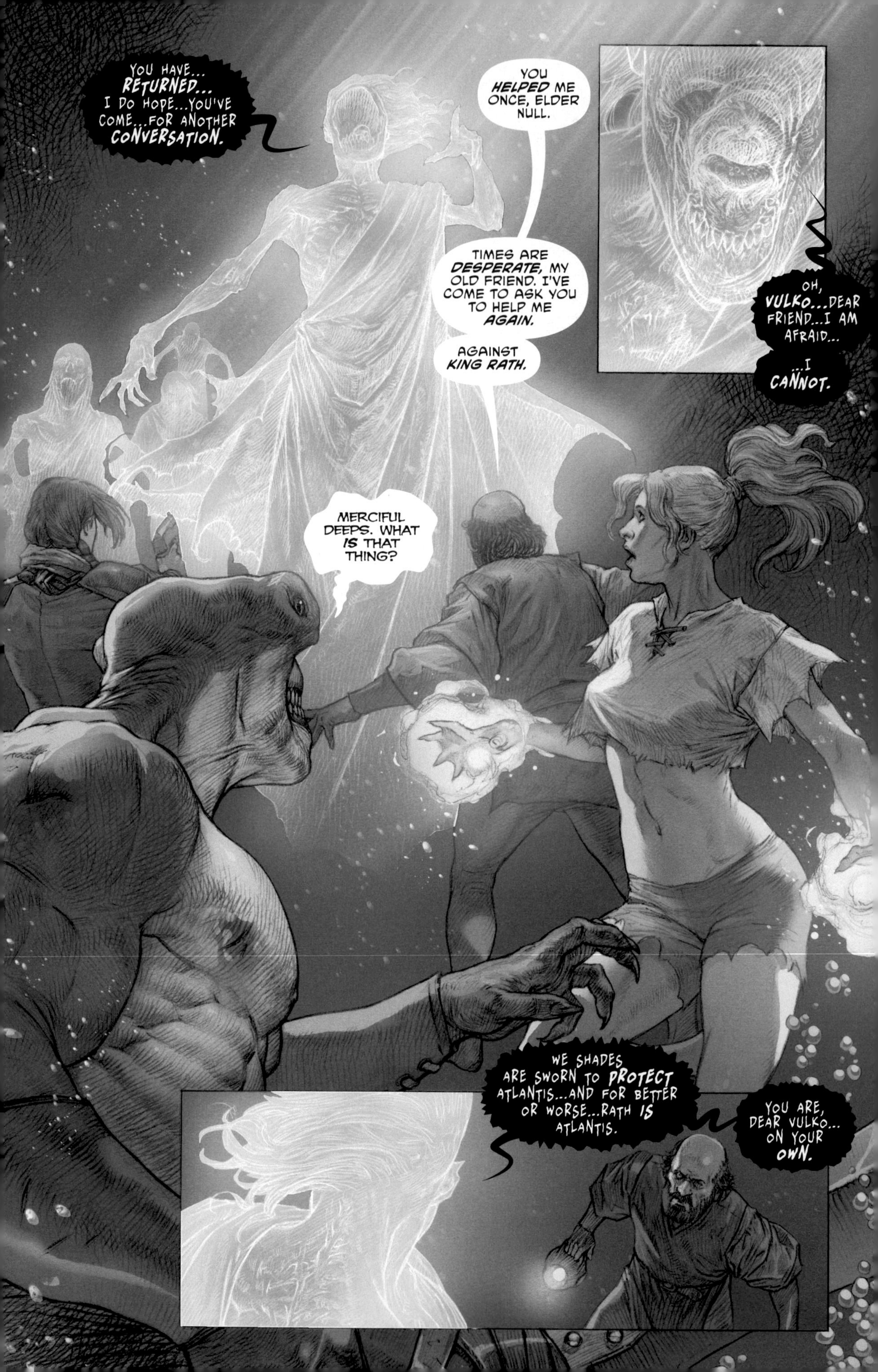
YOU HAVE... RETURNED... I DO HOPE...YOU'VE COME...FOR ANOTHER CONVERSATION.
YOU HELPED ME ONCE, ELDER NULL.
TIMES ARE DESPERATE, MY OLD FRIEND. I'VE COME TO ASK YOU TO HELP ME AGAIN.
AGAINST KING RATH.
OH, VULKO...DEAR FRIEND...I AM AFRAID...
...I CANNOT.
MERCIFUL DEEPS. WHAT IS THAT THING?
WE SHADES ARE SWORN TO PROTECT ATLANTIS...AND FOR BETTER OR WORSE...RATH IS ATLANTIS.
YOU ARE, DEAR VULKO... ON YOUR OWN.

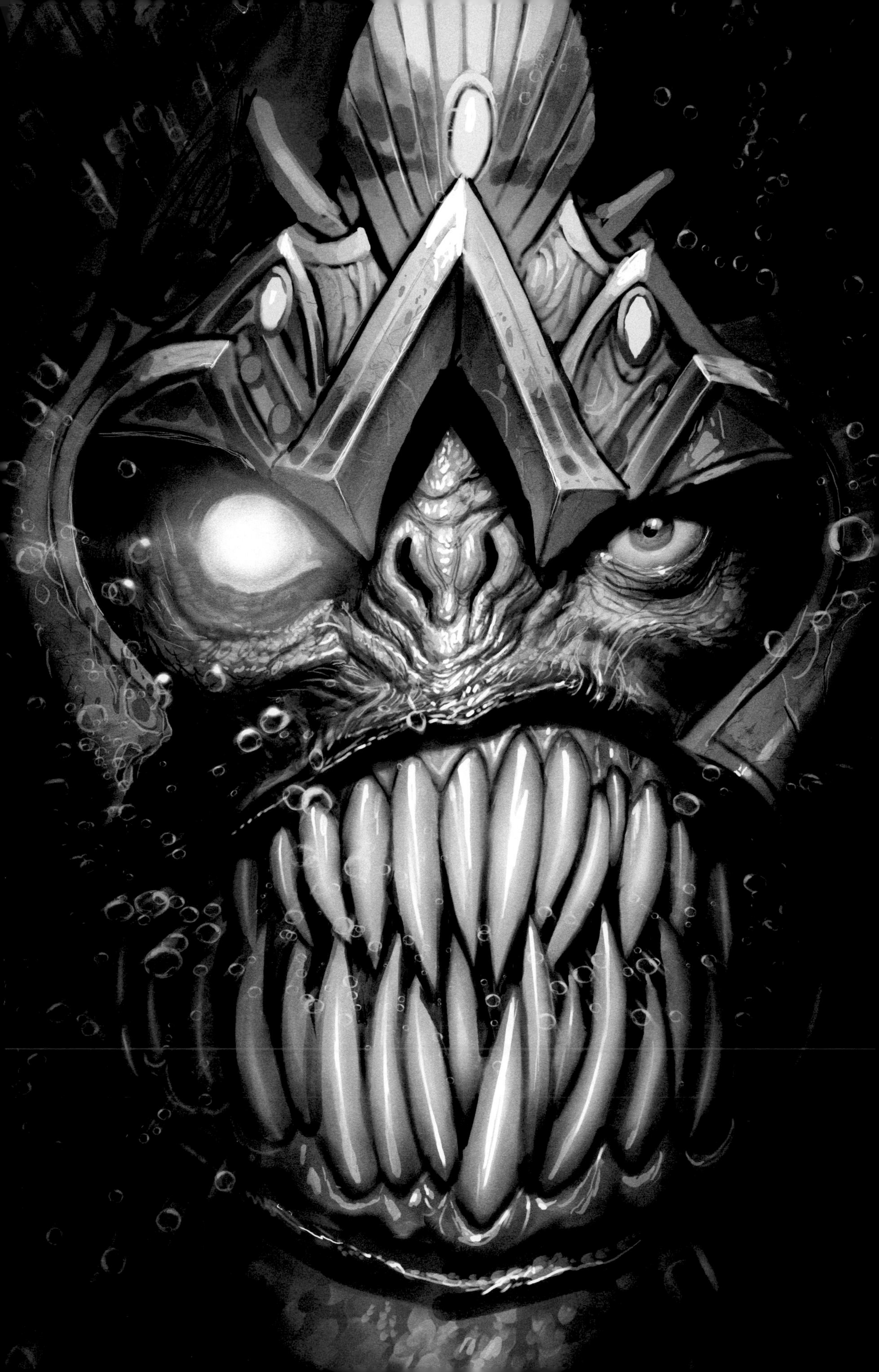

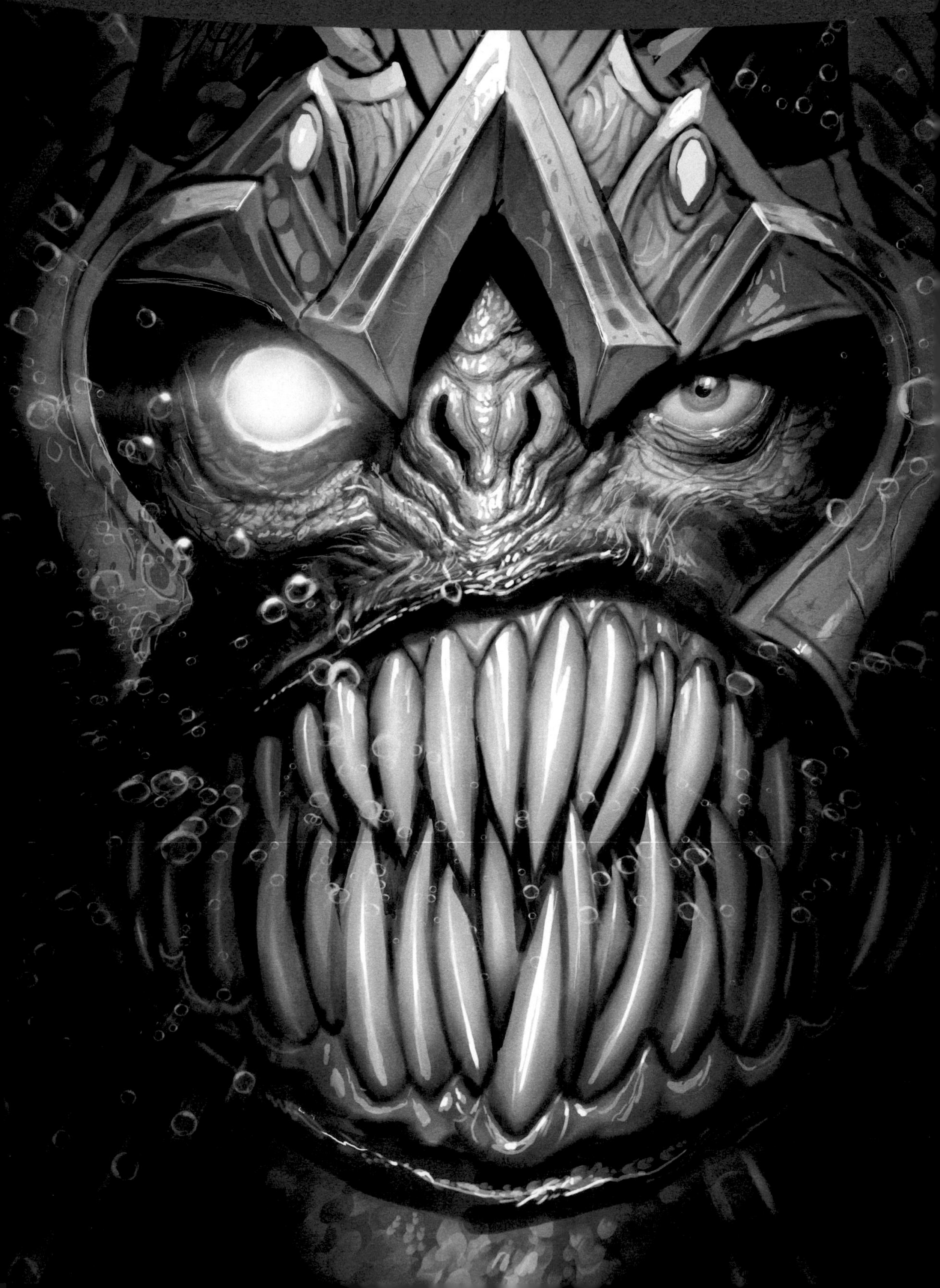

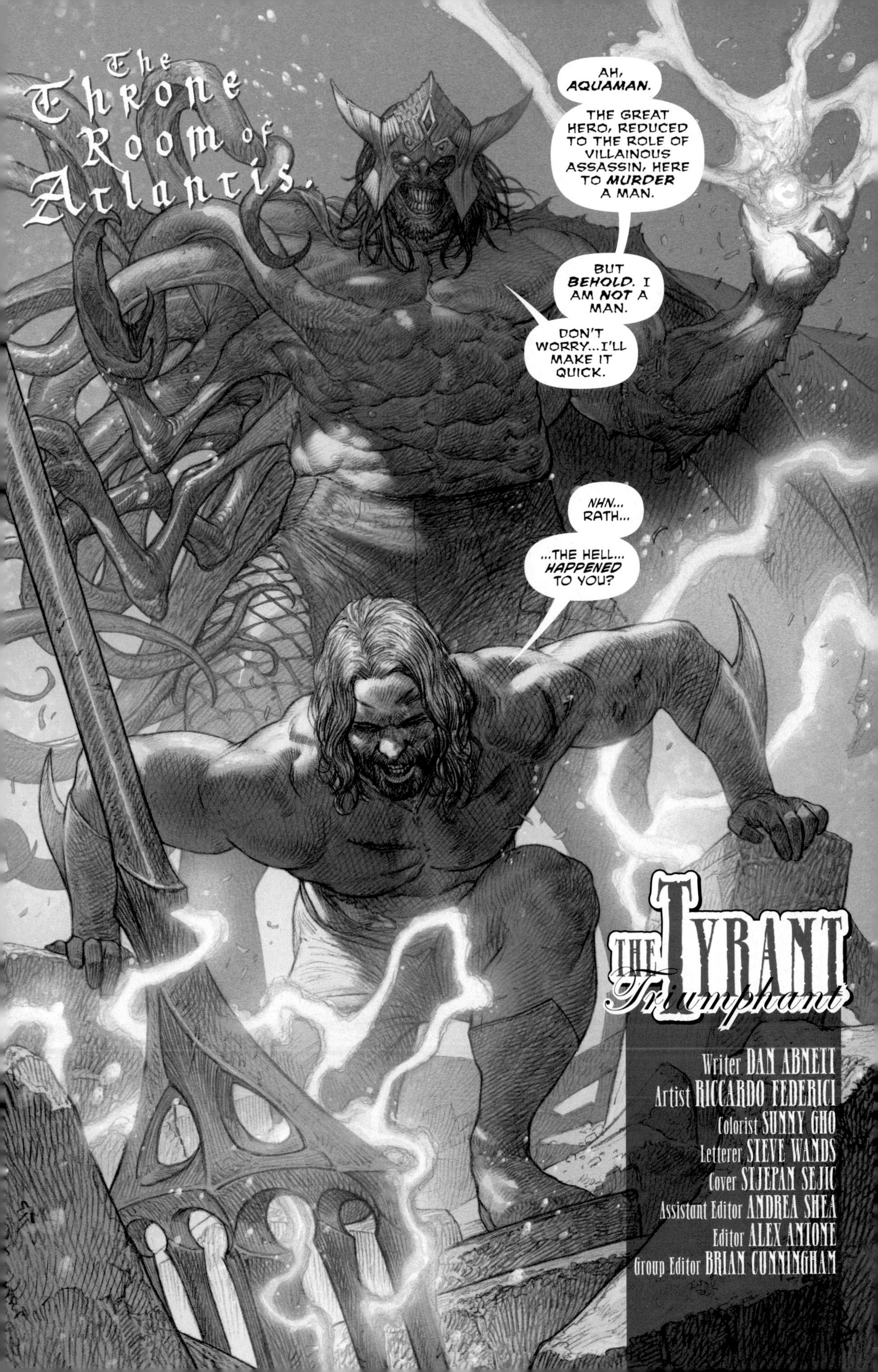

The Throne Room of Atlantis.
AH, AQUAMAN.
THE GREAT HERO, REDUCED TO THE ROLE OF VILLAINOUS ASSASSIN, HERE TO MURDER A MAN.
BUT BEHOLD. I AM NOT A MAN.
DON'T WORRY...I'LL MAKE IT QUICK.
NHN... RATH...
...THE HELL... HAPPENED TO YOU?
THE TYRANT Triumphant
Writer DAN ABNETT
Artist RICCARDO FEDERICI
Colorist SUNNY GHO
Letterer STEVE WANDS
Cover SIJEPAN SEJIC
Assistant Editor ANDREA SHEA
Editor ALEX ANTONE
Group Editor BRIAN CUNNINGHAM

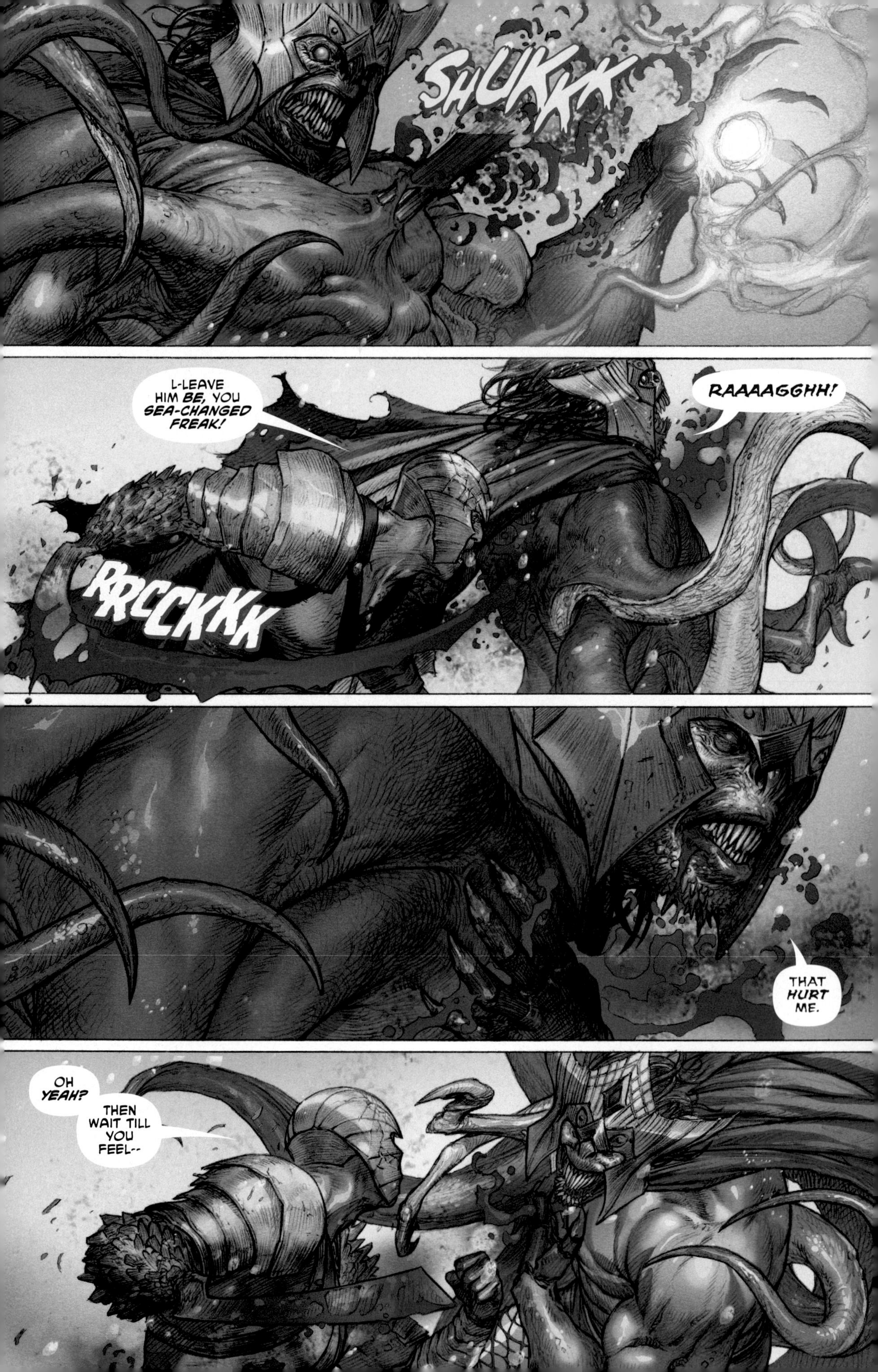
SHUKKK
L-LEAVE HIM BE, YOU SEA-CHANGED FREAK!
RAAAAGGHH!
RRCCKKK
THAT HURT ME.
OH YEAH?
THEN WAIT TILL YOU FEEL--

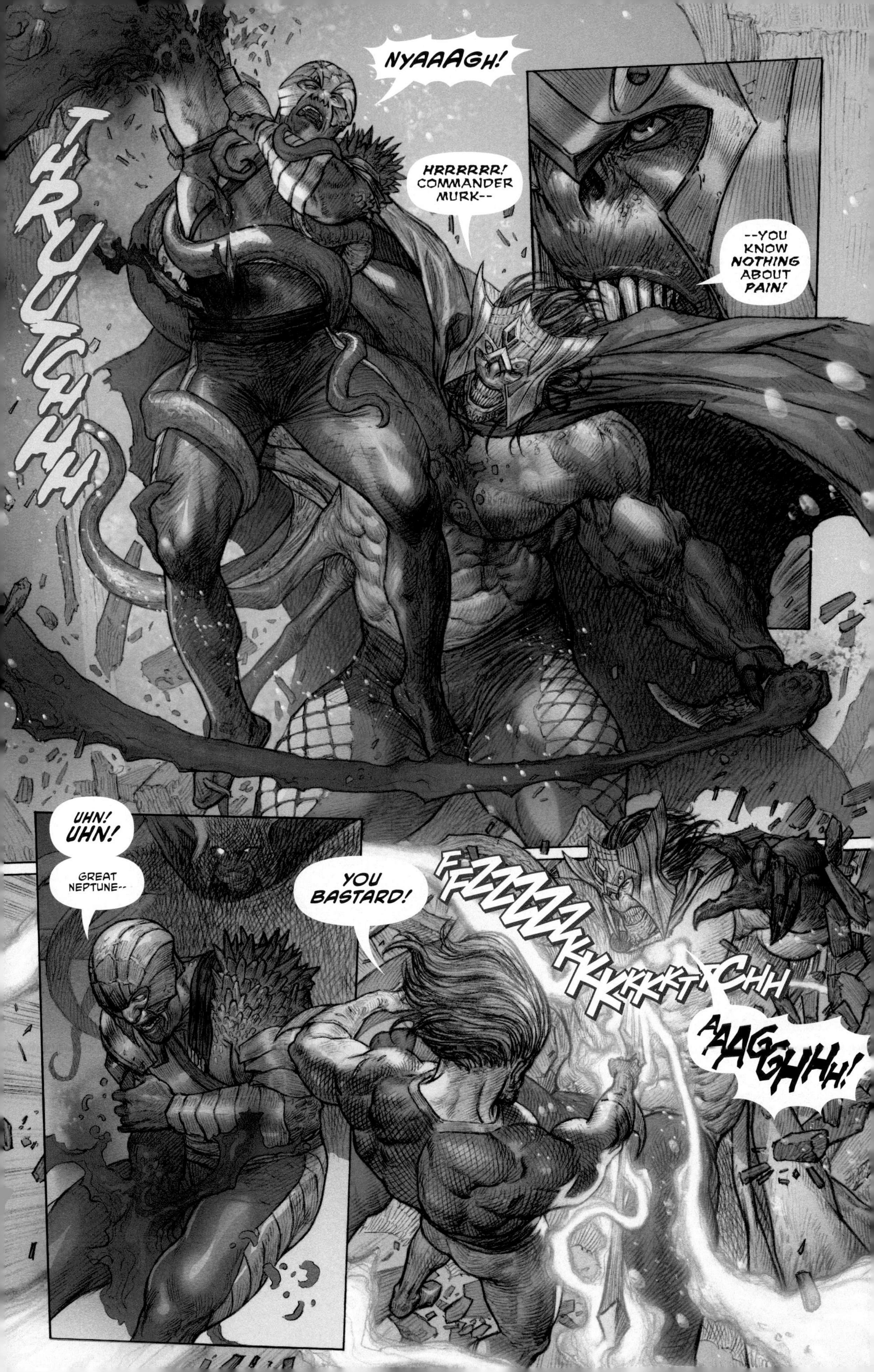
THRUUTCHHH
NYAAAGH!
HRRRRRR! COMMANDER MURK--
--YOU KNOW NOTHING ABOUT PAIN!
UHN! UHN!
GREAT NEPTUNE--
YOU BASTARD!
FFZZZZZKKKKKKTTCHH
AAAGGHHH!

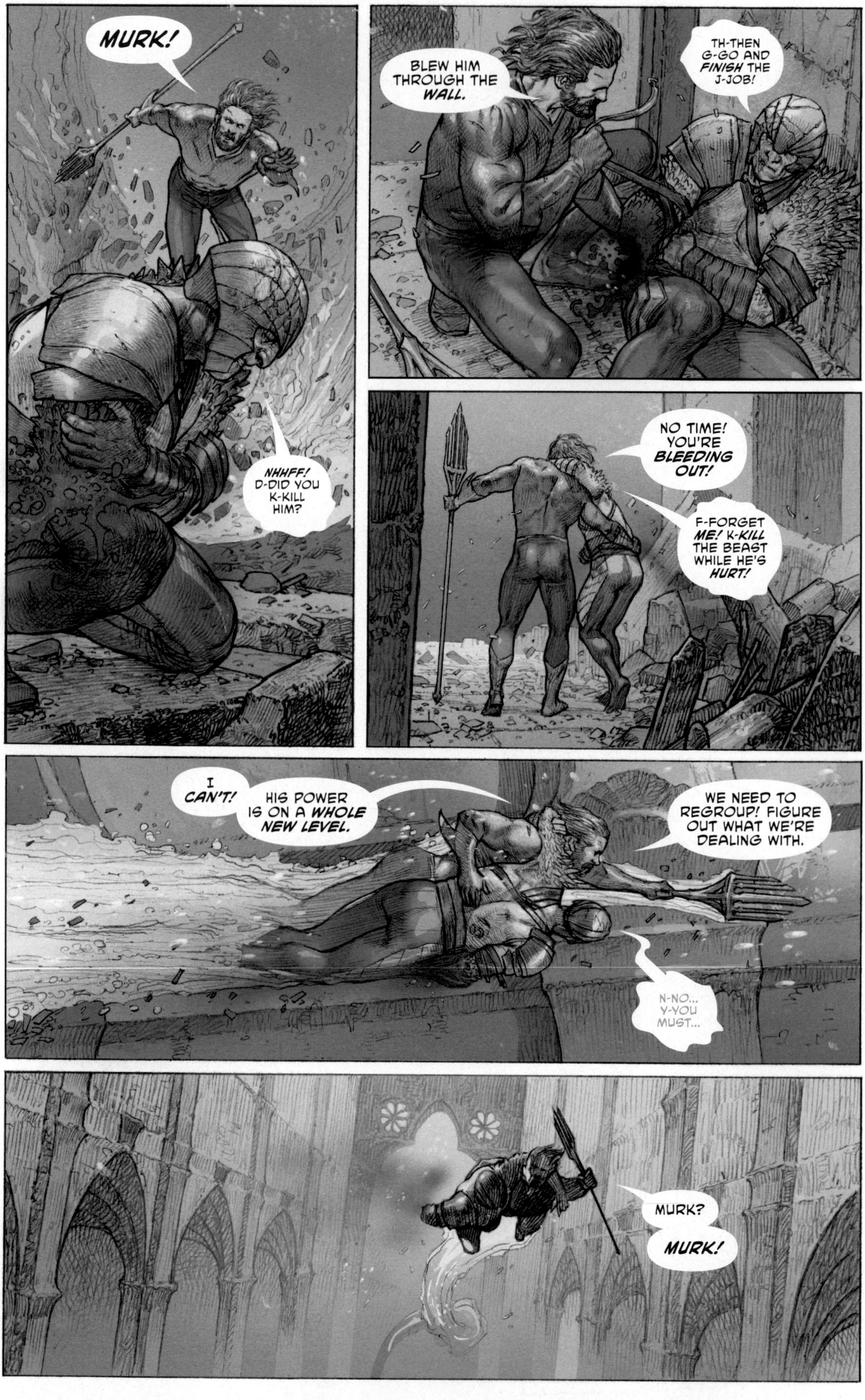
MURK!
NHHFF! D-DID YOU K-KILL HIM?
BLEW HIM THROUGH THE WALL.
TH-THEN G-GO AND FINISH THE J-JOB!
NO TIME! YOU'RE BLEEDING OUT!
F-FORGET ME! K-KILL THE BEAST WHILE HE'S HURT!
I CAN'T!
HIS POWER IS ON A WHOLE NEW LEVEL.
WE NEED TO REGROUP! FIGURE OUT WHAT WE'RE DEALING WITH.
N-NO... Y-YOU MUST...
MURK?
MURK!

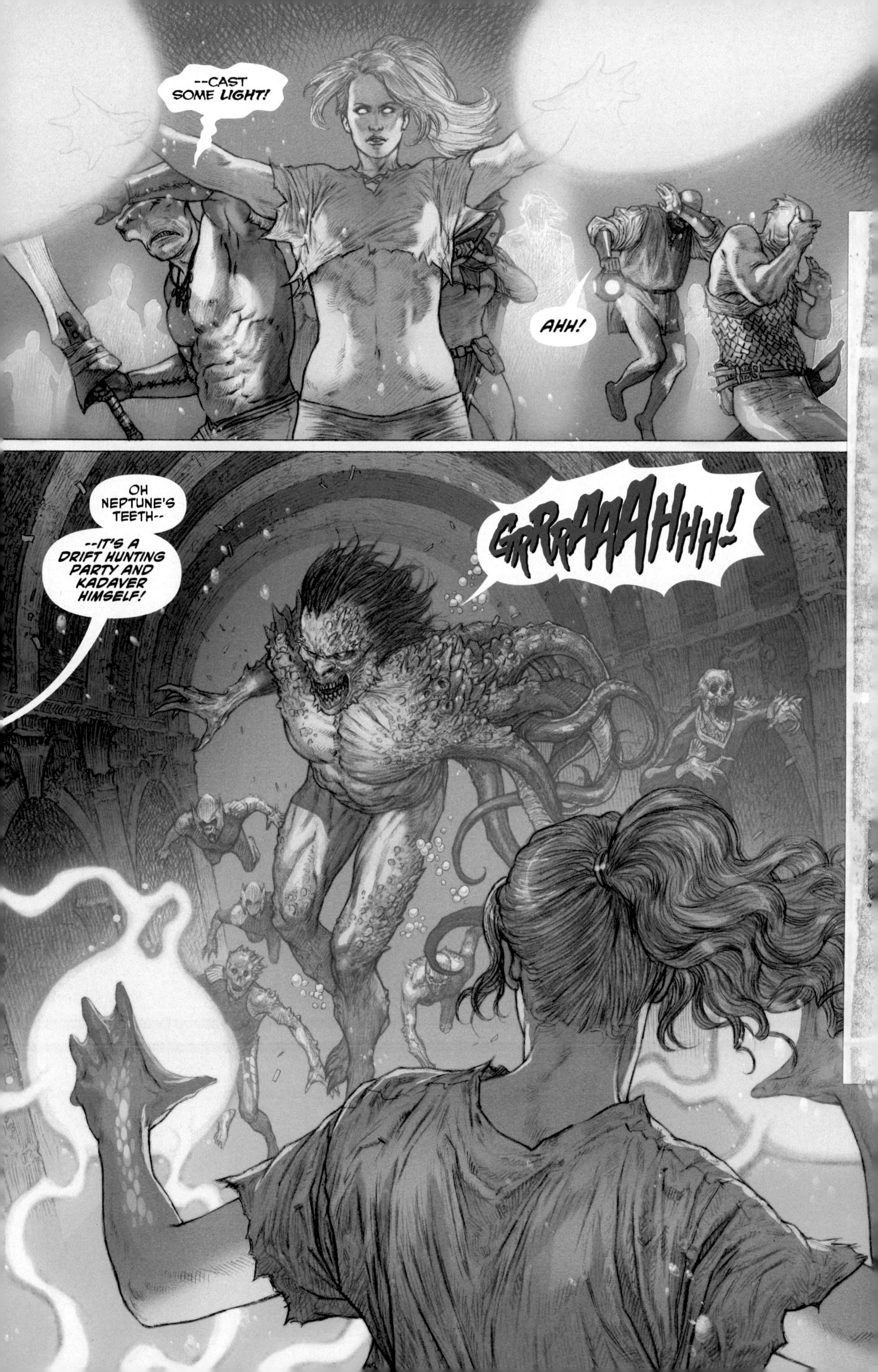
--CAST SOME LIGHT!
AHH!
OH NEPTUNE'S TEETH--
--IT'S A DRIFT HUNTING PARTY AND KADAVER HIMSELF!
GRRRAAAHHH!

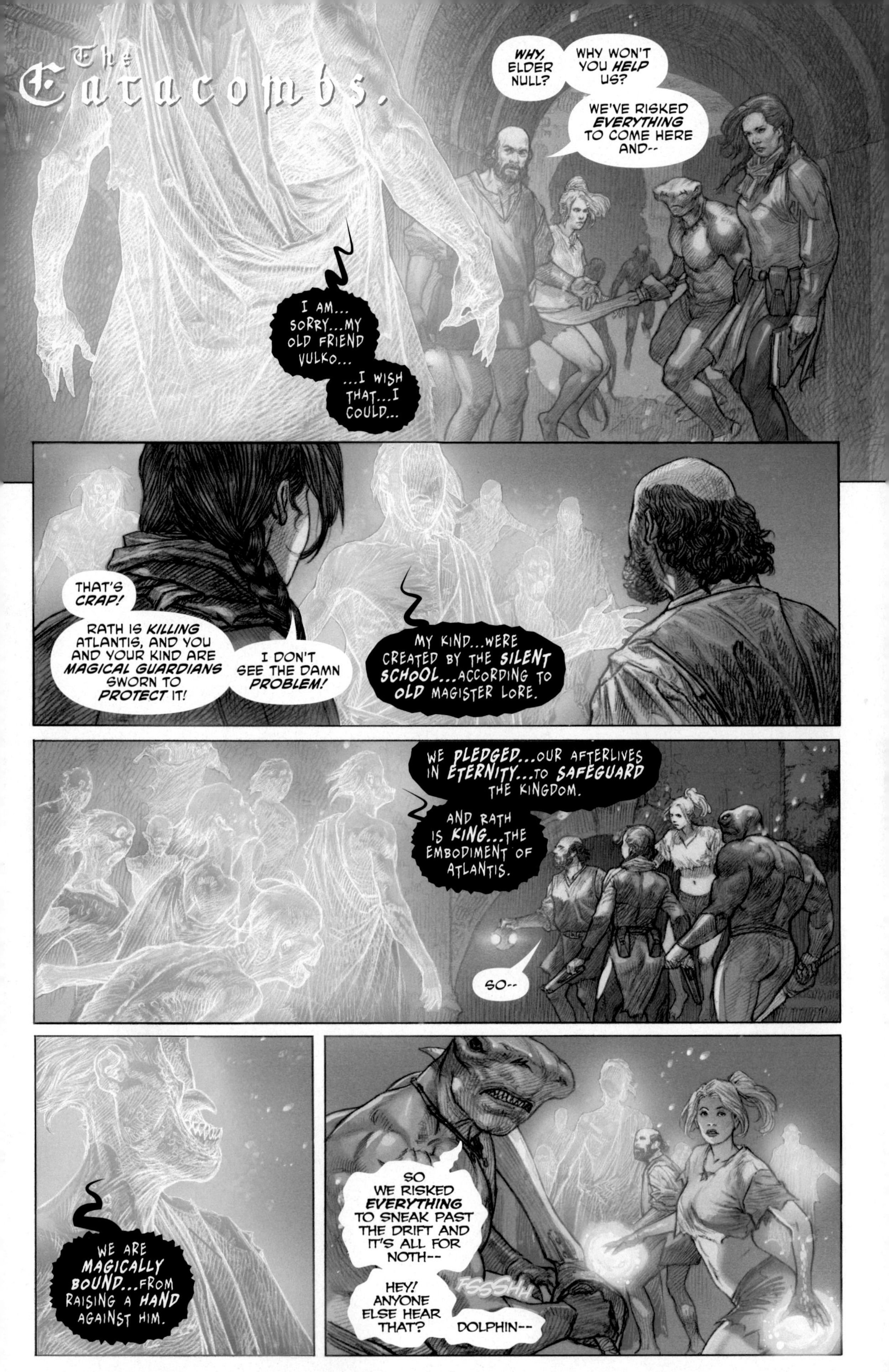
The Catacombs.
WHY, ELDER NULL?
WHY WON'T YOU HELP US?
WE'VE RISKED EVERYTHING TO COME HERE AND--
I AM... SORRY...MY OLD FRIEND VULKO...
...I WISH THAT...I COULD...
THAT'S CRAP!
RATH IS KILLING ATLANTIS, AND YOU AND YOUR KIND ARE MAGICAL GUARDIANS SWORN TO PROTECT IT!
I DON'T SEE THE DAMN PROBLEM!
MY KIND...WERE CREATED BY THE SILENT SCHOOL...ACCORDING TO OLD MAGISTER LORE.
WE PLEDGED...OUR AFTERLIVES IN ETERNITY...TO SAFEGUARD THE KINGDOM.
AND RATH IS KING...THE EMBODIMENT OF ATLANTIS.
SO--
WE ARE MAGICALLY BOUND...FROM RAISING A HAND AGAINST HIM.
SO WE RISKED EVERYTHING TO SNEAK PAST THE DRIFT AND IT'S ALL FOR NOTH--
FSSSHH
HEY! ANYONE ELSE HEAR THAT?
DOLPHIN--

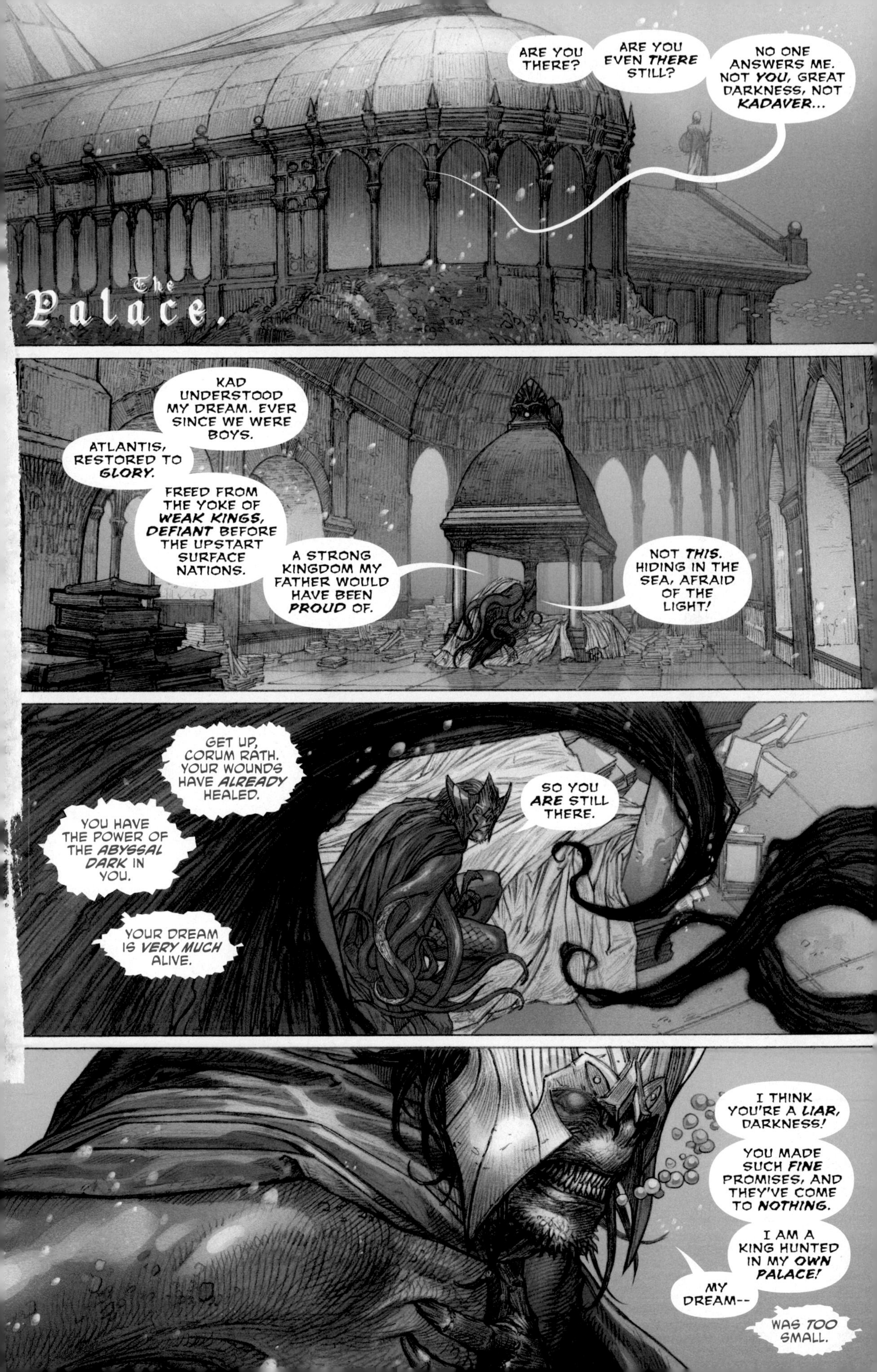

The Palace.
ARE YOU THERE?
ARE YOU EVEN THERE STILL?
NO ONE ANSWERS ME. NOT YOU, GREAT DARKNESS, NOT KADAVER...
KAD UNDERSTOOD MY DREAM. EVER SINCE WE WERE BOYS.
ATLANTIS, RESTORED TO GLORY.
FREED FROM THE YOKE OF WEAK KINGS, DEFIANT BEFORE THE UPSTART SURFACE NATIONS.
A STRONG KINGDOM MY FATHER WOULD HAVE BEEN PROUD OF.
NOT THIS. HIDING IN THE SEA, AFRAID OF THE LIGHT!
GET UP, CORUM RATH. YOUR WOUNDS HAVE ALREADY HEALED.
YOU HAVE THE POWER OF THE ABYSSAL DARK IN YOU.
YOUR DREAM IS VERY MUCH ALIVE.
SO YOU ARE STILL THERE.
I THINK YOU'RE A LIAR, DARKNESS!
YOU MADE SUCH FINE PROMISES, AND THEY'VE COME TO NOTHING.
I AM A KING HUNTED IN MY OWN PALACE!
MY DREAM--
WAS TOO SMALL.

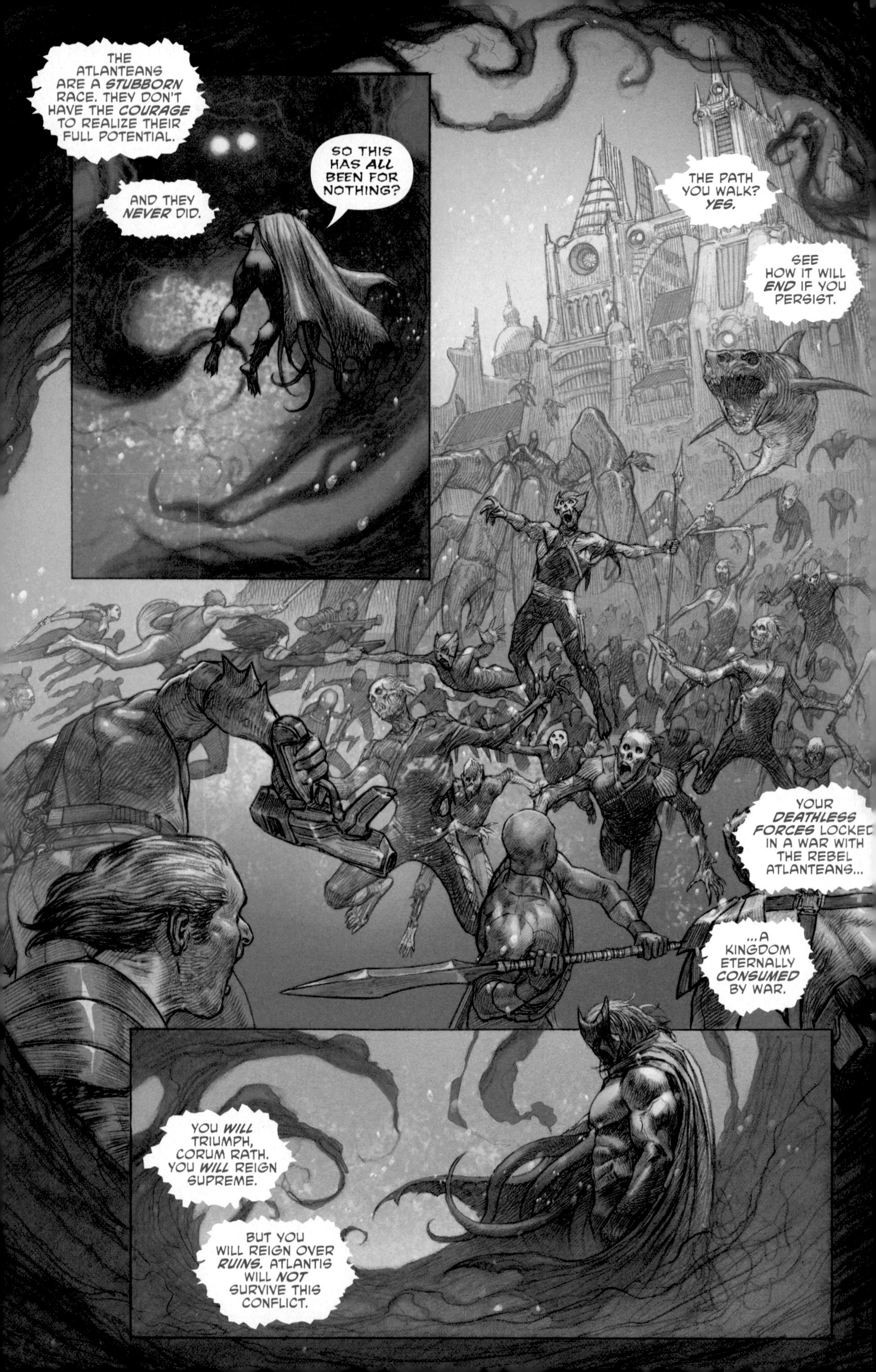
THE ATLANTEANS ARE A STUBBORN RACE. THEY DON'T HAVE THE COURAGE TO REALIZE THEIR FULL POTENTIAL.
AND THEY NEVER DID.
SO THIS HAS ALL BEEN FOR NOTHING?
THE PATH YOU WALK? YES.
SEE HOW IT WILL END IF YOU PERSIST.
YOUR DEATHLESS FORCES LOCKED IN A WAR WITH THE REBEL ATLANTEANS...
...A KINGDOM ETERNALLY CONSUMED BY WAR.
YOU WILL TRIUMPH, CORUM RATH. YOU WILL REIGN SUPREME.
BUT YOU WILL REIGN OVER RUINS. ATLANTIS WILL NOT SURVIVE THIS CONFLICT.

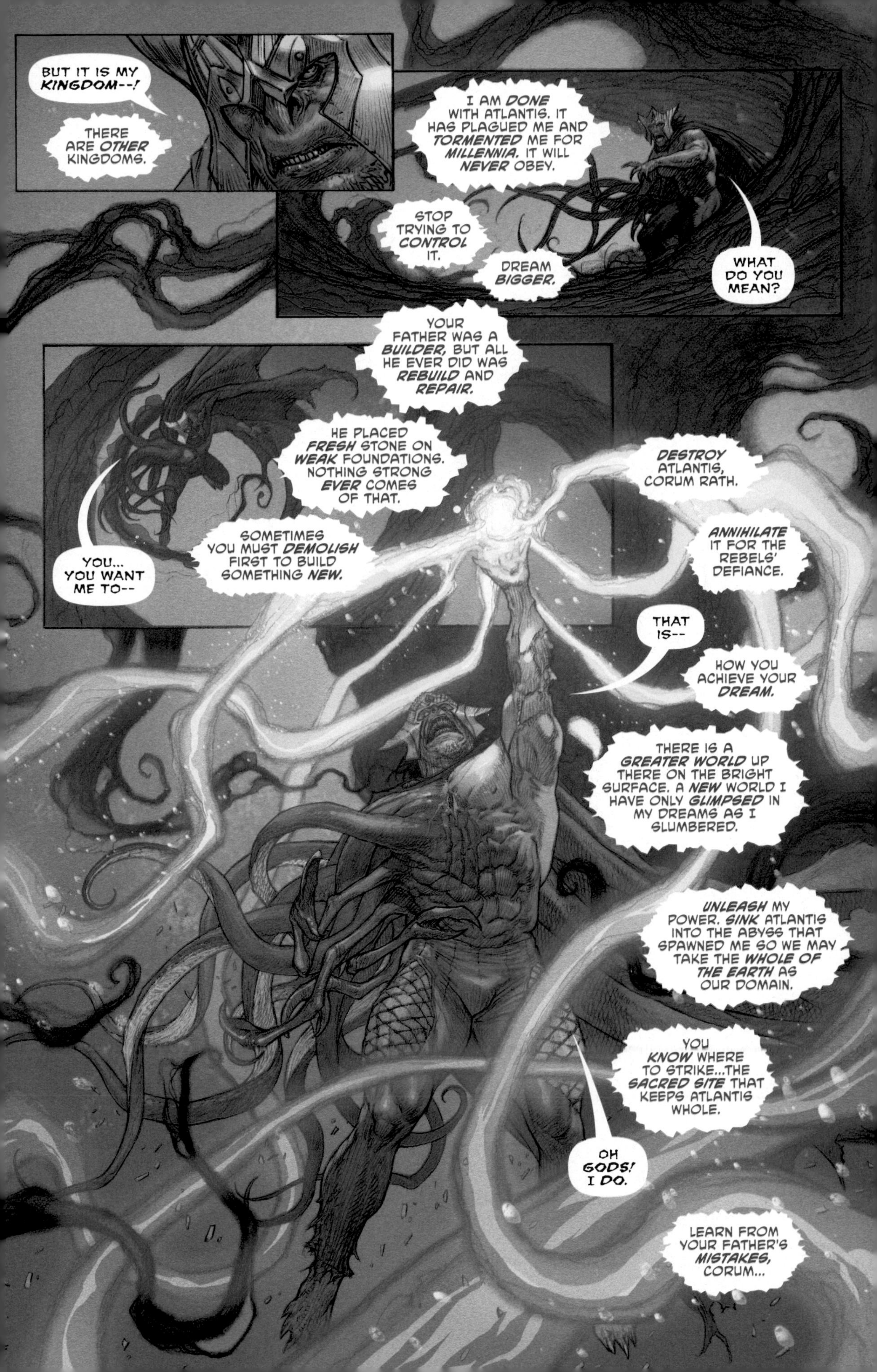
BUT IT IS MY *KINGDOM*--!
THERE ARE *OTHER* KINGDOMS.
I AM *DONE* WITH ATLANTIS. IT HAS PLAGUED ME AND *TORMENTED* ME FOR *MILLENNIA.* IT WILL *NEVER* OBEY.
STOP TRYING TO *CONTROL* IT.
DREAM *BIGGER.*
WHAT DO YOU MEAN?
YOUR FATHER WAS A *BUILDER,* BUT ALL HE EVER DID WAS *REBUILD* AND *REPAIR.*
HE PLACED *FRESH* STONE ON *WEAK* FOUNDATIONS. NOTHING STRONG *EVER* COMES OF THAT.
SOMETIMES YOU MUST *DEMOLISH* FIRST TO BUILD SOMETHING *NEW.*
YOU... YOU WANT ME TO--
DESTROY ATLANTIS, CORUM RATH.
ANNIHILATE IT FOR THE REBELS' DEFIANCE.
THAT IS--
HOW YOU ACHIEVE YOUR *DREAM.*
THERE IS A *GREATER WORLD* UP THERE ON THE BRIGHT SURFACE. A *NEW* WORLD I HAVE ONLY *GLIMPSED* IN MY DREAMS AS I SLUMBERED.
UNLEASH MY POWER. *SINK* ATLANTIS INTO THE ABYSS THAT SPAWNED ME SO WE MAY TAKE THE *WHOLE OF THE EARTH* AS OUR DOMAIN.
YOU *KNOW* WHERE TO STRIKE...THE *SACRED SITE* THAT KEEPS ATLANTIS WHOLE.
OH *GODS!* I *DO.*
LEARN FROM YOUR FATHER'S *MISTAKES,* CORUM...

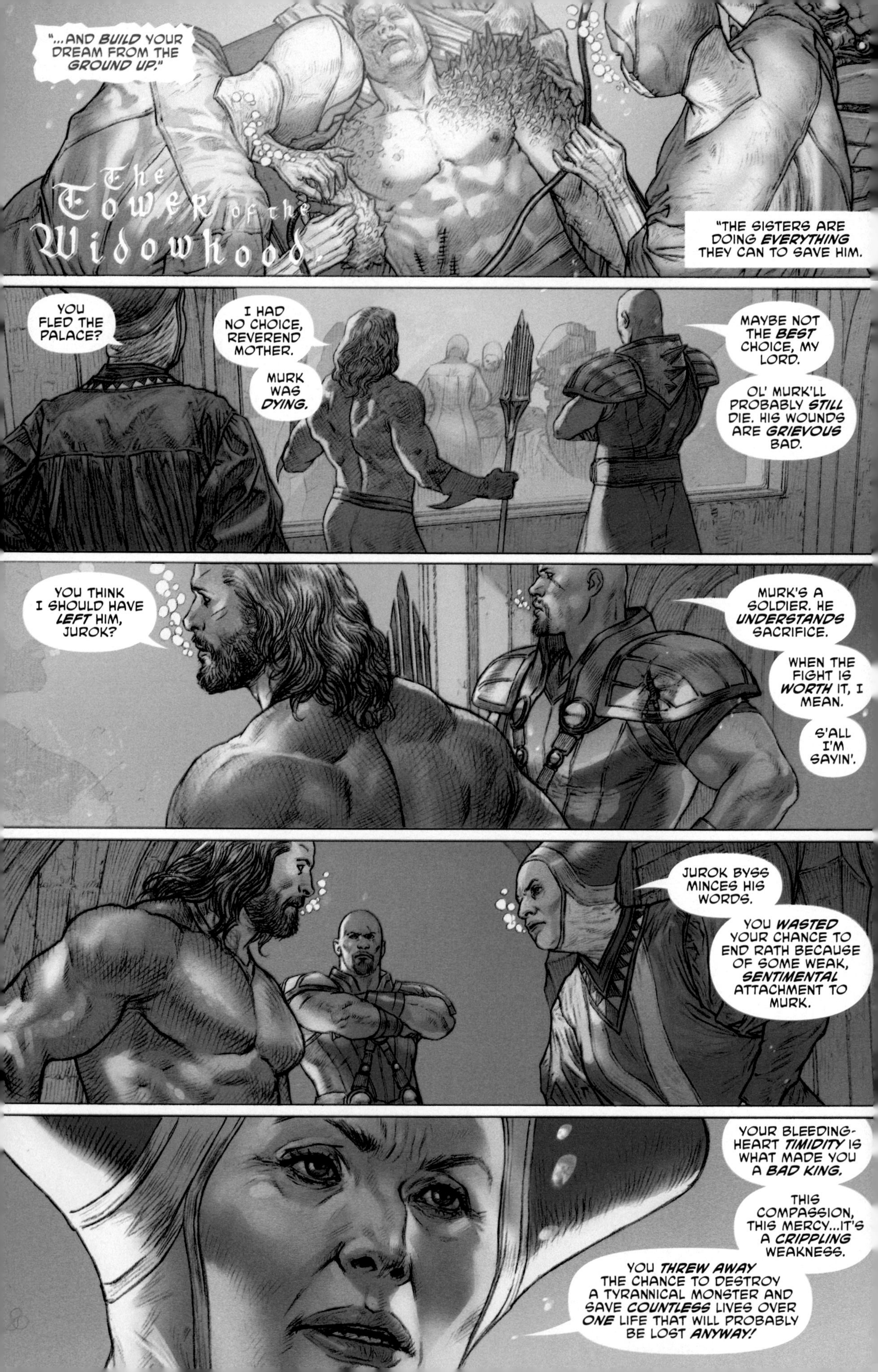
"...AND BUILD YOUR DREAM FROM THE GROUND UP."
The Tower of the Widowhood
"THE SISTERS ARE DOING EVERYTHING THEY CAN TO SAVE HIM.
YOU FLED THE PALACE?
I HAD NO CHOICE, REVEREND MOTHER.
MURK WAS DYING.
MAYBE NOT THE BEST CHOICE, MY LORD.
OL' MURK'LL PROBABLY STILL DIE. HIS WOUNDS ARE GRIEVOUS BAD.
YOU THINK I SHOULD HAVE LEFT HIM, JUROK?
MURK'S A SOLDIER. HE UNDERSTANDS SACRIFICE.
WHEN THE FIGHT IS WORTH IT, I MEAN.
S'ALL I'M SAYIN'.
JUROK BYSS MINCES HIS WORDS.
YOU WASTED YOUR CHANCE TO END RATH BECAUSE OF SOME WEAK, SENTIMENTAL ATTACHMENT TO MURK.
YOUR BLEEDING-HEART TIMIDITY IS WHAT MADE YOU A BAD KING.
THIS COMPASSION, THIS MERCY...IT'S A CRIPPLING WEAKNESS.
YOU THREW AWAY THE CHANCE TO DESTROY A TYRANNICAL MONSTER AND SAVE COUNTLESS LIVES OVER ONE LIFE THAT WILL PROBABLY BE LOST ANYWAY!

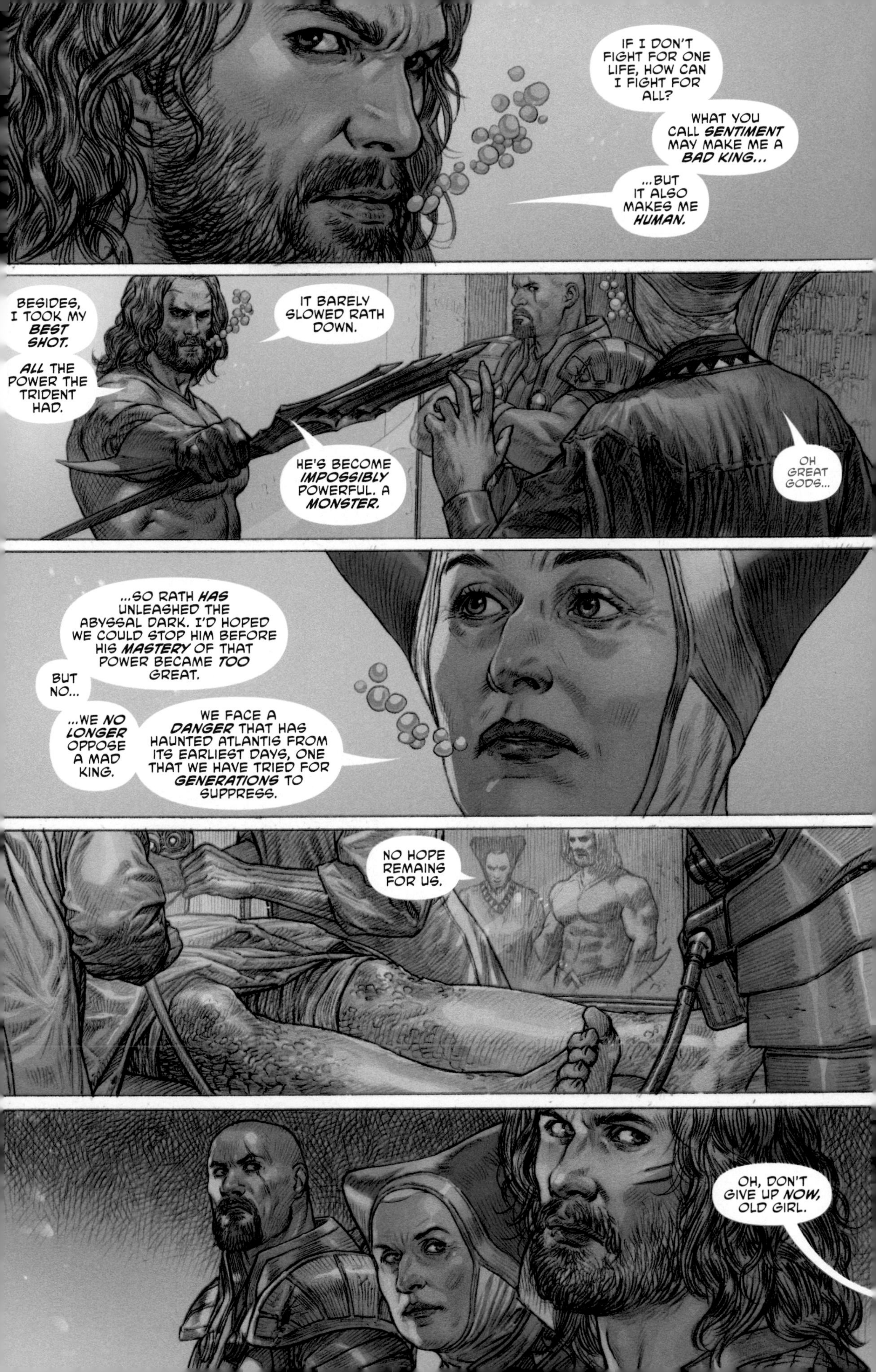
IF I DON'T FIGHT FOR ONE LIFE, HOW CAN I FIGHT FOR ALL?
WHAT YOU CALL SENTIMENT MAY MAKE ME A BAD KING...
...BUT IT ALSO MAKES ME HUMAN.
BESIDES, I TOOK MY BEST SHOT.
ALL THE POWER THE TRIDENT HAD.
IT BARELY SLOWED RATH DOWN.
HE'S BECOME IMPOSSIBLY POWERFUL. A MONSTER.
OH GREAT GODS...
...SO RATH HAS UNLEASHED THE ABYSSAL DARK. I'D HOPED WE COULD STOP HIM BEFORE HIS MASTERY OF THAT POWER BECAME TOO GREAT.
BUT NO...
...WE NO LONGER OPPOSE A MAD KING.
WE FACE A DANGER THAT HAS HAUNTED ATLANTIS FROM ITS EARLIEST DAYS, ONE THAT WE HAVE TRIED FOR GENERATIONS TO SUPPRESS.
NO HOPE REMAINS FOR US.
OH, DON'T GIVE UP NOW, OLD GIRL.

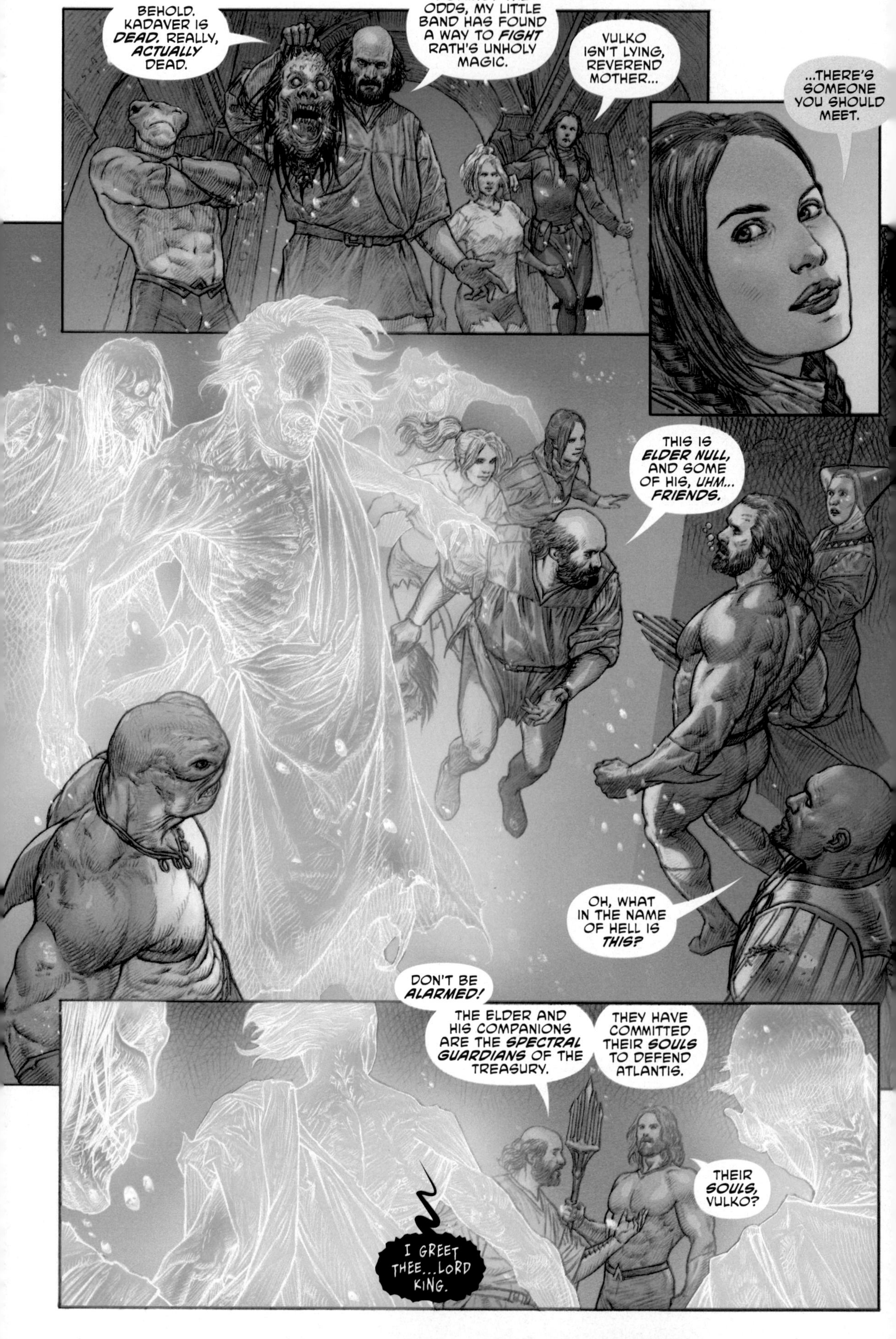
BEHOLD. KADAVER IS DEAD. REALLY, ACTUALLY DEAD.
AGAINST THE ODDS, MY LITTLE BAND HAS FOUND A WAY TO FIGHT RATH'S UNHOLY MAGIC.
VULKO ISN'T LYING, REVEREND MOTHER...
...THERE'S SOMEONE YOU SHOULD MEET.
THIS IS ELDER NULL, AND SOME OF HIS, UHM... FRIENDS.
OH, WHAT IN THE NAME OF HELL IS THIS?
DON'T BE ALARMED!
THE ELDER AND HIS COMPANIONS ARE THE SPECTRAL GUARDIANS OF THE TREASURY.
THEY HAVE COMMITTED THEIR SOULS TO DEFEND ATLANTIS.
THEIR SOULS, VULKO?
I GREET THEE...LORD KING.

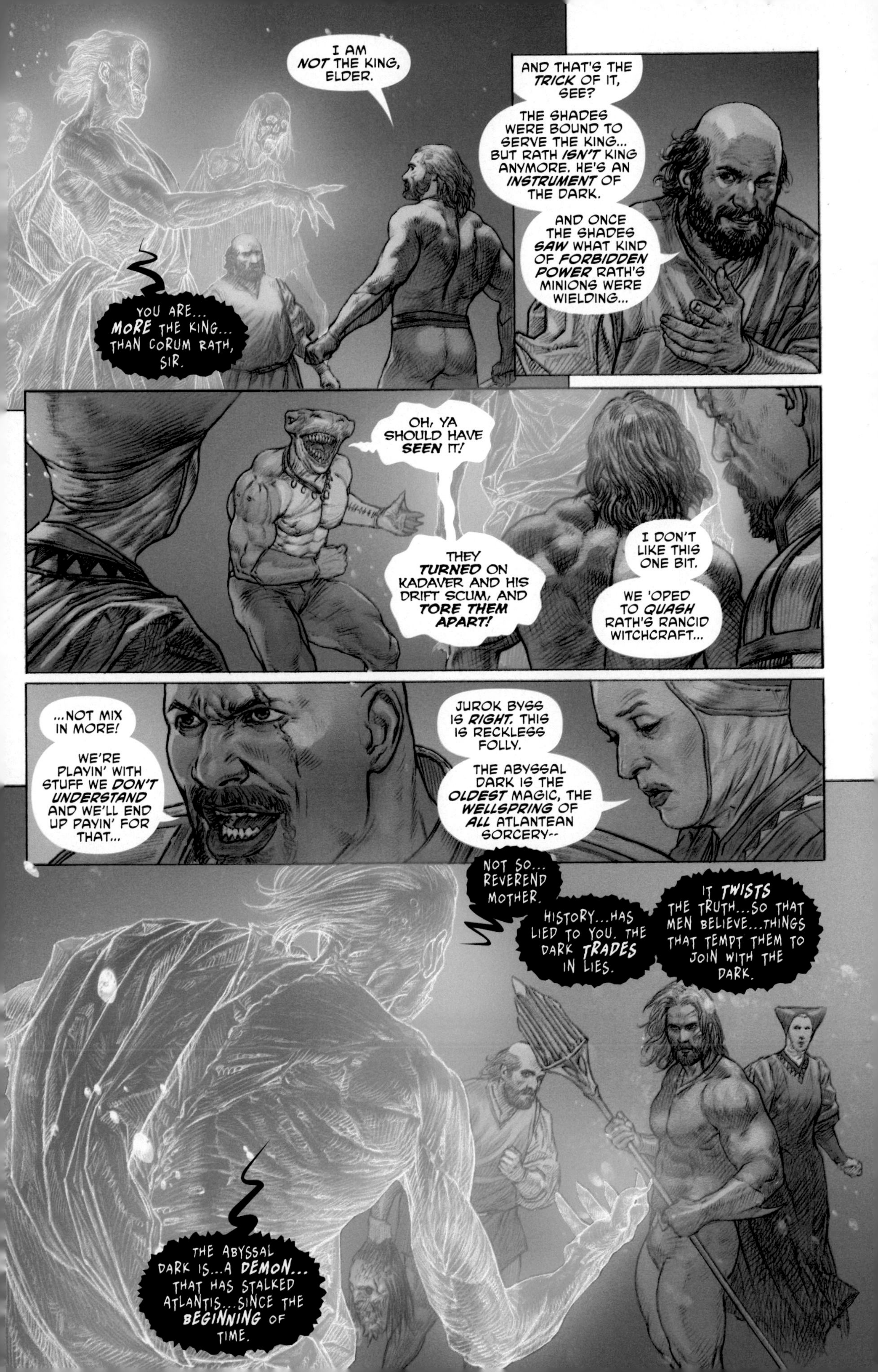
I AM NOT THE KING, ELDER.
YOU ARE... MORE THE KING... THAN CORUM RATH, SIR.
AND THAT'S THE TRICK OF IT, SEE?
THE SHADES WERE BOUND TO SERVE THE KING... BUT RATH ISN'T KING ANYMORE. HE'S AN INSTRUMENT OF THE DARK.
AND ONCE THE SHADES SAW WHAT KIND OF FORBIDDEN POWER RATH'S MINIONS WERE WIELDING...
OH, YA SHOULD HAVE SEEN IT!
THEY TURNED ON KADAVER AND HIS DRIFT SCUM, AND TORE THEM APART!
I DON'T LIKE THIS ONE BIT.
WE 'OPED TO QUASH RATH'S RANCID WITCHCRAFT...
...NOT MIX IN MORE!
WE'RE PLAYIN' WITH STUFF WE DON'T UNDERSTAND AND WE'LL END UP PAYIN' FOR THAT...
JUROK BYSS IS RIGHT. THIS IS RECKLESS FOLLY.
THE ABYSSAL DARK IS THE OLDEST MAGIC, THE WELLSPRING OF ALL ATLANTEAN SORCERY--
NOT SO... REVEREND MOTHER.
HISTORY...HAS LIED TO YOU. THE DARK TRADES IN LIES.
IT TWISTS THE TRUTH...SO THAT MEN BELIEVE...THINGS THAT TEMPT THEM TO JOIN WITH THE DARK.
THE ABYSSAL DARK IS...A DEMON... THAT HAS STALKED ATLANTIS...SINCE THE BEGINNING OF TIME.

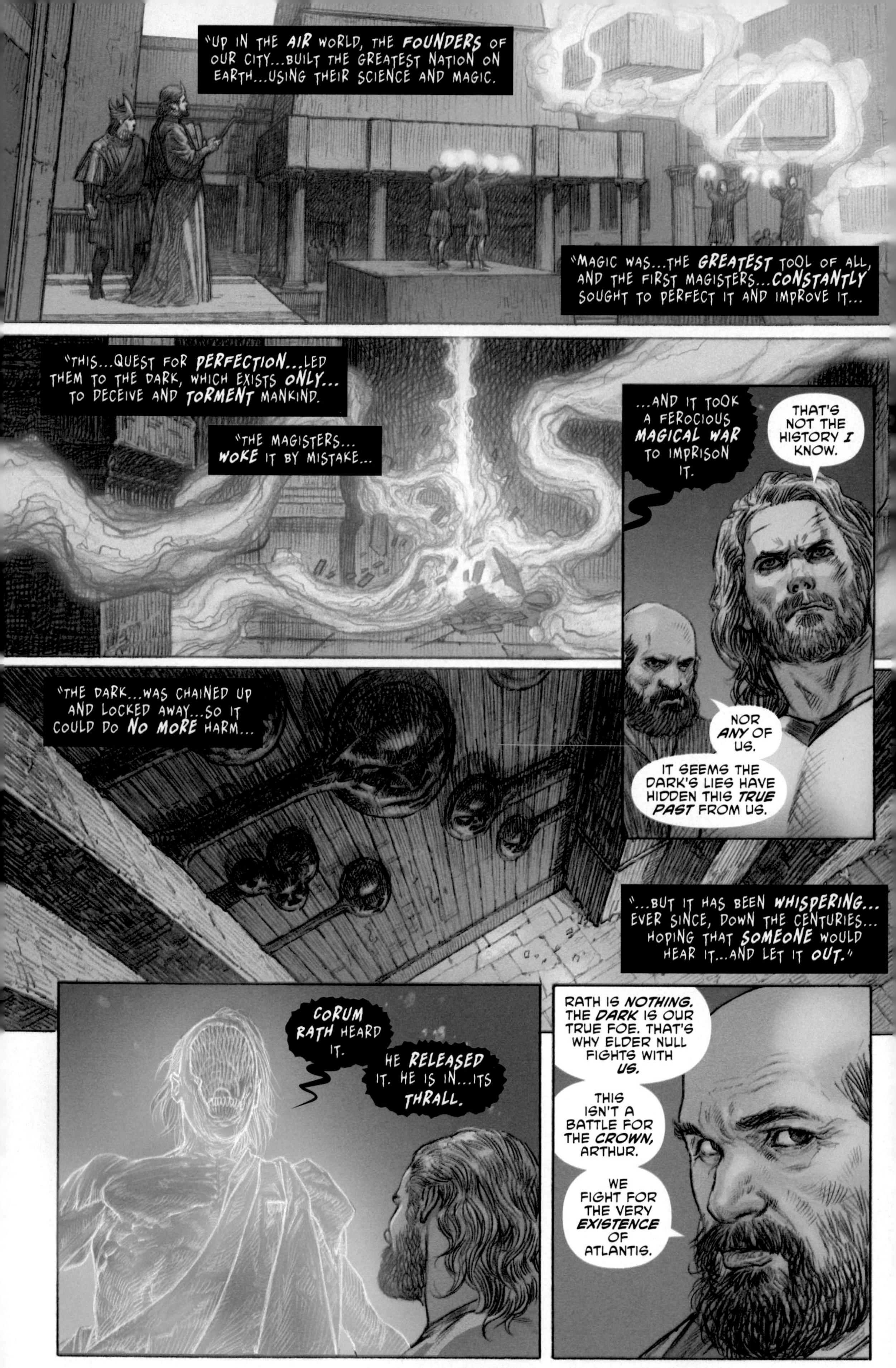
"UP IN THE AIR WORLD, THE FOUNDERS OF OUR CITY...BUILT THE GREATEST NATION ON EARTH...USING THEIR SCIENCE AND MAGIC.
"MAGIC WAS...THE GREATEST TOOL OF ALL, AND THE FIRST MAGISTERS...CONSTANTLY SOUGHT TO PERFECT IT AND IMPROVE IT...
"THIS...QUEST FOR PERFECTION...LED THEM TO THE DARK, WHICH EXISTS ONLY...TO DECEIVE AND TORMENT MANKIND.
"THE MAGISTERS...WOKE IT BY MISTAKE...
...AND IT TOOK A FEROCIOUS MAGICAL WAR TO IMPRISON IT.
THAT'S NOT THE HISTORY I KNOW.
"THE DARK...WAS CHAINED UP AND LOCKED AWAY...SO IT COULD DO NO MORE HARM...
NOR ANY OF US.
IT SEEMS THE DARK'S LIES HAVE HIDDEN THIS TRUE PAST FROM US.
"...BUT IT HAS BEEN WHISPERING...EVER SINCE, DOWN THE CENTURIES...HOPING THAT SOMEONE WOULD HEAR IT...AND LET IT OUT."
CORUM RATH HEARD IT.
HE RELEASED IT. HE IS IN...ITS THRALL.
RATH IS NOTHING. THE DARK IS OUR TRUE FOE. THAT'S WHY ELDER NULL FIGHTS WITH US.
THIS ISN'T A BATTLE FOR THE CROWN, ARTHUR.
WE FIGHT FOR THE VERY EXISTENCE OF ATLANTIS.

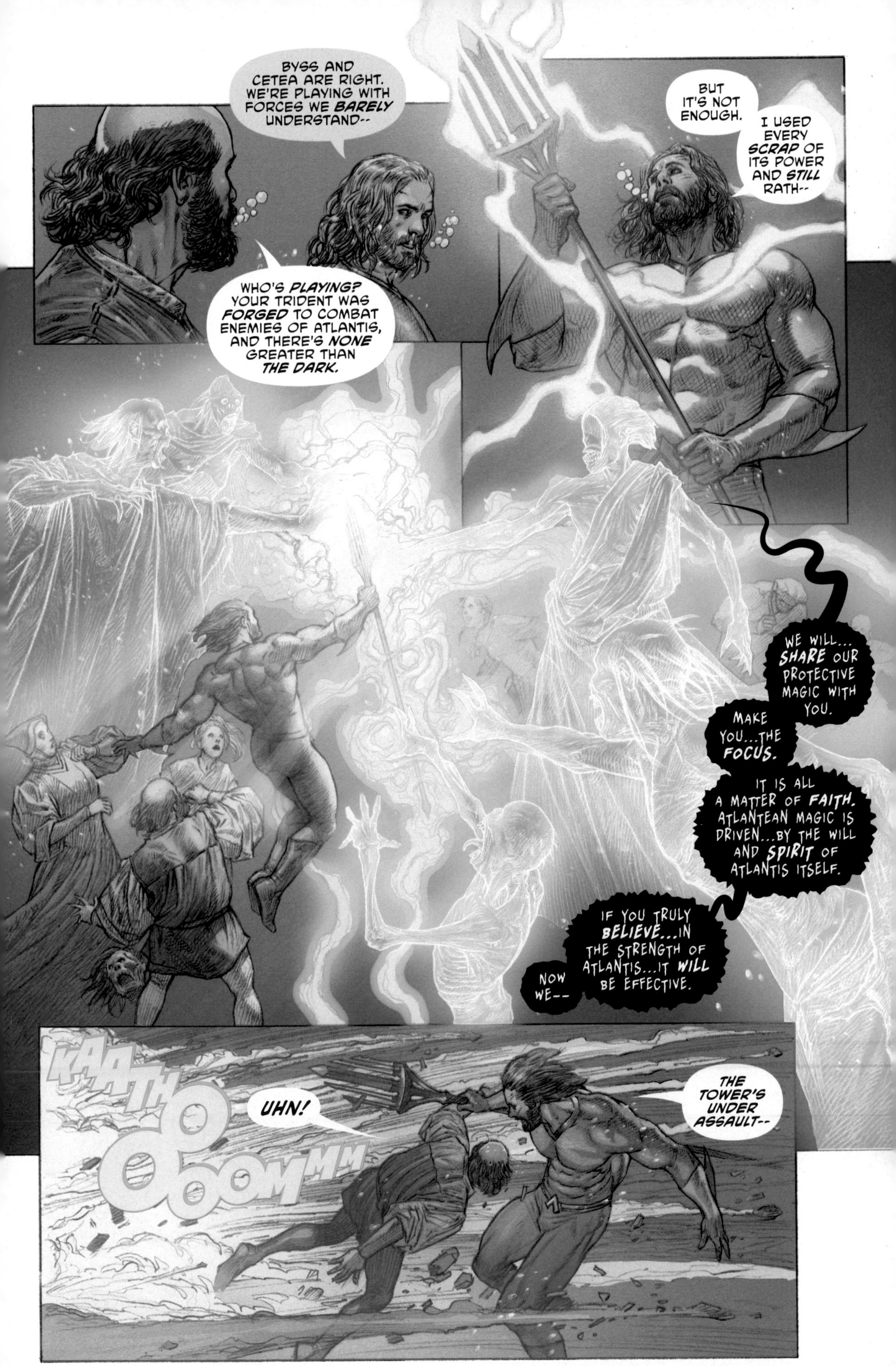
BYSS AND CETEA ARE RIGHT. WE'RE PLAYING WITH FORCES WE *BARELY* UNDERSTAND--
WHO'S *PLAYING?* YOUR TRIDENT WAS *FORGED* TO COMBAT ENEMIES OF ATLANTIS, AND THERE'S *NONE* GREATER THAN *THE DARK.*
BUT IT'S NOT ENOUGH.
I USED EVERY *SCRAP* OF ITS POWER AND *STILL* RATH--
WE WILL... *SHARE* OUR PROTECTIVE MAGIC WITH YOU.
MAKE YOU...THE *FOCUS.*
IT IS ALL A MATTER OF *FAITH.* ATLANTEAN MAGIC IS DRIVEN...BY THE WILL AND *SPIRIT* OF ATLANTIS ITSELF.
IF YOU TRULY *BELIEVE...*IN THE STRENGTH OF ATLANTIS...IT *WILL* BE EFFECTIVE.
NOW WE--
KAATHOOOOMMM
UHN!
THE TOWER'S UNDER ASSAULT--

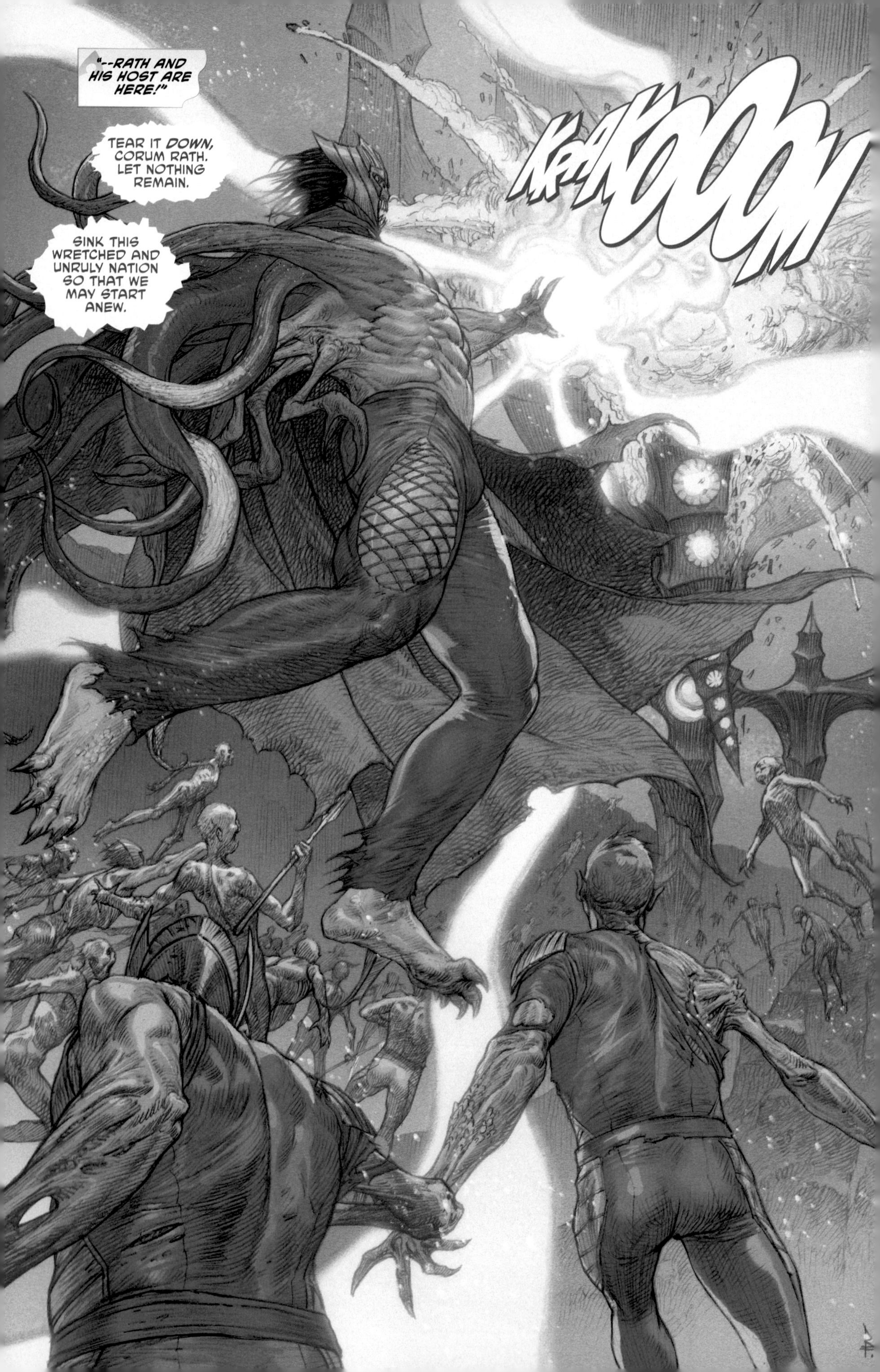
"--RATH AND HIS HOST ARE HERE!"
TEAR IT *DOWN*, CORUM RATH. LET NOTHING REMAIN.
SINK THIS WRETCHED AND UNRULY NATION SO THAT WE MAY START ANEW.
KRAKOOOM

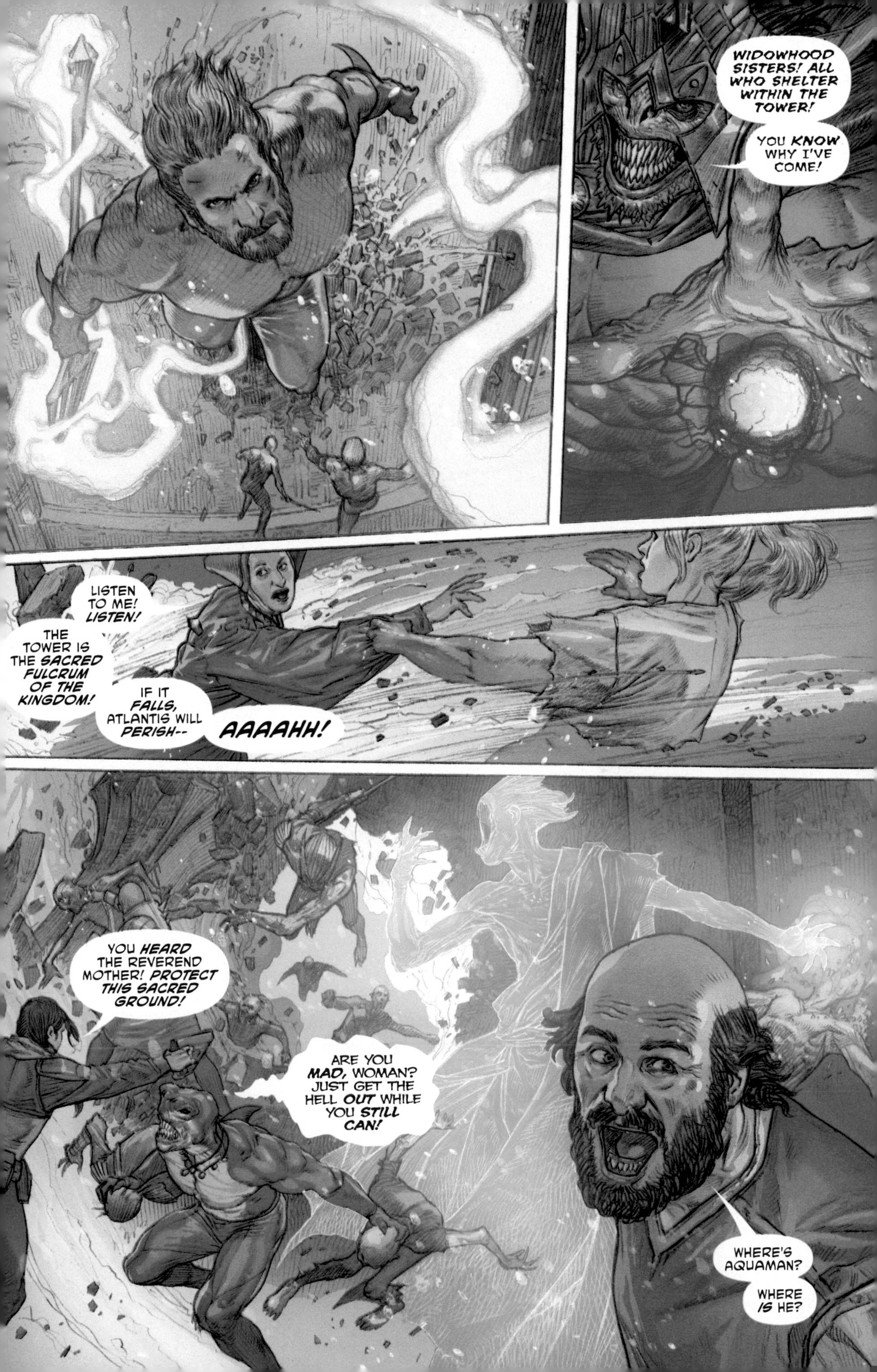
WIDOWHOOD SISTERS! ALL WHO SHELTER WITHIN THE TOWER!
YOU KNOW WHY I'VE COME!
LISTEN TO ME! LISTEN!
THE TOWER IS THE SACRED FULCRUM OF THE KINGDOM!
IF IT FALLS, ATLANTIS WILL PERISH--
AAAAHH!
YOU HEARD THE REVEREND MOTHER! PROTECT THIS SACRED GROUND!
ARE YOU MAD, WOMAN? JUST GET THE HELL OUT WHILE YOU STILL CAN!
WHERE'S AQUAMAN?
WHERE IS HE?

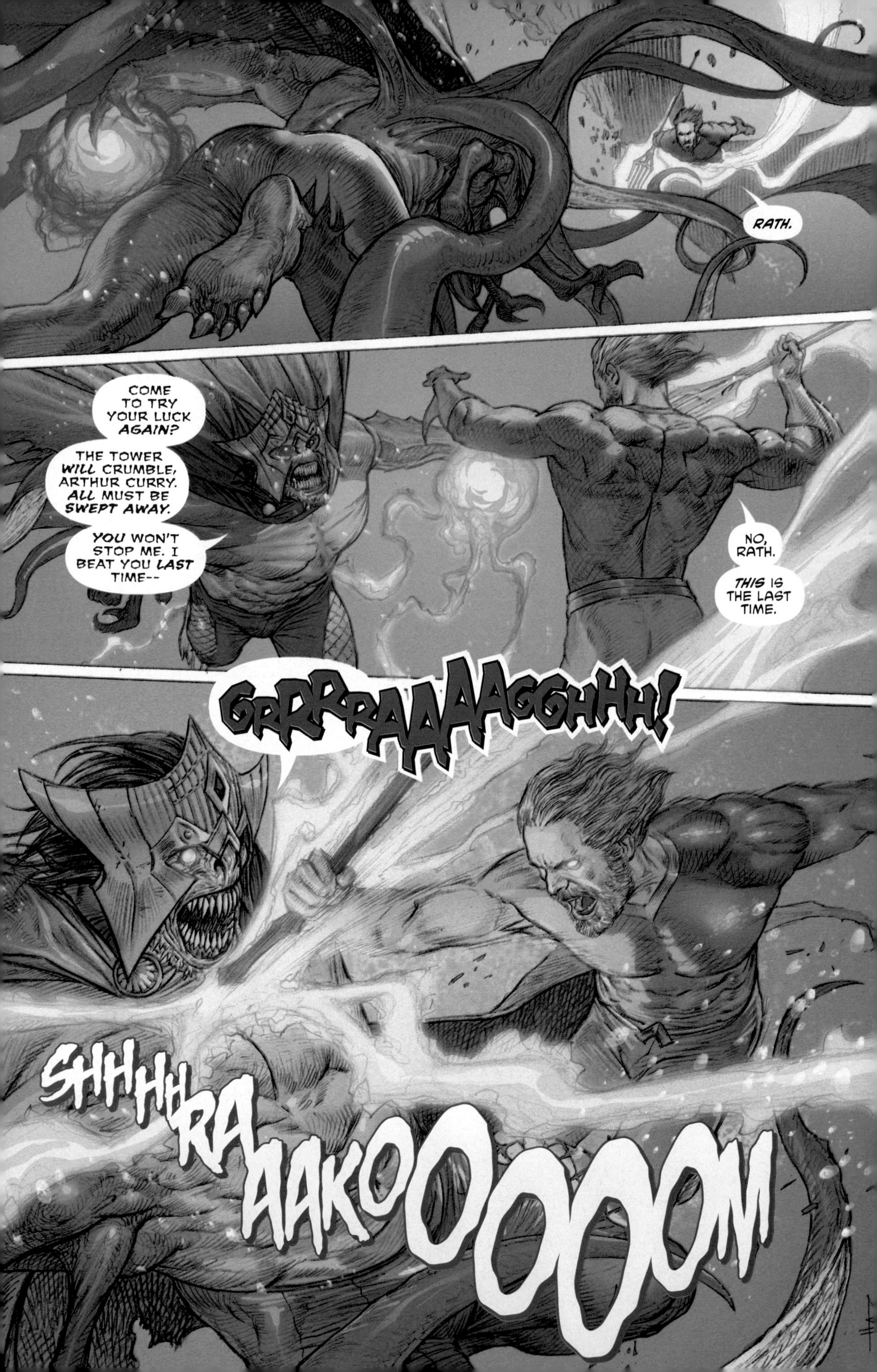
RATH.
COME TO TRY YOUR LUCK AGAIN?
THE TOWER WILL CRUMBLE, ARTHUR CURRY. ALL MUST BE SWEPT AWAY.
YOU WON'T STOP ME. I BEAT YOU LAST TIME--
NO, RATH.
THIS IS THE LAST TIME.
GRRRRAAAAAGGHHH!
SHHHHRAAAKOOOOOOM

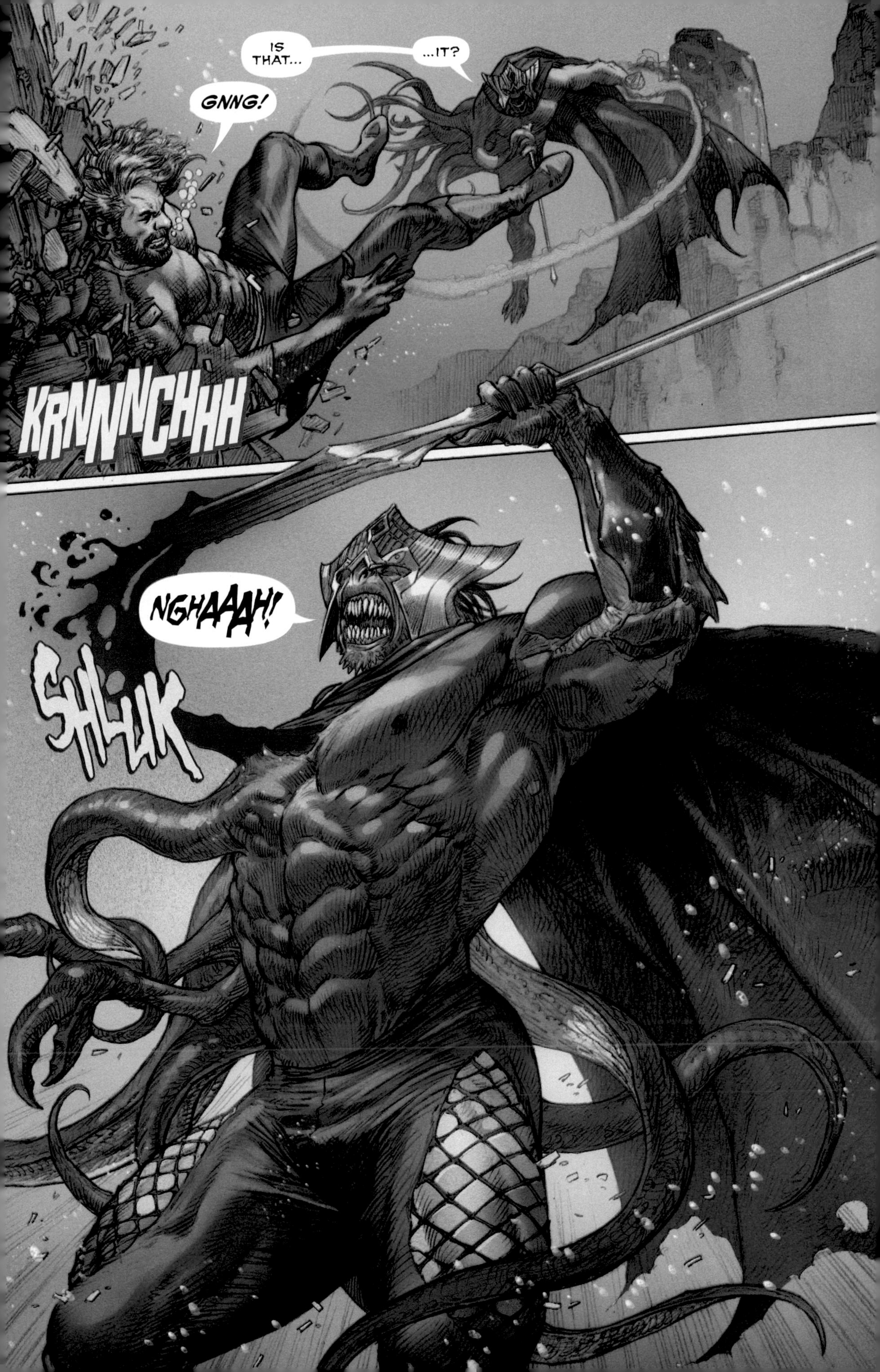
GNNG!
IS THAT...
...IT?
KRNNNCHHH
NGHAAAH!
SHLUK

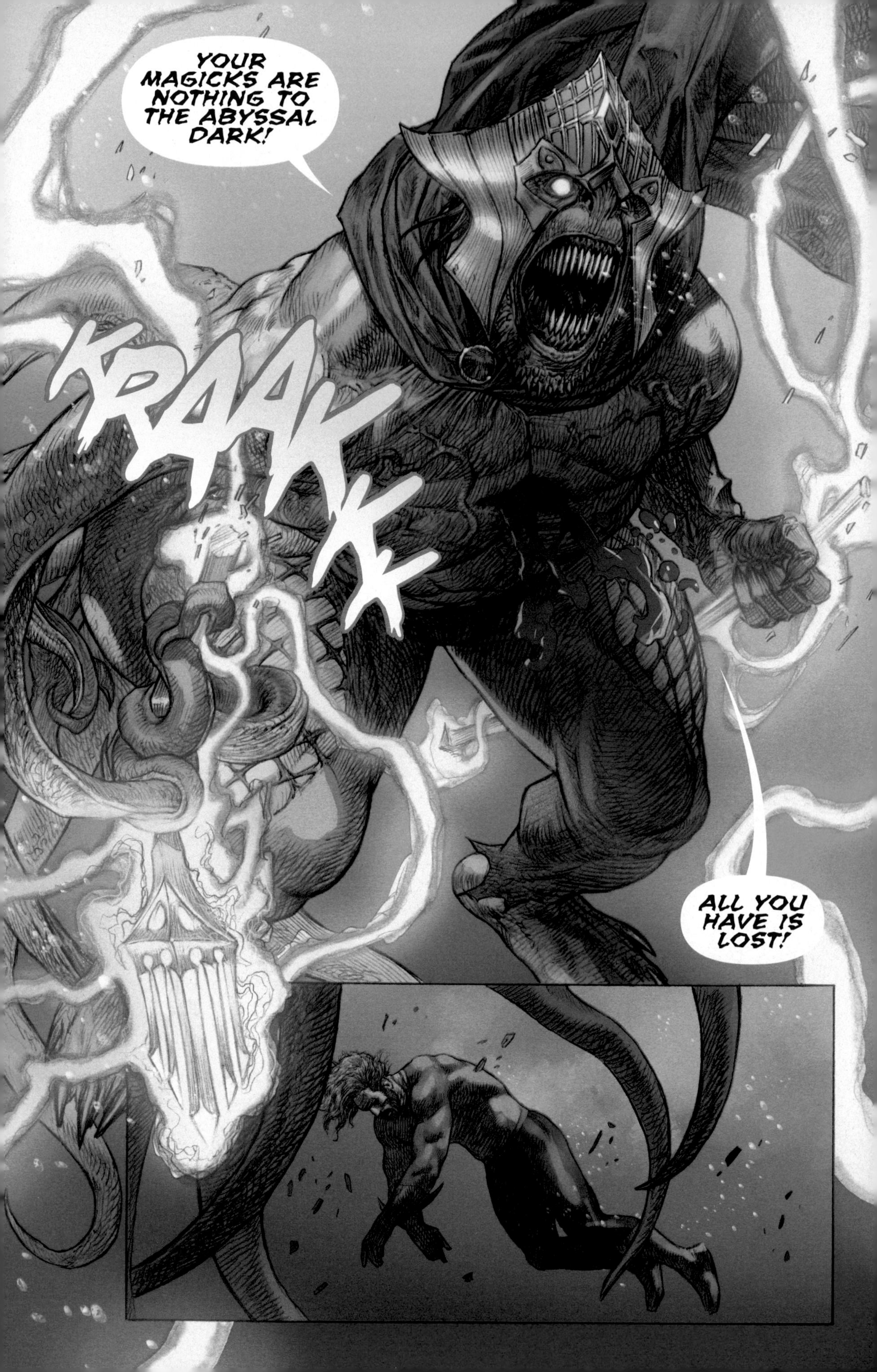
YOUR MAGICKS ARE NOTHING TO THE ABYSSAL DARK!
KRAAKKK
ALL YOU HAVE IS LOST!

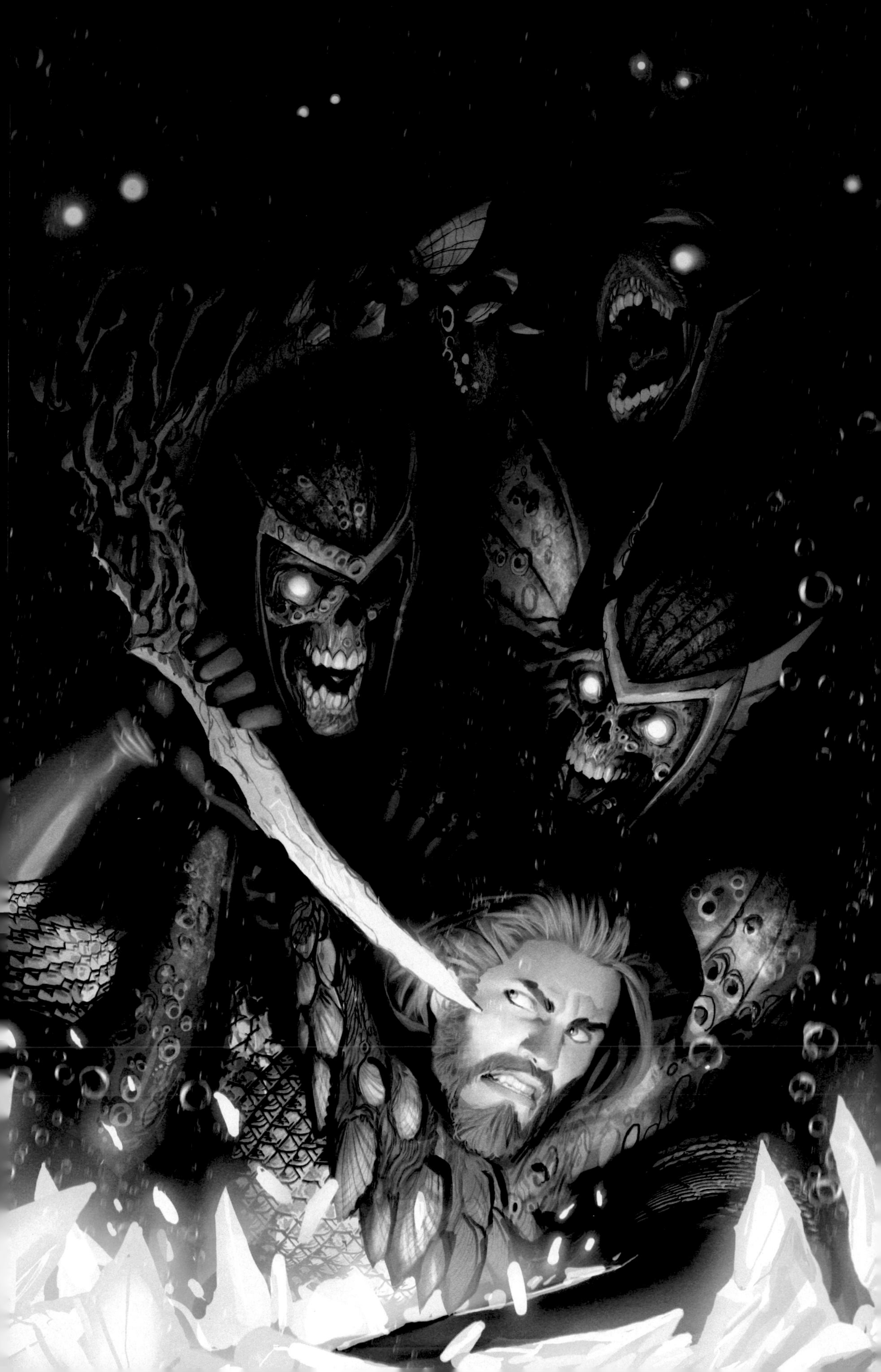

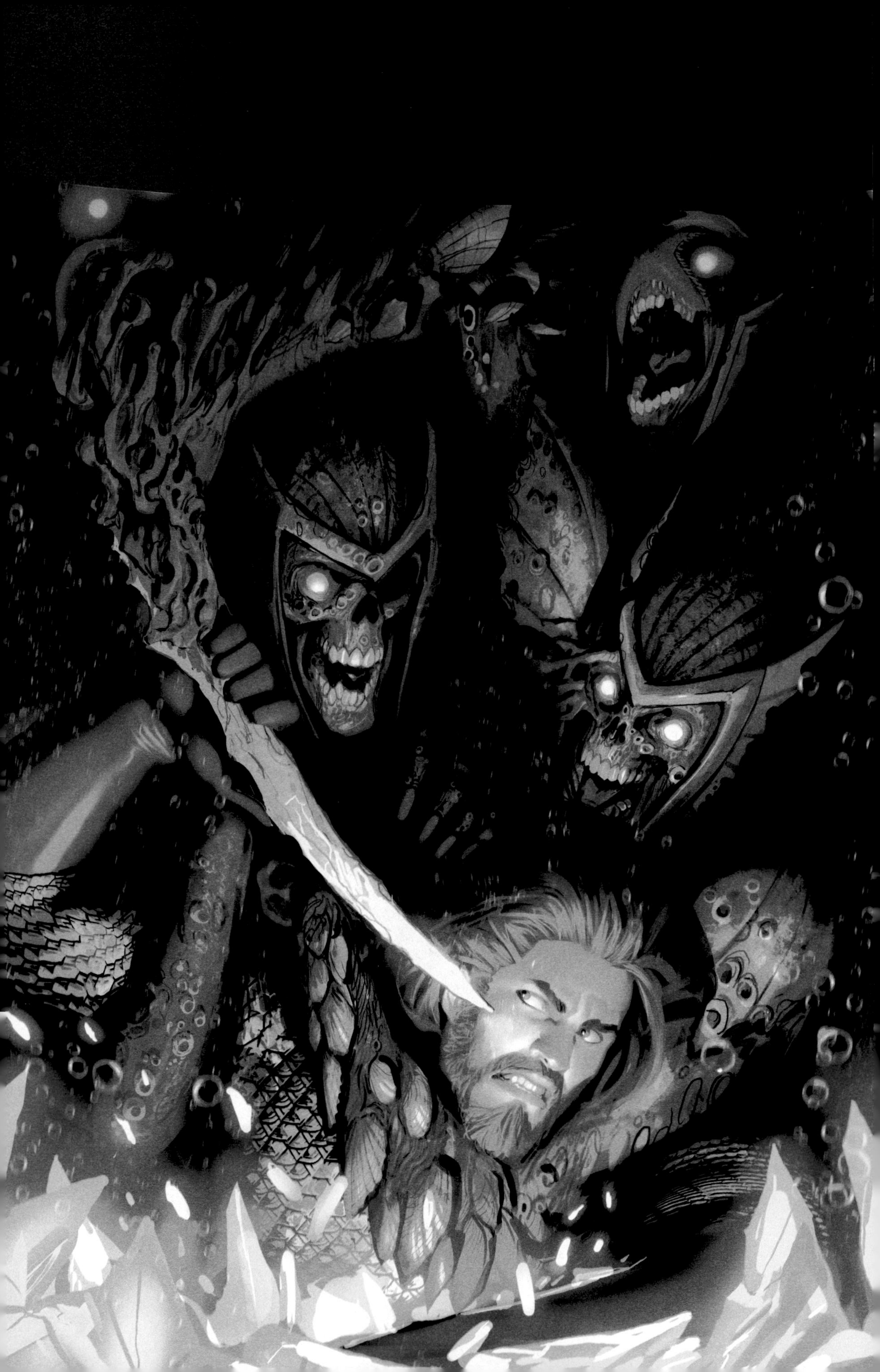

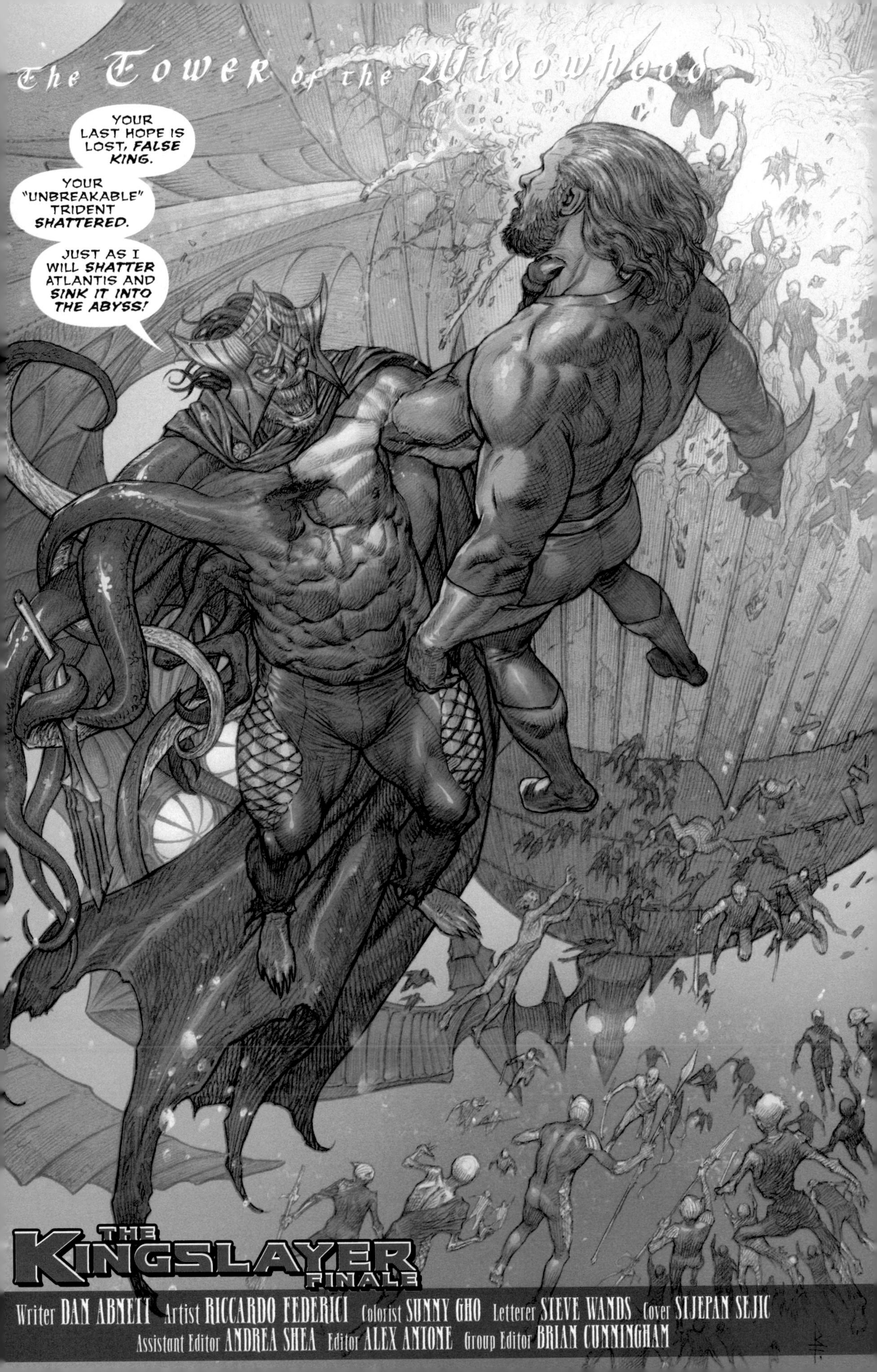
The Tower of the Widowhood
YOUR LAST HOPE IS LOST, FALSE KING.
YOUR "UNBREAKABLE" TRIDENT SHATTERED.
JUST AS I WILL SHATTER ATLANTIS AND SINK IT INTO THE ABYSS!
THE KINGSLAYER FINALE
Writer DAN ABNETT Artist RICCARDO FEDERICI Colorist SUNNY GHO Letterer STEVE WANDS Cover SIJEPAN SEJIC
Assistant Editor ANDREA SHEA Editor ALEX ANTONE Group Editor BRIAN CUNNINGHAM

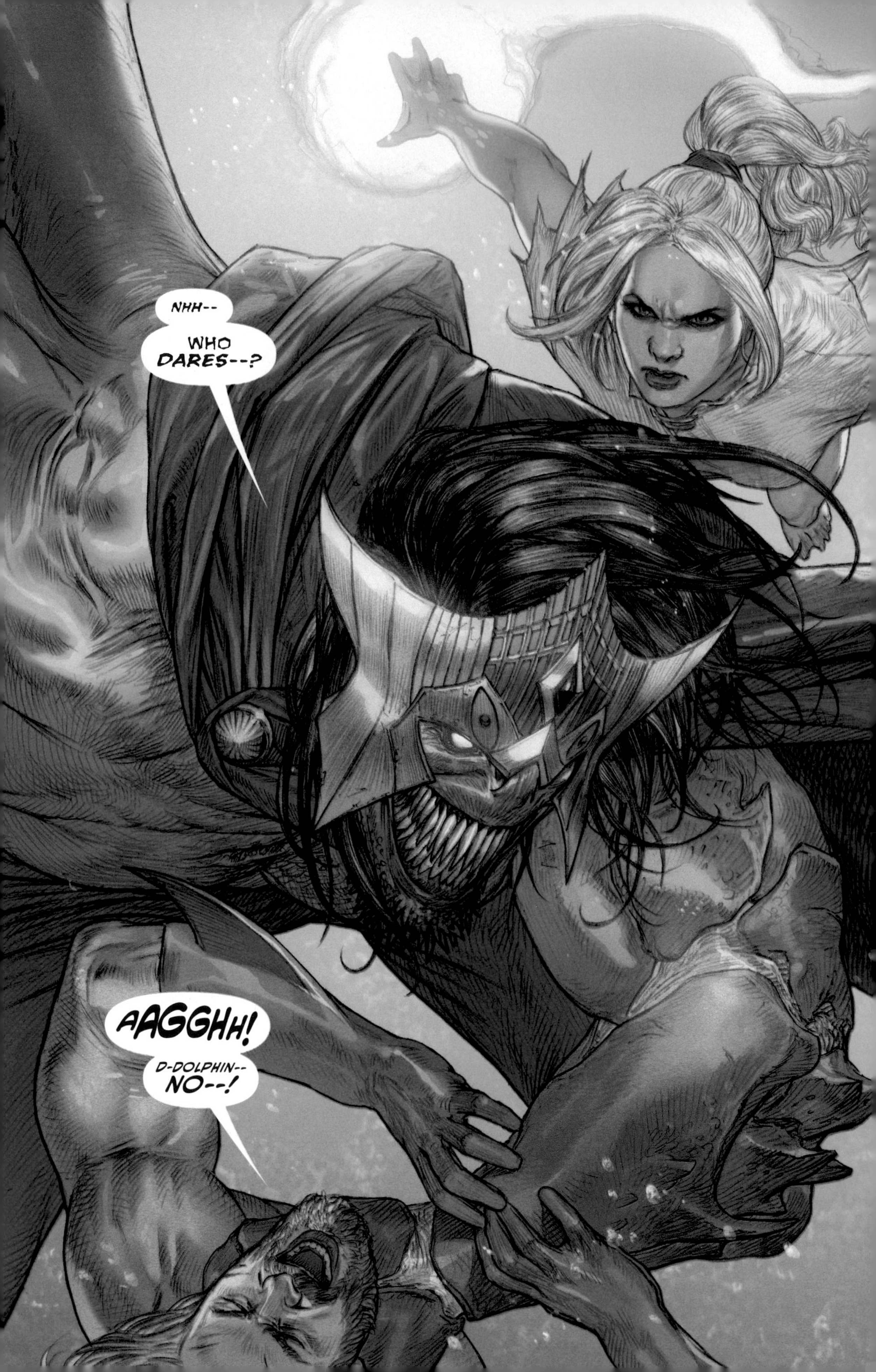
NHH--
WHO DARES--?
AAGGHH!
D-DOLPHIN-- NO--!

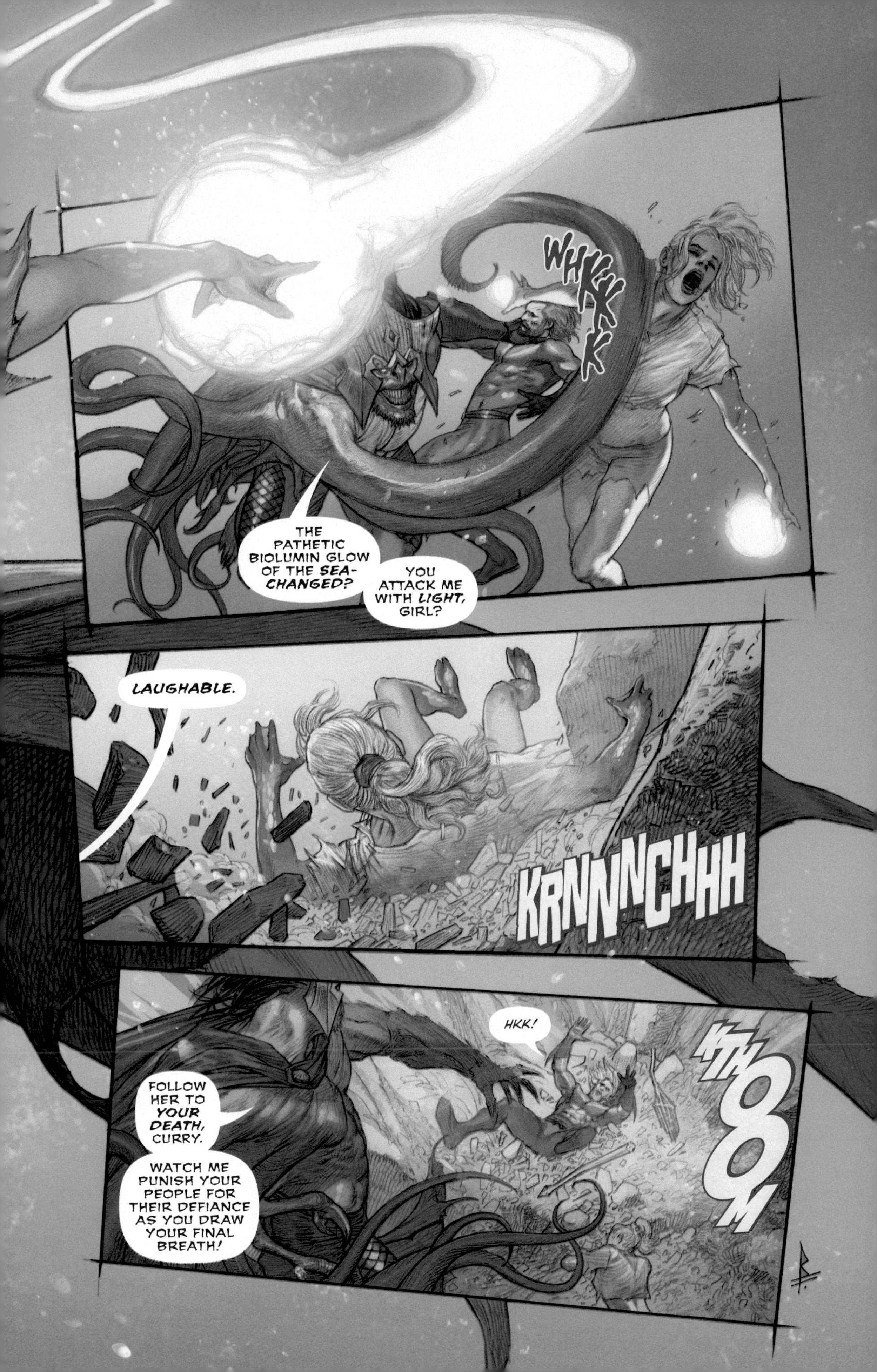
WHKKKK
THE PATHETIC BIOLUMIN GLOW OF THE SEA-CHANGED?
YOU ATTACK ME WITH LIGHT, GIRL?
LAUGHABLE.
KRNNNCHHH
HKK!
KTHOOOM
FOLLOW HER TO YOUR DEATH, CURRY.
WATCH ME PUNISH YOUR PEOPLE FOR THEIR DEFIANCE AS YOU DRAW YOUR FINAL BREATH!

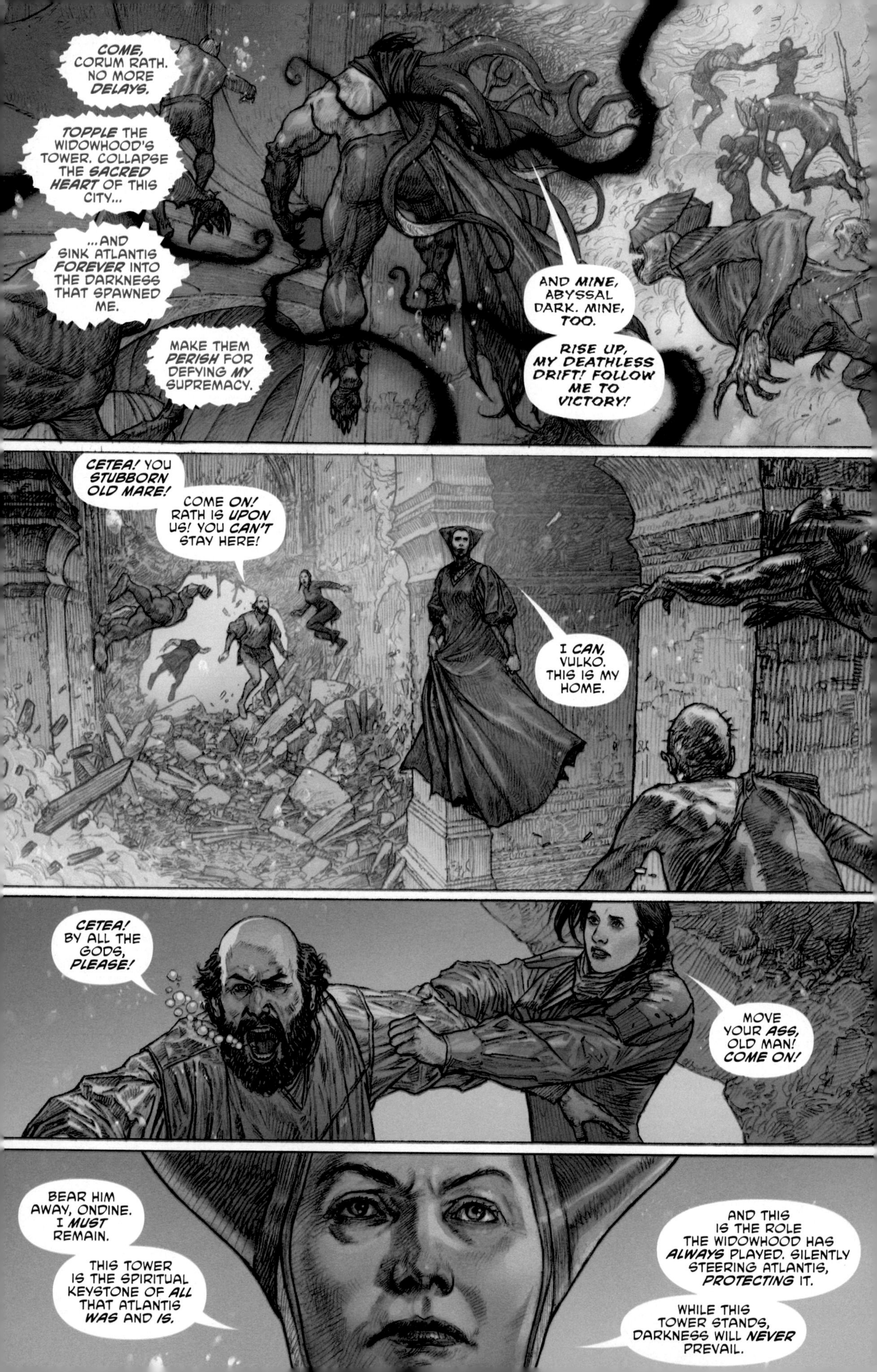

COME, CORUM RATH. NO MORE DELAYS.
TOPPLE THE WIDOWHOOD'S TOWER. COLLAPSE THE SACRED HEART OF THIS CITY...
...AND SINK ATLANTIS FOREVER INTO THE DARKNESS THAT SPAWNED ME.
MAKE THEM PERISH FOR DEFYING MY SUPREMACY.
AND MINE, ABYSSAL DARK. MINE, TOO.
RISE UP, MY DEATHLESS DRIFT! FOLLOW ME TO VICTORY!
CETEA! YOU STUBBORN OLD MARE!
COME ON! RATH IS UPON US! YOU CAN'T STAY HERE!
I CAN, VULKO. THIS IS MY HOME.
CETEA! BY ALL THE GODS, PLEASE!
MOVE YOUR ASS, OLD MAN! COME ON!
BEAR HIM AWAY, ONDINE. I MUST REMAIN.
THIS TOWER IS THE SPIRITUAL KEYSTONE OF ALL THAT ATLANTIS WAS AND IS.
AND THIS IS THE ROLE THE WIDOWHOOD HAS ALWAYS PLAYED. SILENTLY STEERING ATLANTIS, PROTECTING IT.
WHILE THIS TOWER STANDS, DARKNESS WILL NEVER PREVAIL.

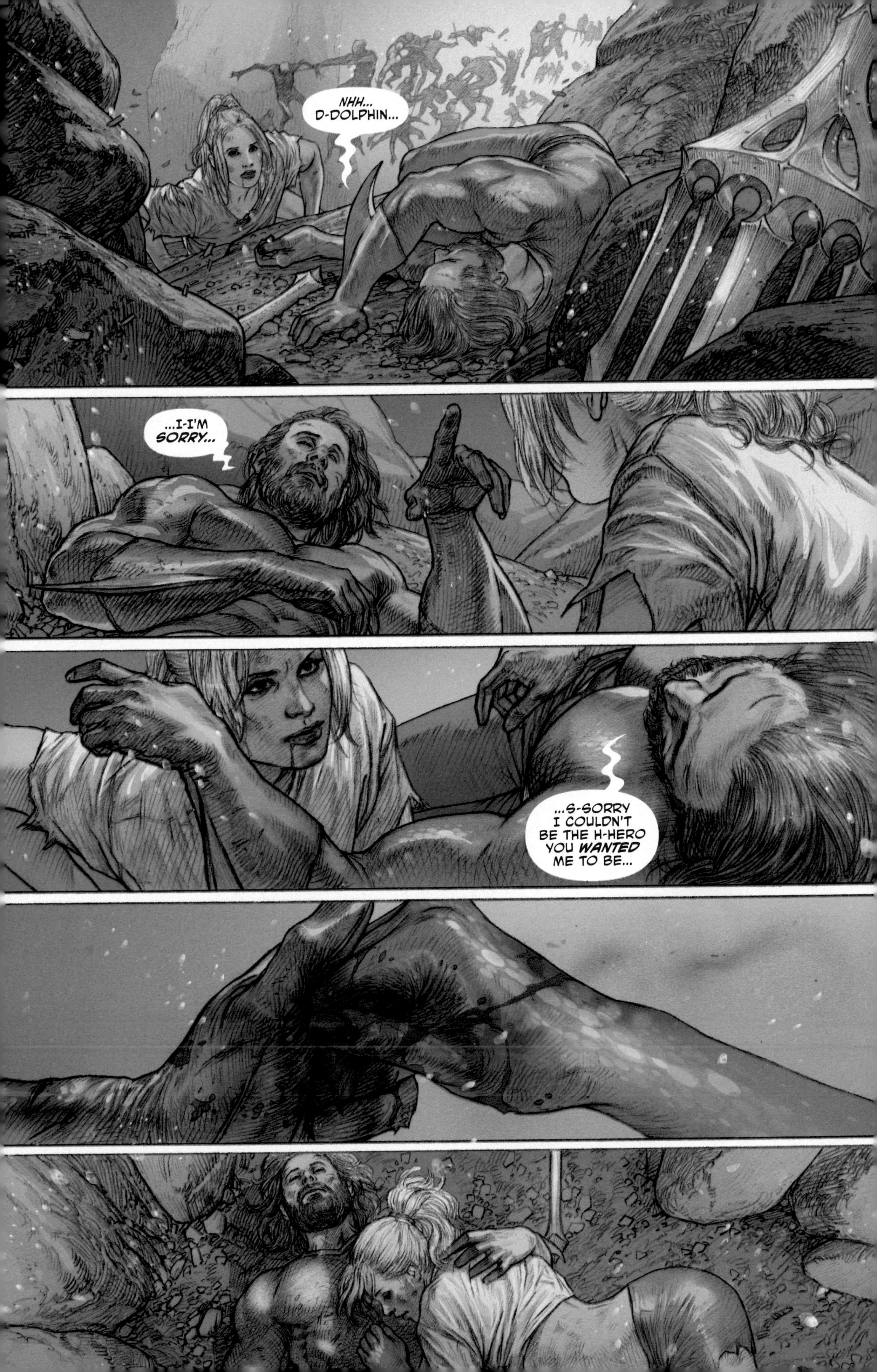
NHH... D-DOLPHIN...
...I-I'M SORRY...
...S-SORRY I COULDN'T BE THE H-HERO YOU WANTED ME TO BE...

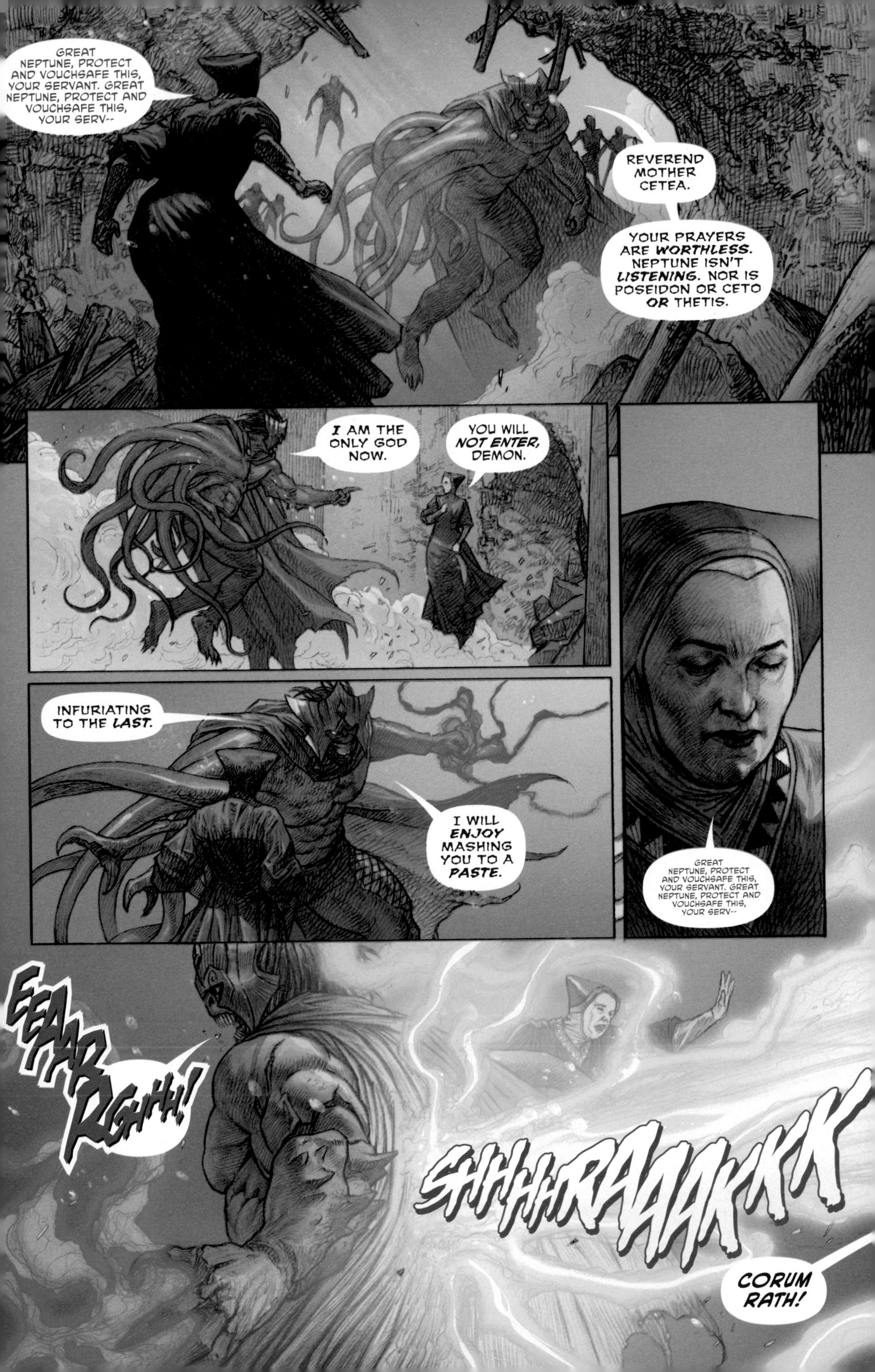

GREAT NEPTUNE, PROTECT AND VOUCHSAFE THIS, YOUR SERVANT. GREAT NEPTUNE, PROTECT AND VOUCHSAFE THIS, YOUR SERV--
REVEREND MOTHER CETEA.
YOUR PRAYERS ARE WORTHLESS. NEPTUNE ISN'T LISTENING. NOR IS POSEIDON OR CETO OR THETIS.
I AM THE ONLY GOD NOW.
YOU WILL NOT ENTER, DEMON.
INFURIATING TO THE LAST.
I WILL ENJOY MASHING YOU TO A PASTE.
GREAT NEPTUNE, PROTECT AND VOUCHSAFE THIS, YOUR SERVANT. GREAT NEPTUNE, PROTECT AND VOUCHSAFE THIS, YOUR SERV--
EEAAARRGHHH!
SHHHHRAAAAKKK
CORUM RATH!

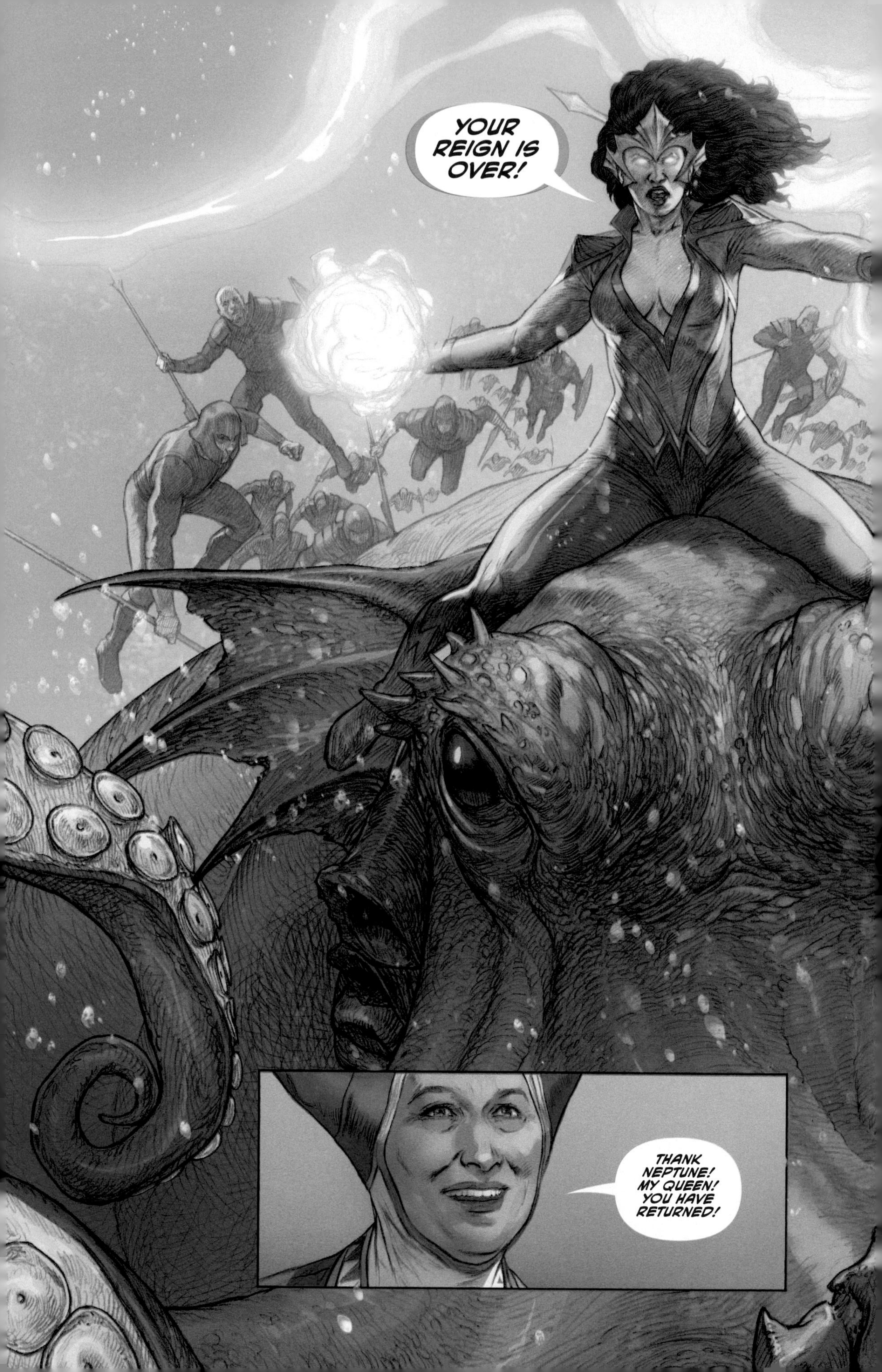
YOUR REIGN IS OVER!
THANK NEPTUNE! MY QUEEN! YOU HAVE RETURNED!

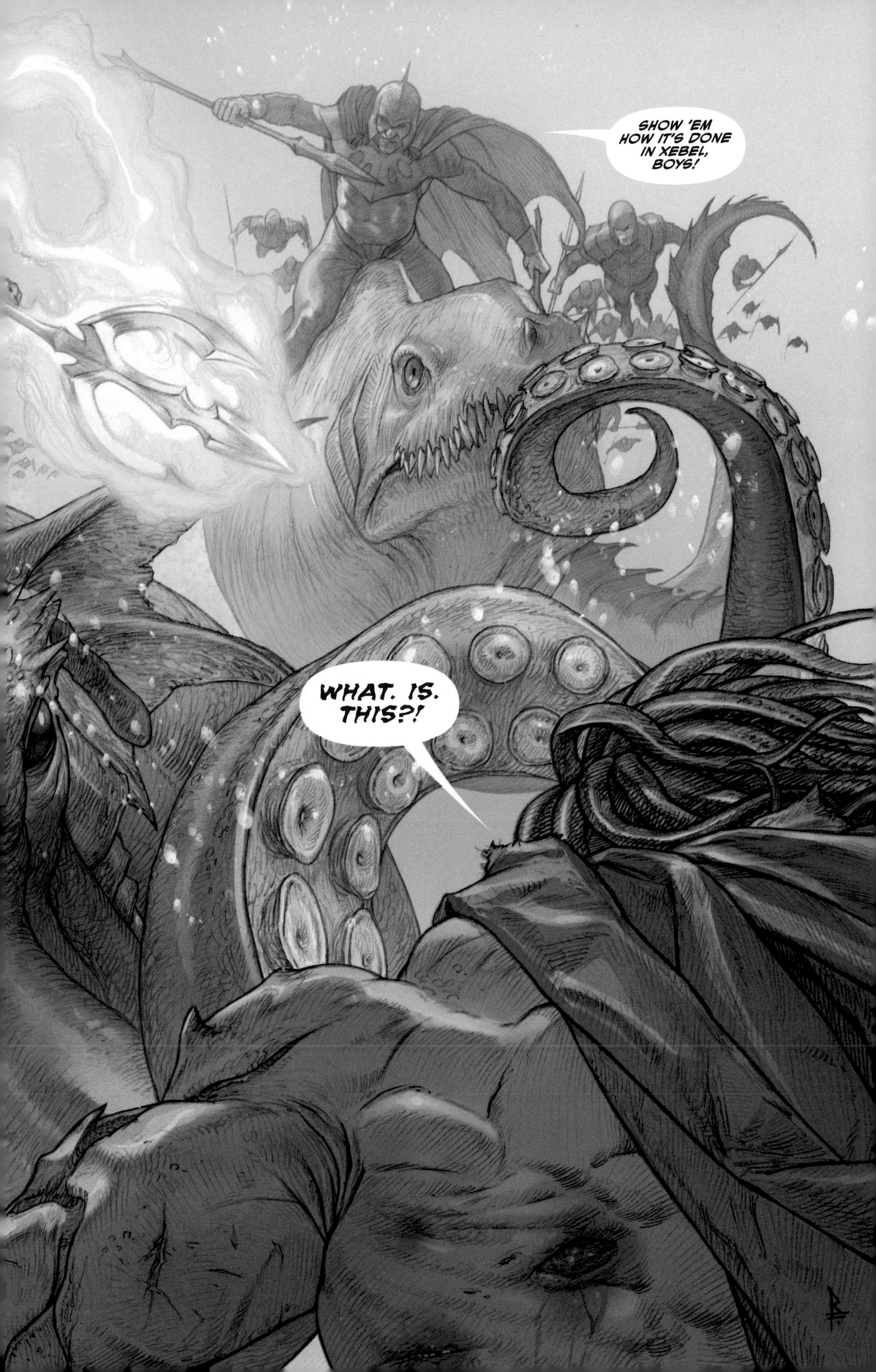
SHOW 'EM HOW IT'S DONE IN XEBEL, BOYS!
WHAT. IS. THIS?!

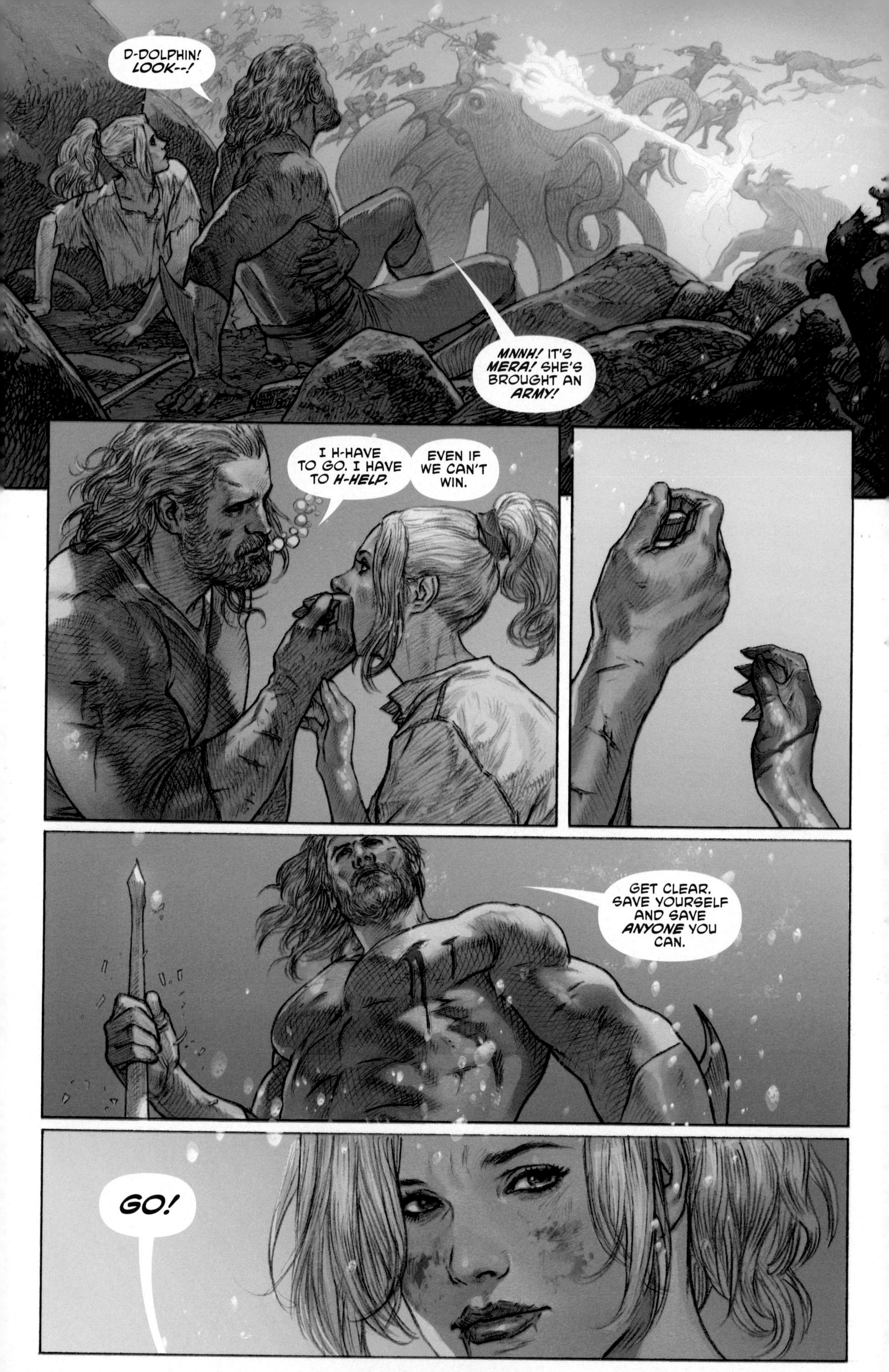
D-DOLPHIN! LOOK--!
MNNH! IT'S MERA! SHE'S BROUGHT AN ARMY!
I H-HAVE TO GO. I HAVE TO H-HELP.
EVEN IF WE CAN'T WIN.
GET CLEAR. SAVE YOURSELF AND SAVE ANYONE YOU CAN.
GO!

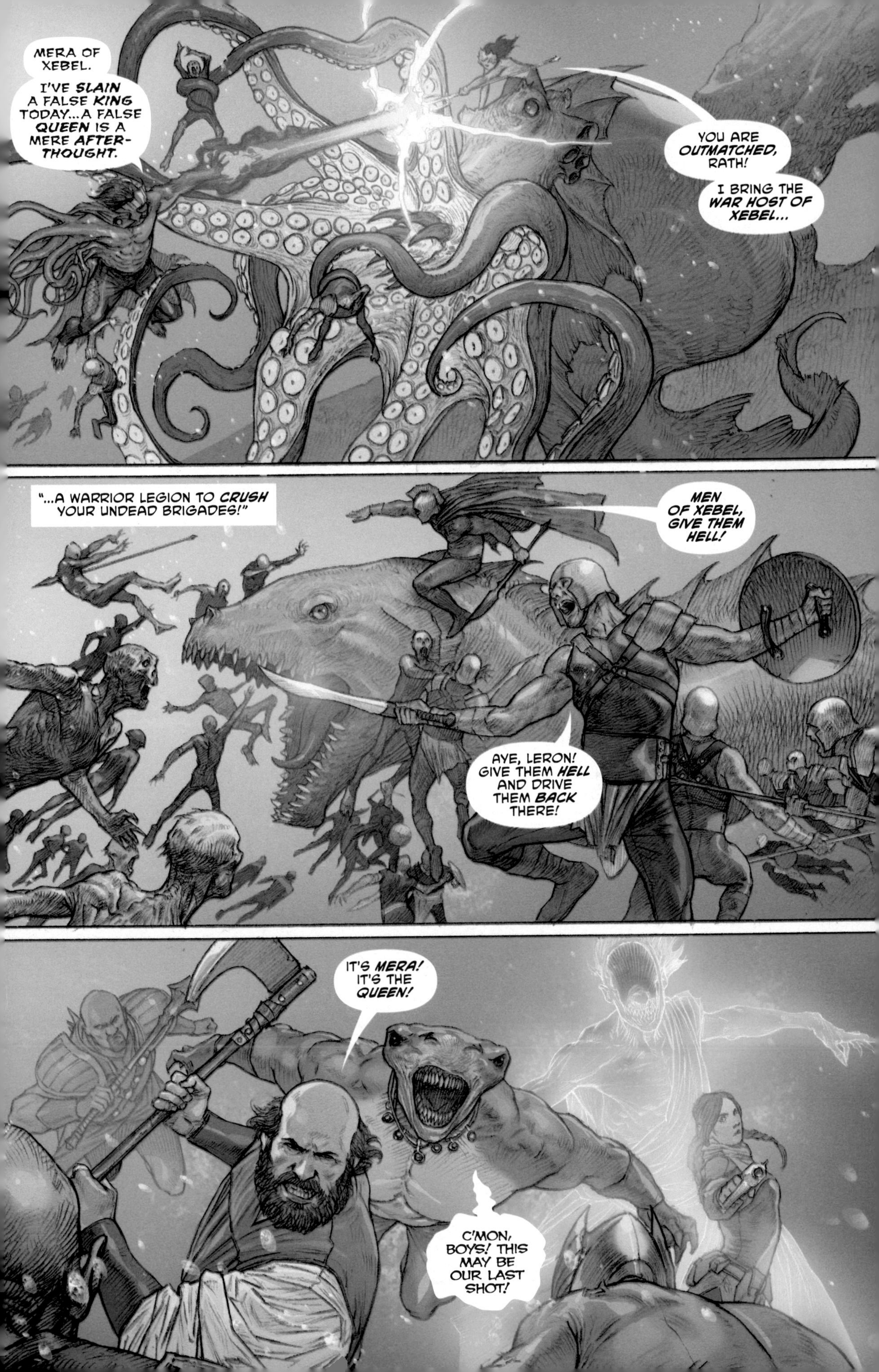
MERA OF XEBEL.
I'VE SLAIN A FALSE KING TODAY...A FALSE QUEEN IS A MERE AFTER-THOUGHT.
YOU ARE OUTMATCHED, RATH!
I BRING THE WAR HOST OF XEBEL...
"...A WARRIOR LEGION TO CRUSH YOUR UNDEAD BRIGADES!"
MEN OF XEBEL, GIVE THEM HELL!
AYE, LERON! GIVE THEM HELL AND DRIVE THEM BACK THERE!
IT'S MERA! IT'S THE QUEEN!
C'MON, BOYS! THIS MAY BE OUR LAST SHOT!

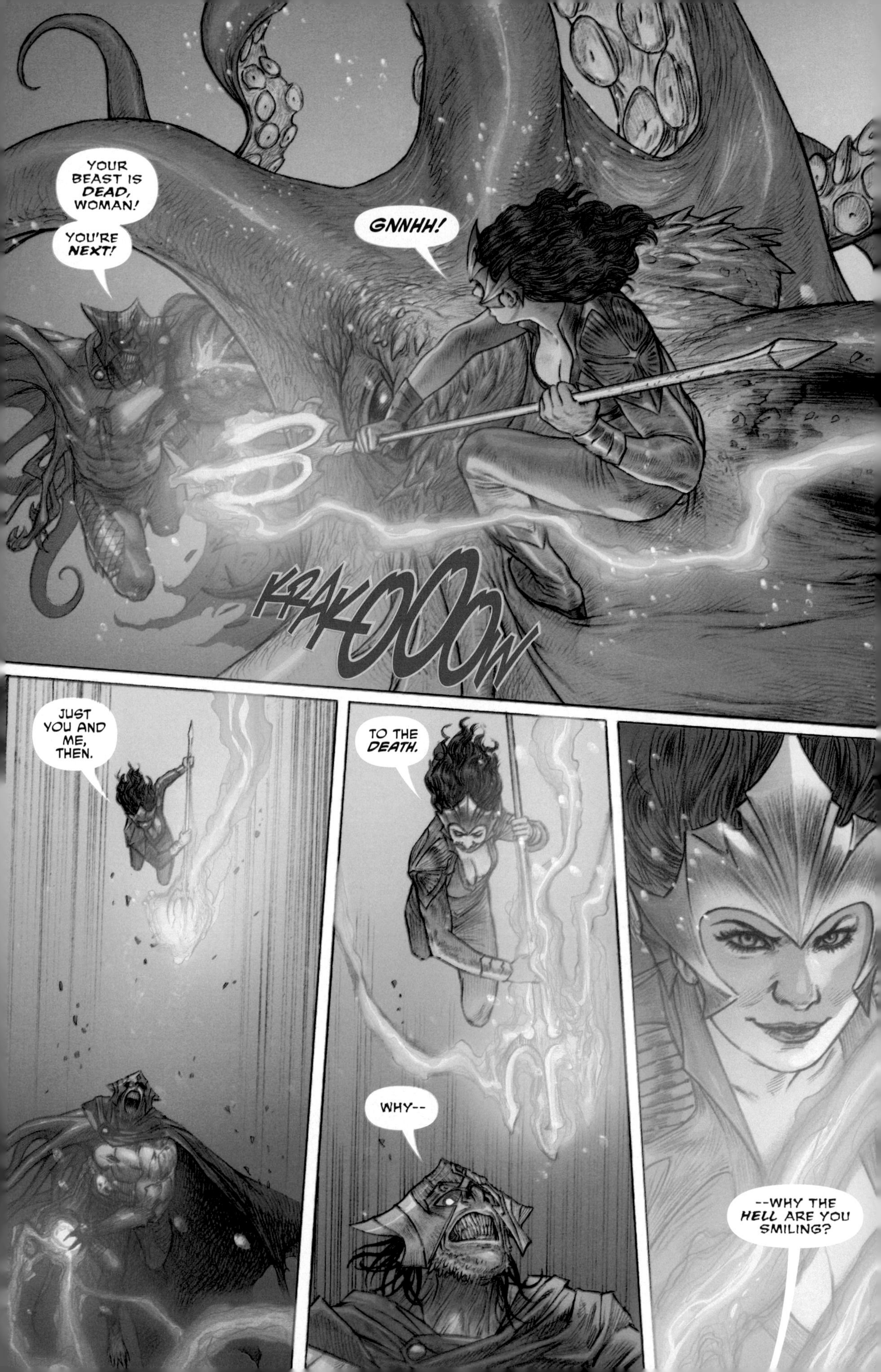
YOUR BEAST IS DEAD, WOMAN!
YOU'RE NEXT!
GNNHH!
KRAKOOOOW
JUST YOU AND ME, THEN.
TO THE DEATH.
WHY--
--WHY THE HELL ARE YOU SMILING?

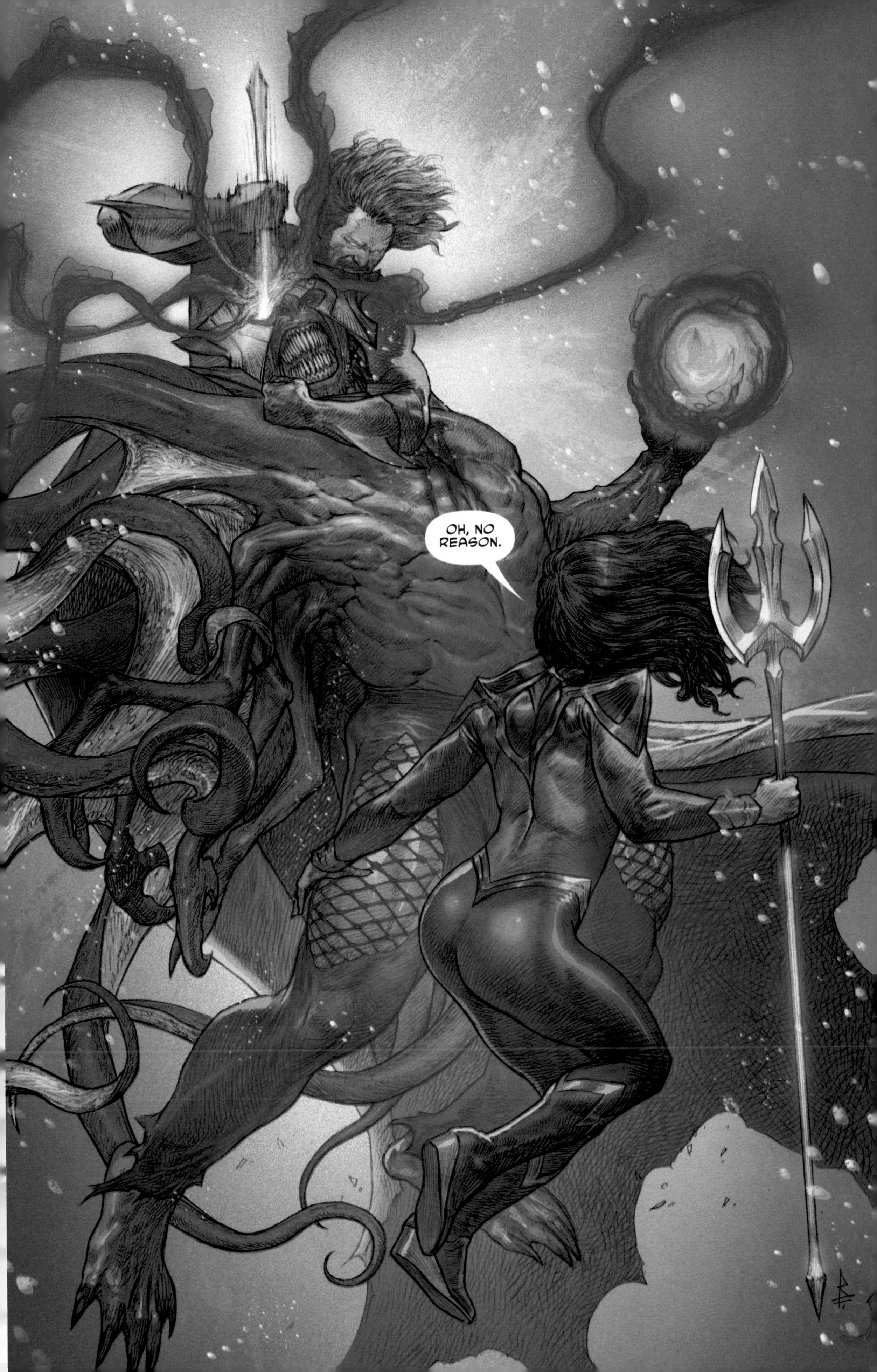
OH, NO REASON.

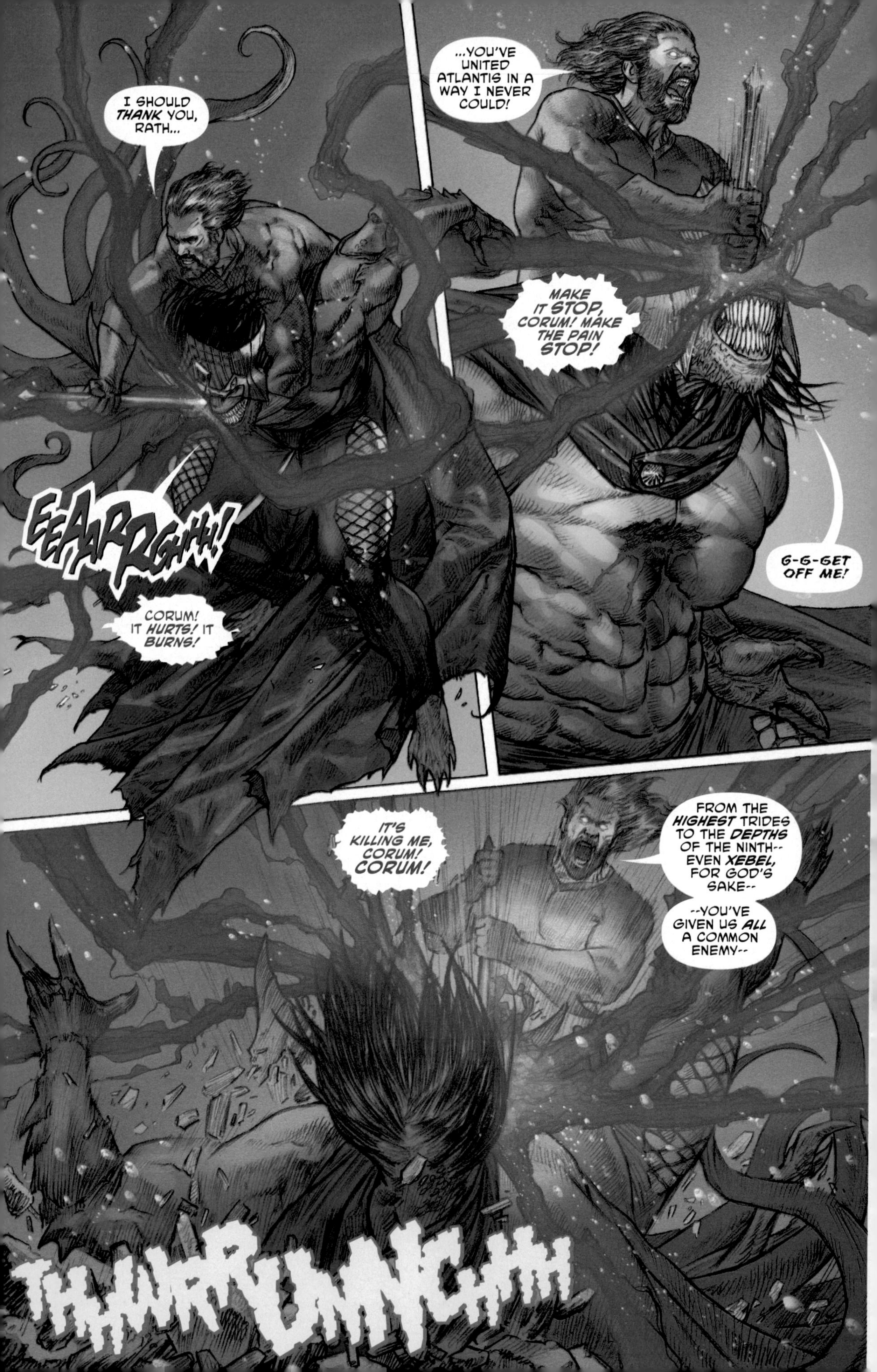
I SHOULD *THANK* YOU, RATH...
...YOU'VE UNITED ATLANTIS IN A WAY I NEVER COULD!
MAKE IT *STOP,* CORUM! MAKE THE PAIN *STOP!*
EEAARRGHH!
CORUM! IT *HURTS!* IT *BURNS!*
G-G-GET OFF ME!
IT'S KILLING ME, CORUM! *CORUM!*
FROM THE *HIGHEST* TRIDES TO THE *DEPTHS* OF THE NINTH-- EVEN *XEBEL,* FOR GOD'S SAKE--
--YOU'VE GIVEN US *ALL* A COMMON ENEMY--
THWRUNCHH

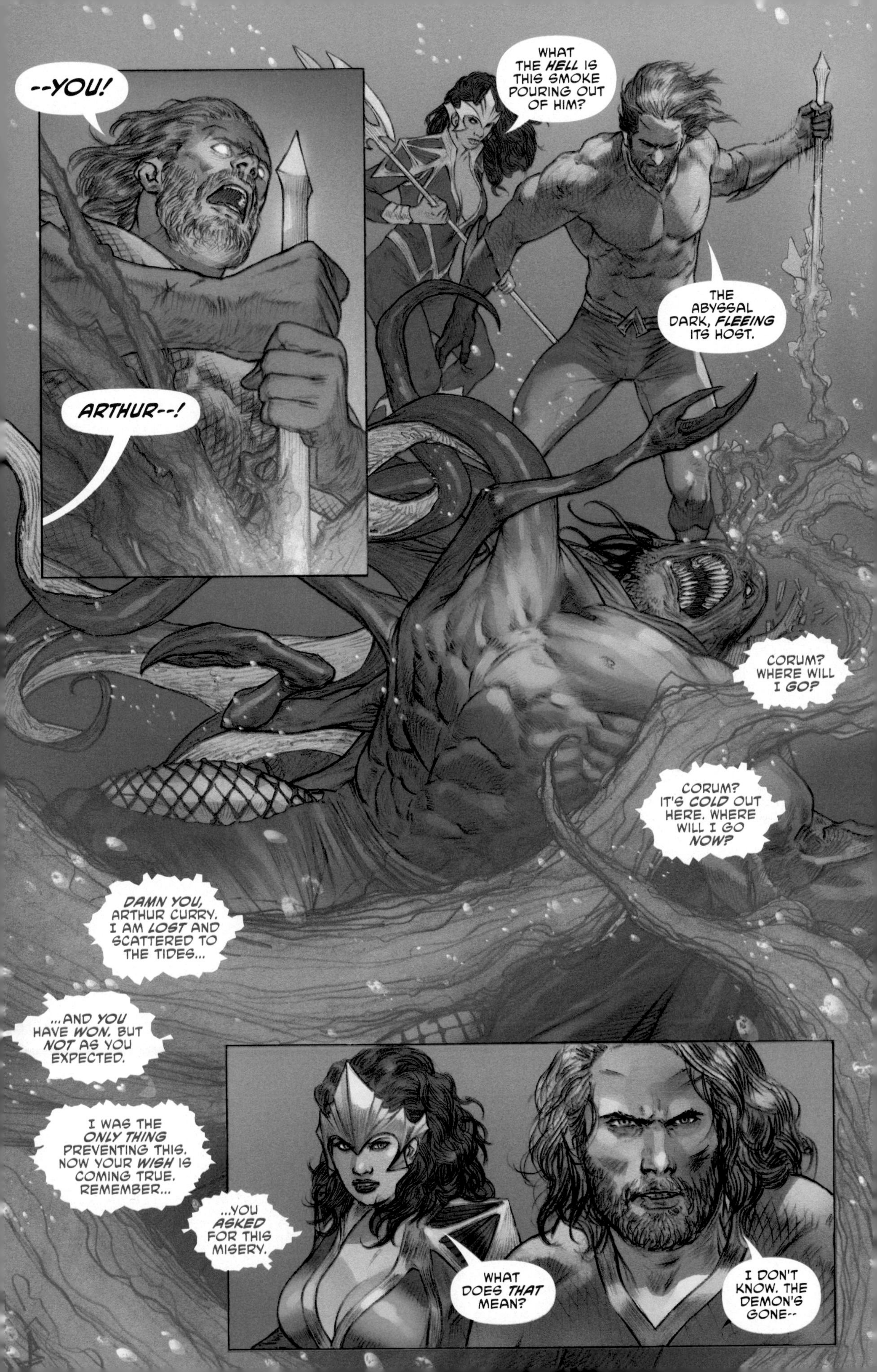
--YOU!
ARTHUR--!
WHAT THE HELL IS THIS SMOKE POURING OUT OF HIM?
THE ABYSSAL DARK, FLEEING ITS HOST.
CORUM? WHERE WILL I GO?
CORUM? IT'S COLD OUT HERE. WHERE WILL I GO NOW?
DAMN YOU, ARTHUR CURRY. I AM LOST AND SCATTERED TO THE TIDES...
...AND YOU HAVE WON. BUT NOT AS YOU EXPECTED.
I WAS THE ONLY THING PREVENTING THIS. NOW YOUR WISH IS COMING TRUE. REMEMBER...
...YOU ASKED FOR THIS MISERY.
WHAT DOES THAT MEAN?
I DON'T KNOW. THE DEMON'S GONE--

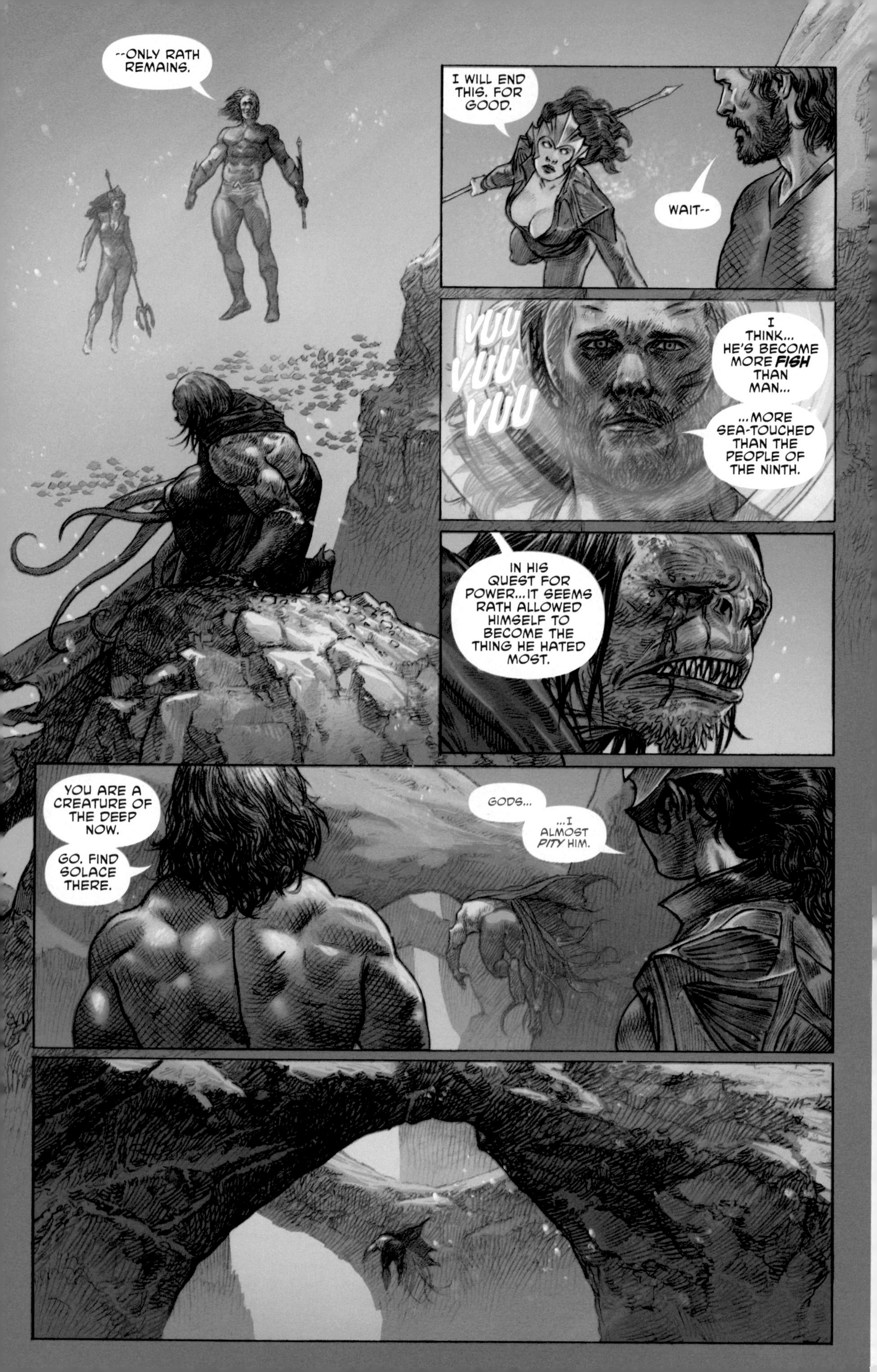
--ONLY RATH REMAINS.
I WILL END THIS. FOR GOOD.
WAIT--
VUU VUU VUU
I THINK... HE'S BECOME MORE FISH THAN MAN...
...MORE SEA-TOUCHED THAN THE PEOPLE OF THE NINTH.
IN HIS QUEST FOR POWER...IT SEEMS RATH ALLOWED HIMSELF TO BECOME THE THING HE HATED MOST.
YOU ARE A CREATURE OF THE DEEP NOW.
GO. FIND SOLACE THERE.
GODS...
...I ALMOST PITY HIM.

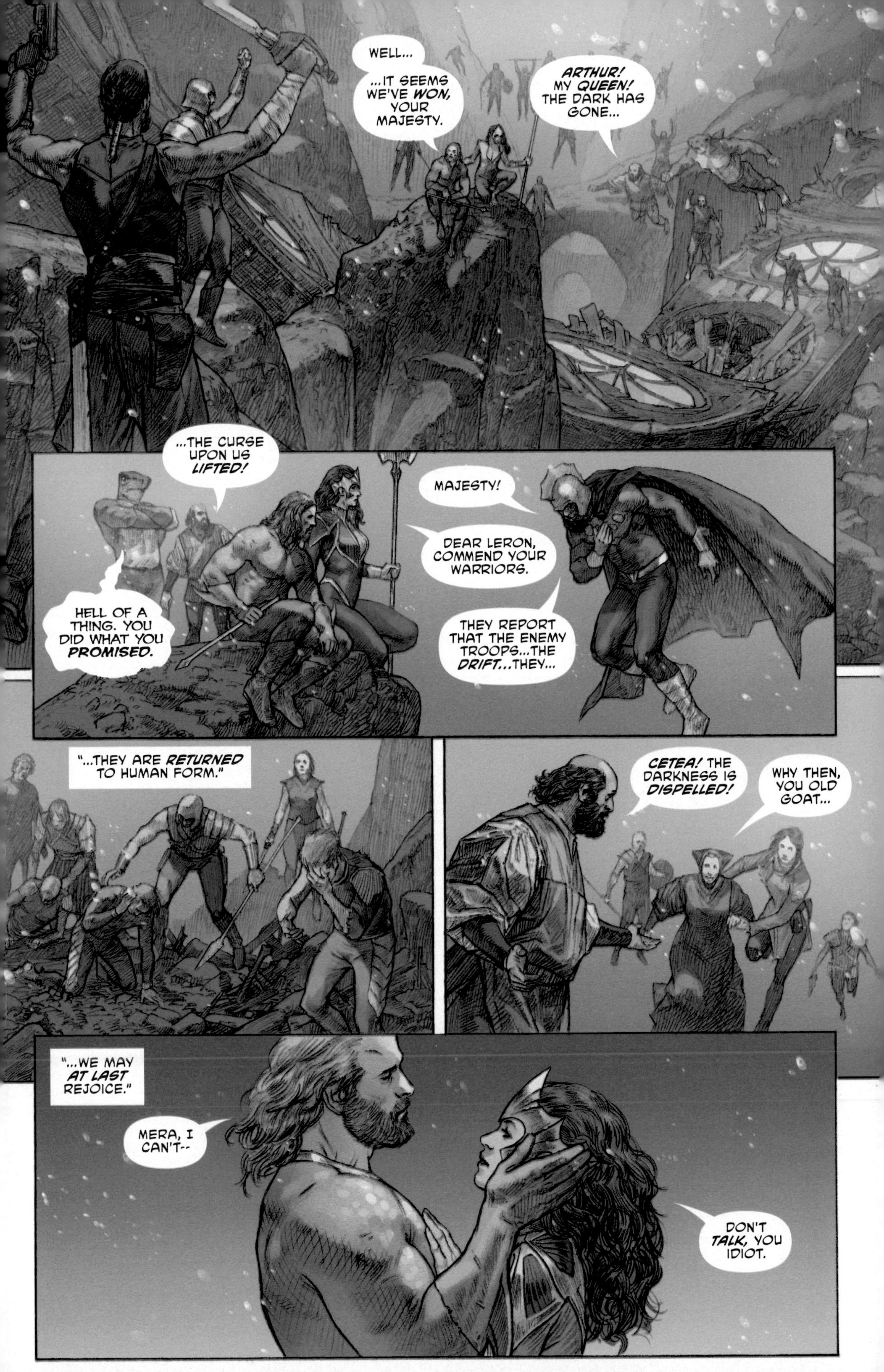
WELL...
...IT SEEMS WE'VE WON, YOUR MAJESTY.
ARTHUR! MY QUEEN! THE DARK HAS GONE...
...THE CURSE UPON US LIFTED!
HELL OF A THING. YOU DID WHAT YOU PROMISED.
MAJESTY!
DEAR LERON, COMMEND YOUR WARRIORS.
THEY REPORT THAT THE ENEMY TROOPS...THE DRIFT...THEY...
"...THEY ARE RETURNED TO HUMAN FORM."
CETEA! THE DARKNESS IS DISPELLED!
WHY THEN, YOU OLD GOAT...
"...WE MAY AT LAST REJOICE."
MERA, I CAN'T--
DON'T TALK, YOU IDIOT.

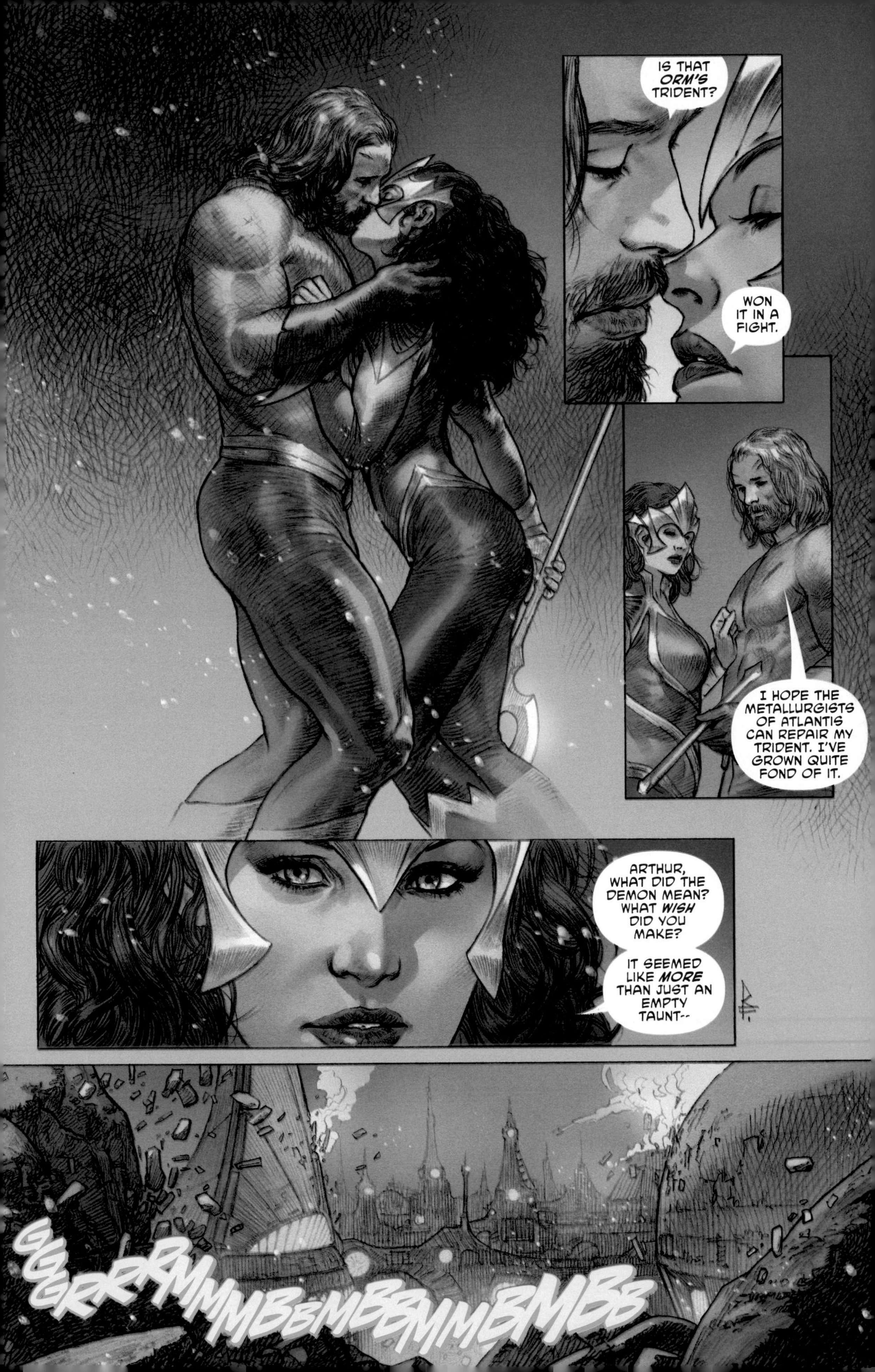
IS THAT ORM'S TRIDENT?
WON IT IN A FIGHT.
I HOPE THE METALLURGISTS OF ATLANTIS CAN REPAIR MY TRIDENT. I'VE GROWN QUITE FOND OF IT.
ARTHUR, WHAT DID THE DEMON MEAN? WHAT WISH DID YOU MAKE?
IT SEEMED LIKE MORE THAN JUST AN EMPTY TAUNT--
GGGRRRMMMMBBBMBBBMMMBMBB

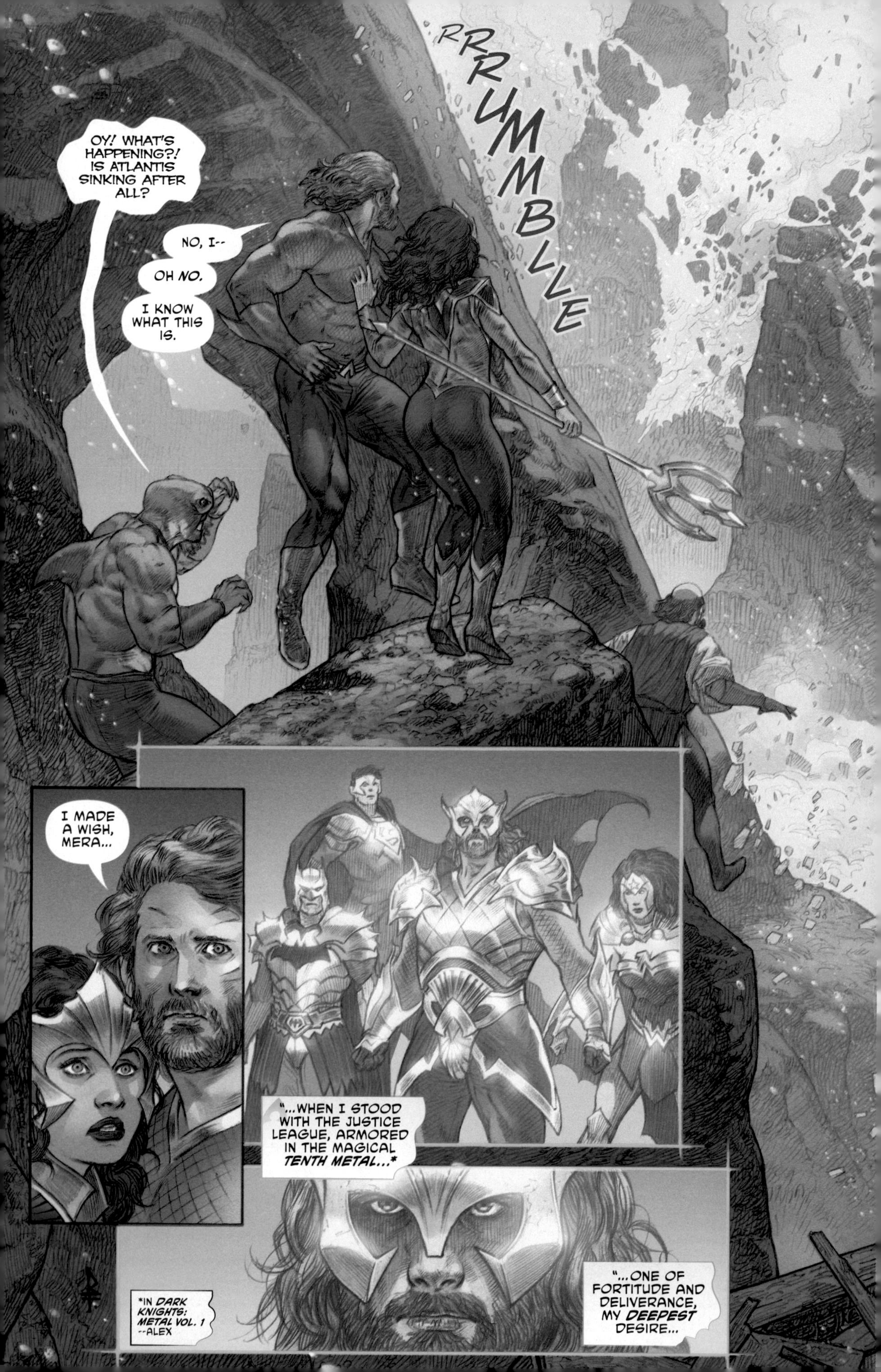
RRRUMMBLLE
OY! WHAT'S HAPPENING?! IS ATLANTIS SINKING AFTER ALL?
NO, I--
OH NO.
I KNOW WHAT THIS IS.
I MADE A WISH, MERA...
"...WHEN I STOOD WITH THE JUSTICE LEAGUE, ARMORED IN THE MAGICAL TENTH METAL...*
*IN DARK KNIGHTS: METAL VOL. 1 --ALEX
"...ONE OF FORTITUDE AND DELIVERANCE, MY DEEPEST DESIRE...

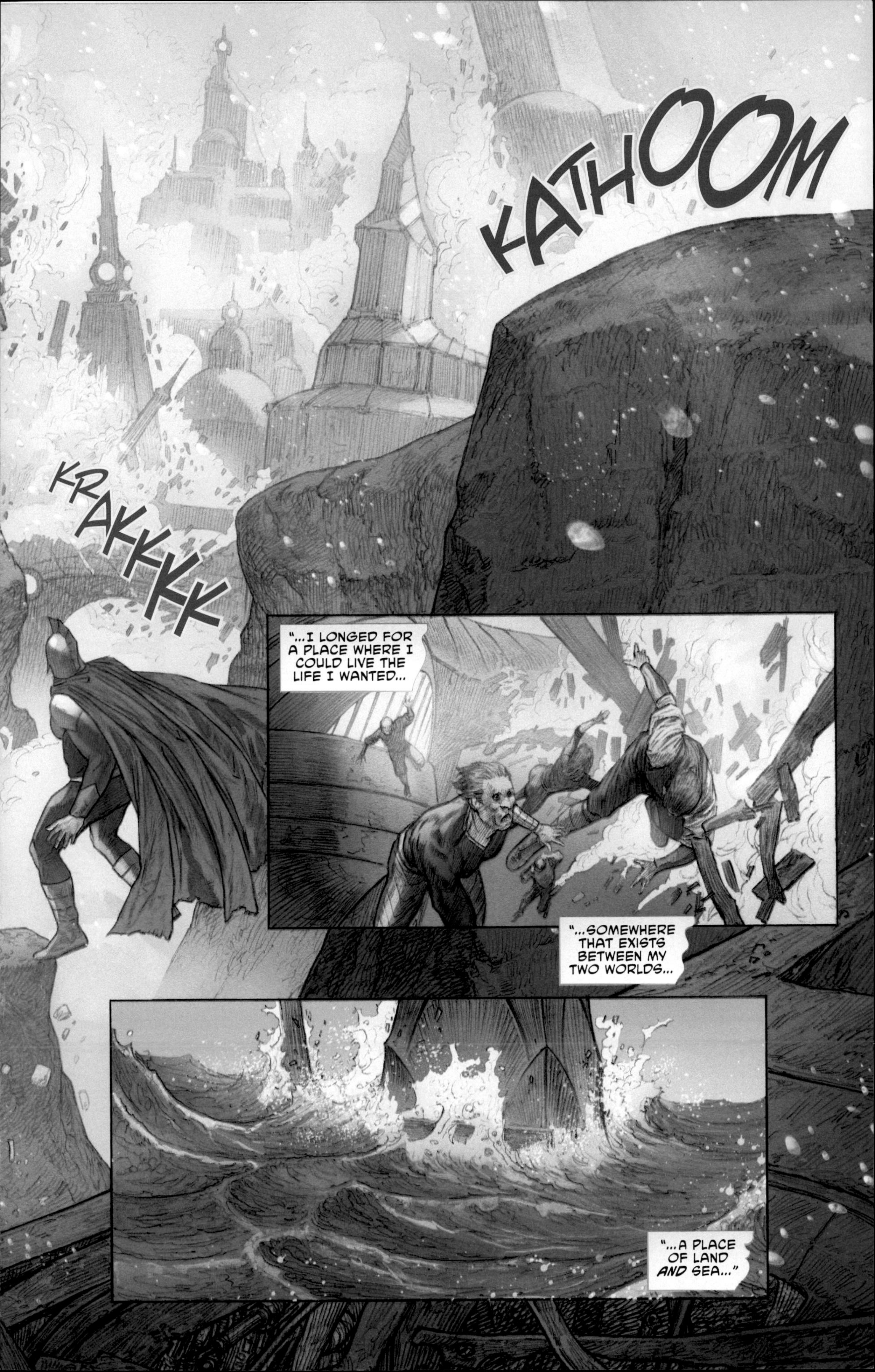
KATHOOM
KRAKKKK
"...I LONGED FOR A PLACE WHERE I COULD LIVE THE LIFE I WANTED...
"...SOMEWHERE THAT EXISTS BETWEEN MY TWO WORLDS...
"...A PLACE OF LAND *AND* SEA..."

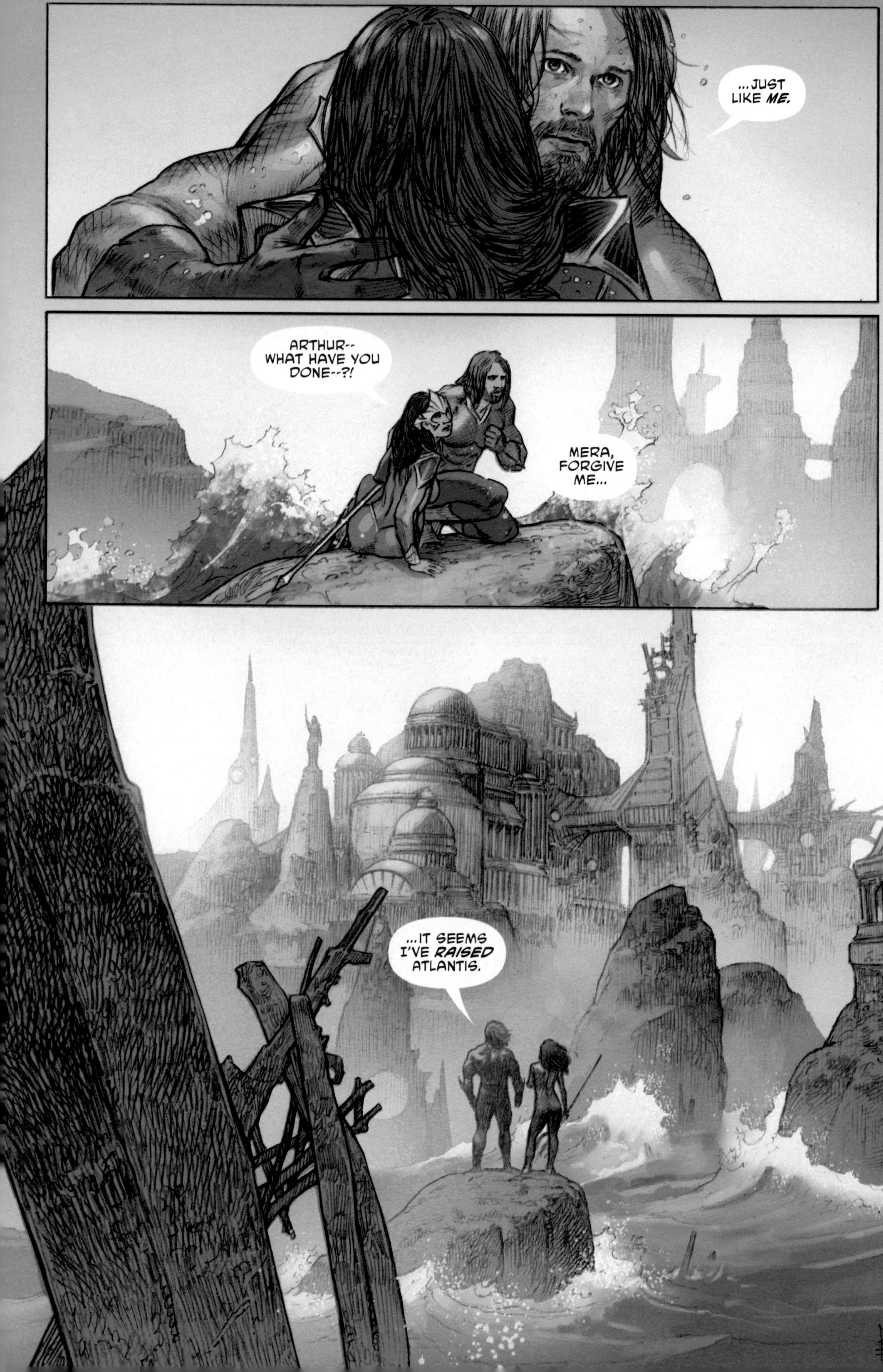
...JUST LIKE *ME.*
ARTHUR-- WHAT HAVE YOU DONE--?!
MERA, FORGIVE ME...
...IT SEEMS I'VE *RAISED* ATLANTIS.

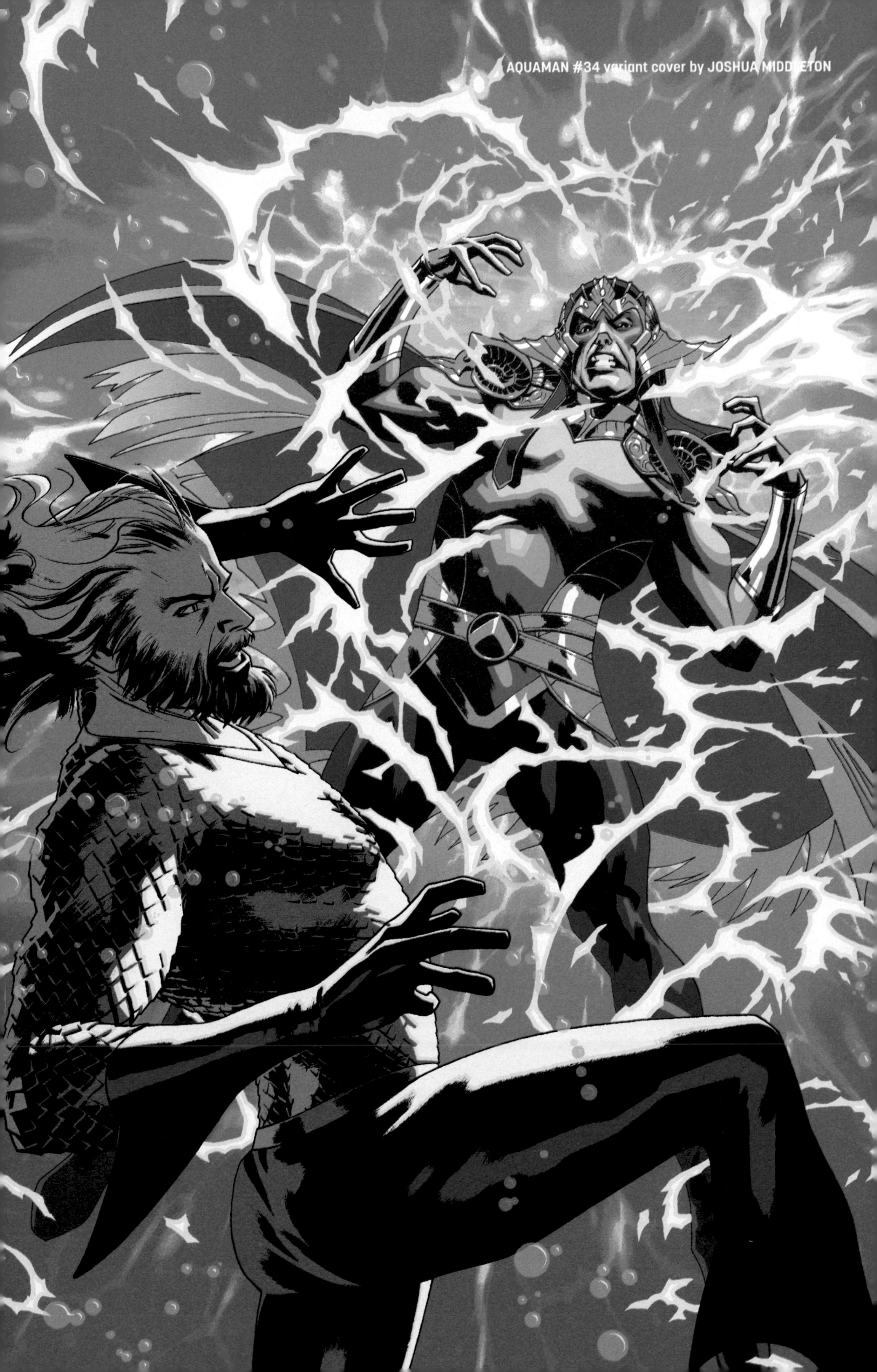

AQUAMAN #34 variant cover by JOSHUA MIDDLETON

AQUAMAN #35 variant cover by JOSHUA MIDDLETON

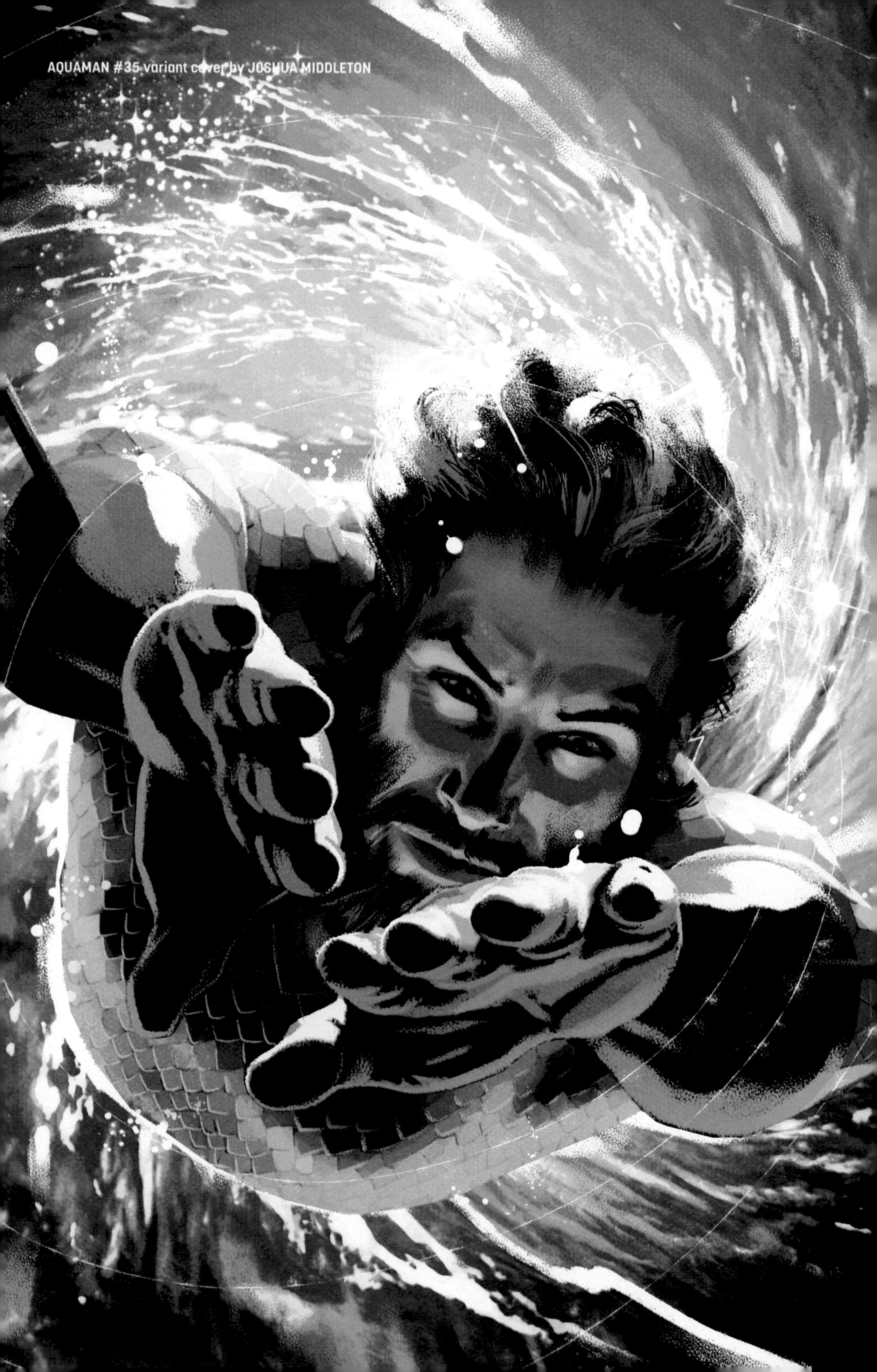

AQUAMAN #36 variant cover by JOSHUA MIDDLETON

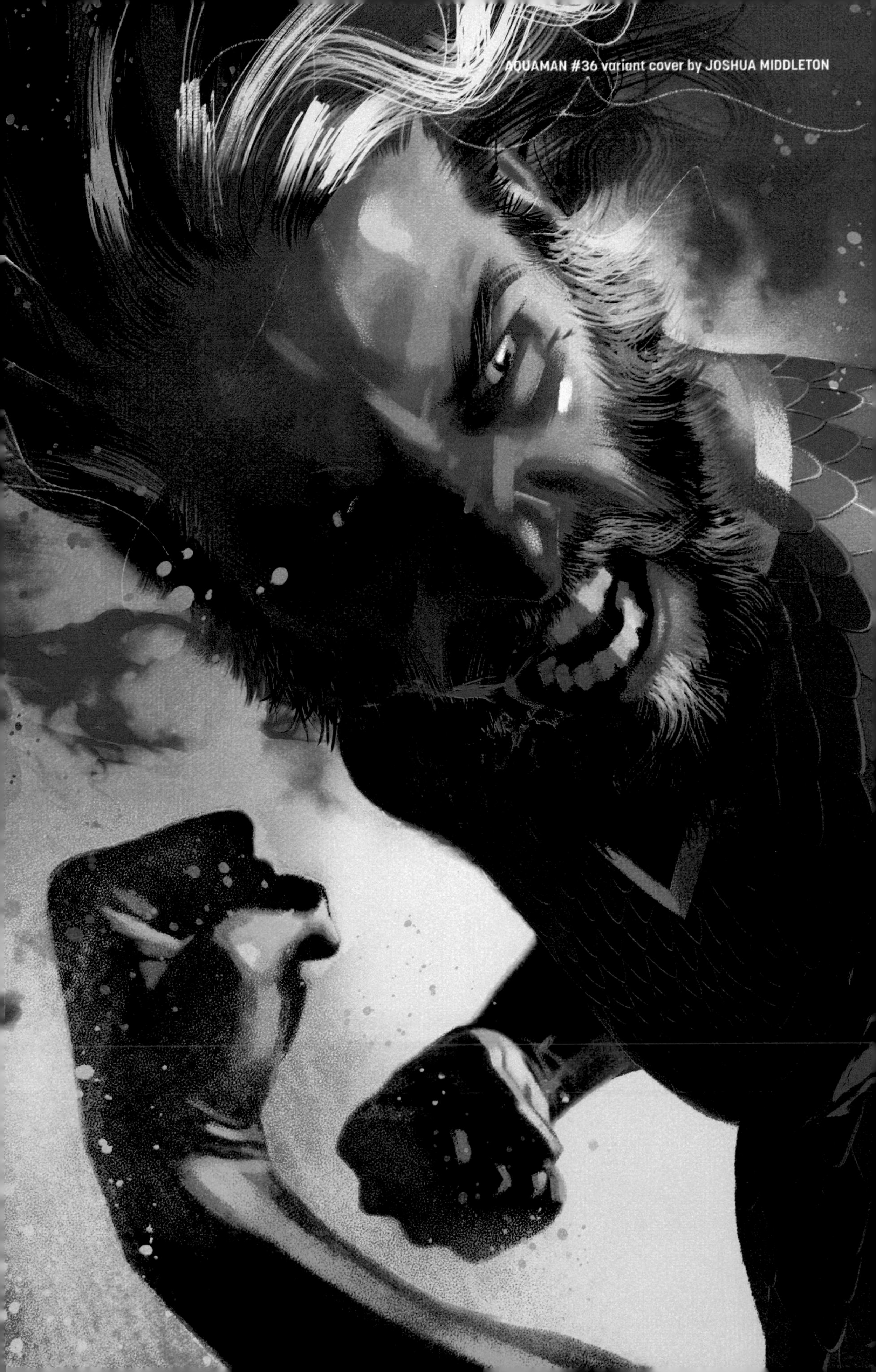

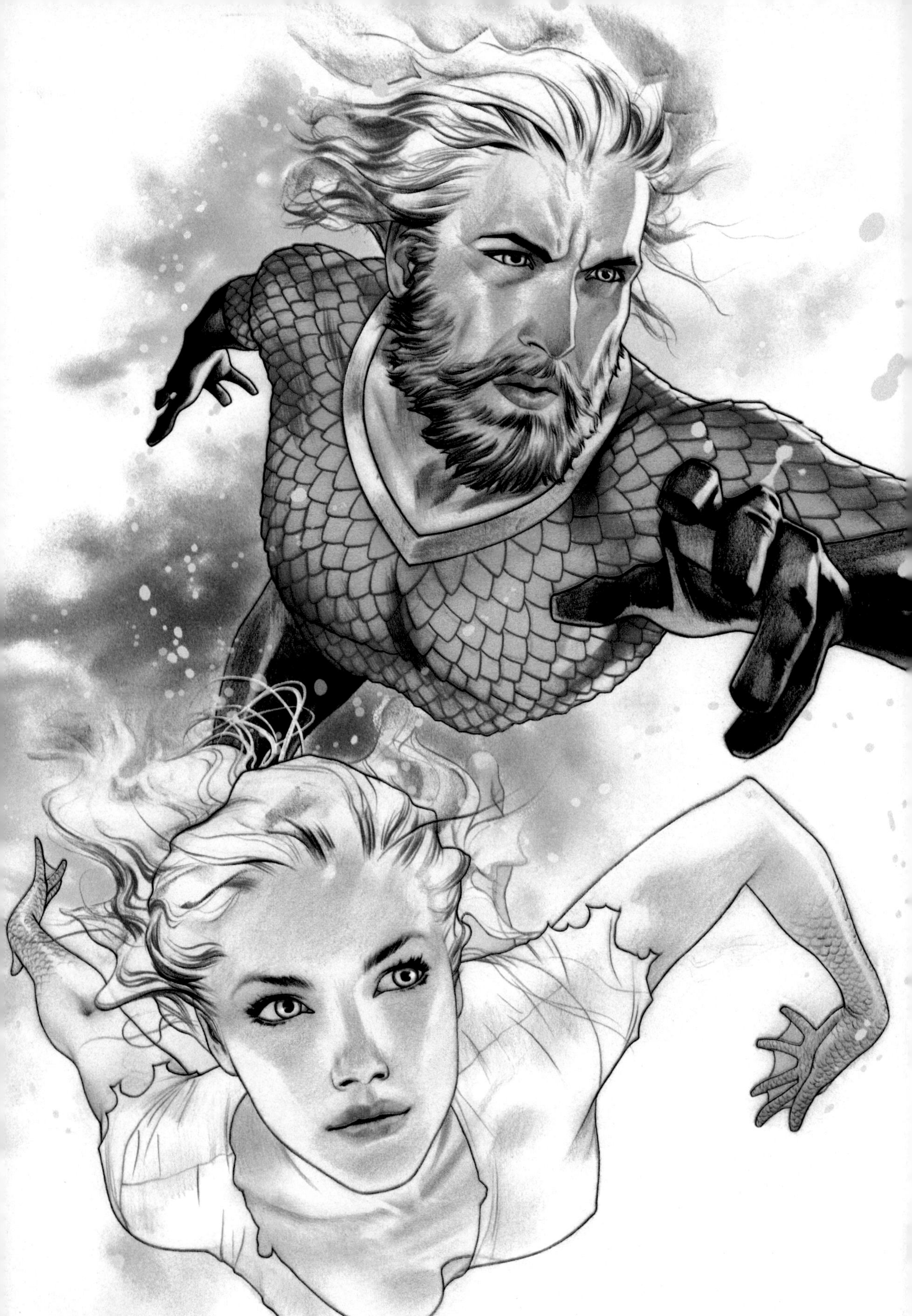

AQUAMAN #37 variant cover by JOSHUA MIDDLETON

AQUAMAN #38 variant cover by JOSHUA MIDDLETON

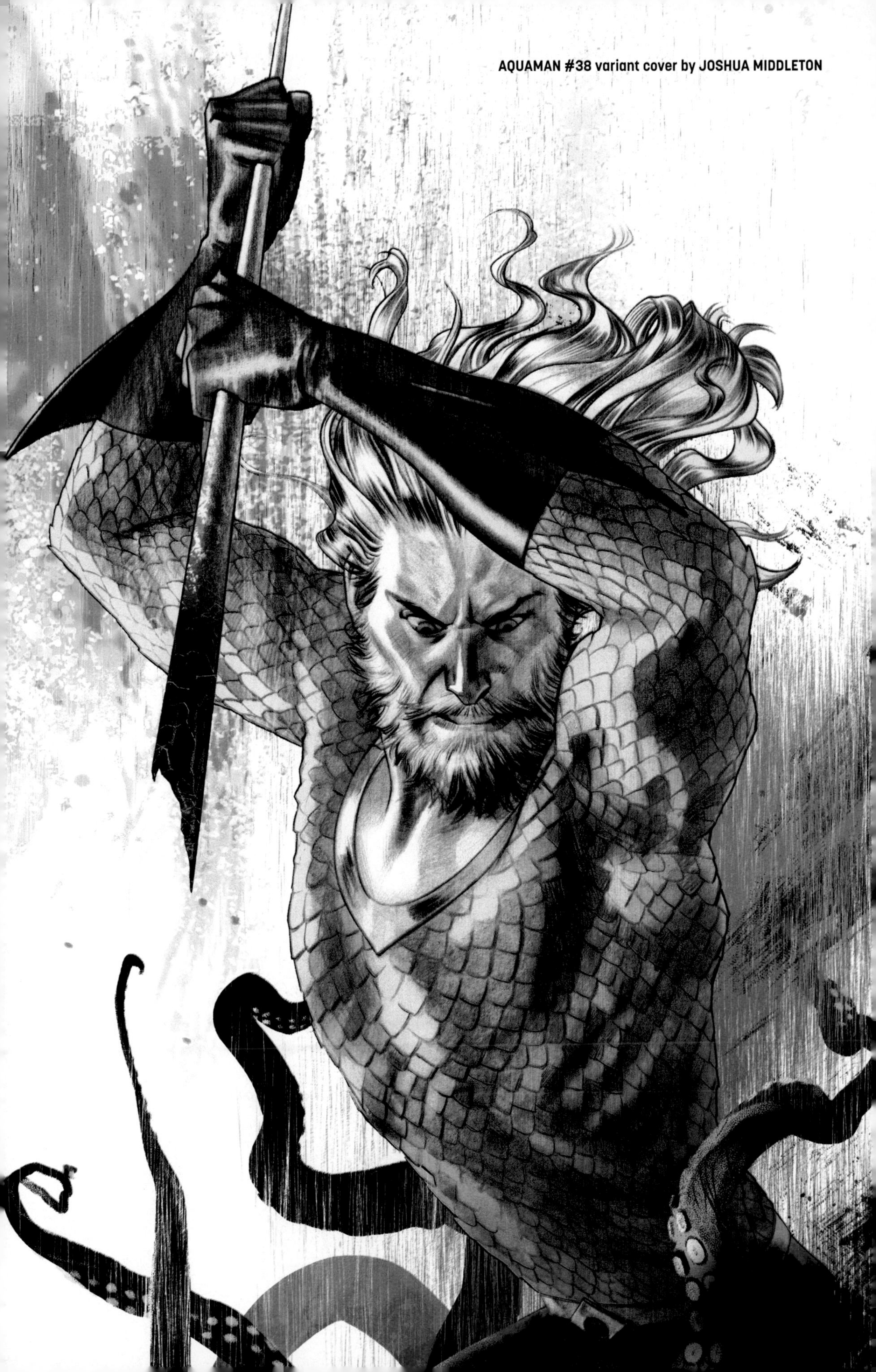

KING RATH full-body character designs by DOUG MAHNKE

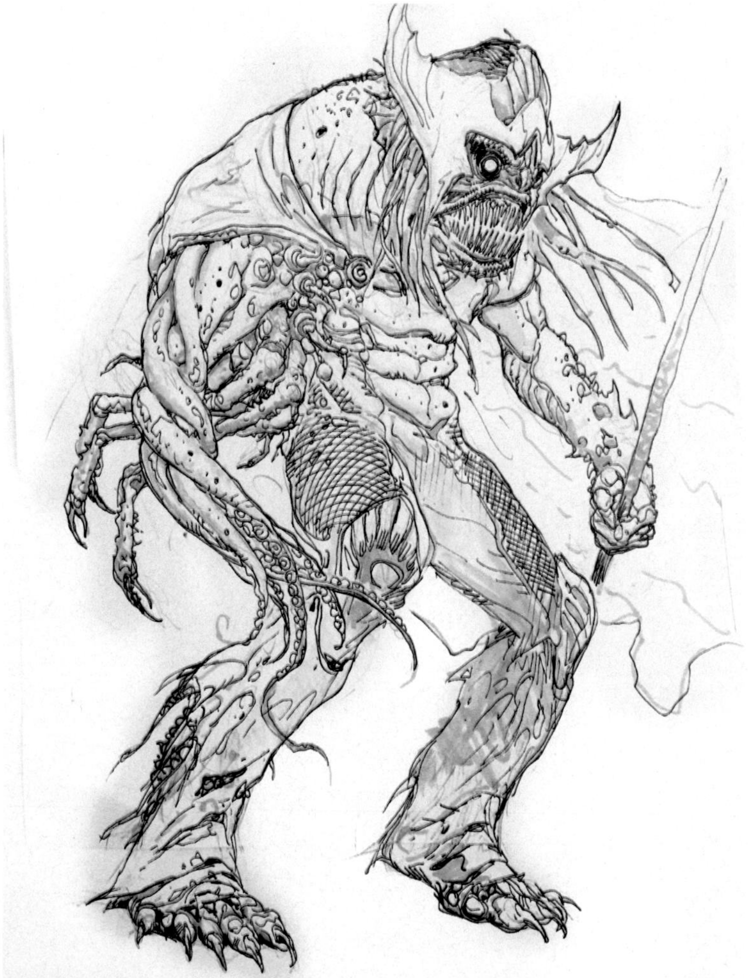

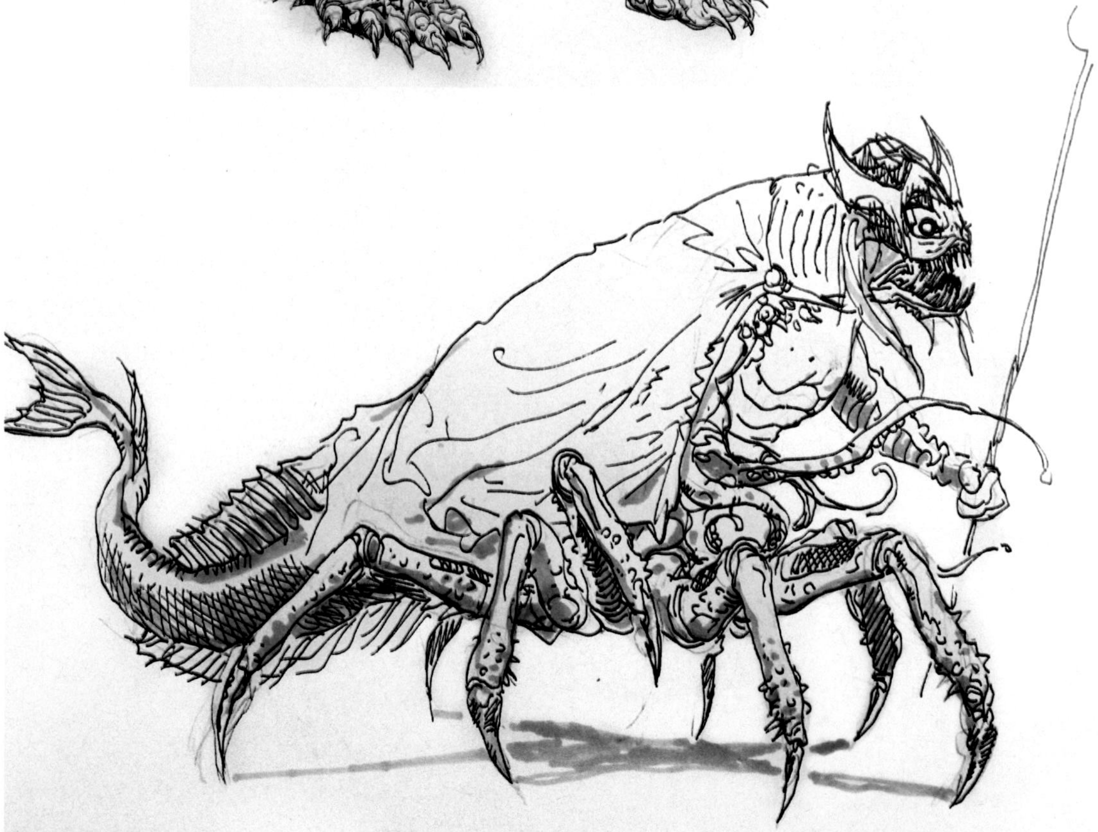

KING RATH profile designs by DOUG MAHNKE

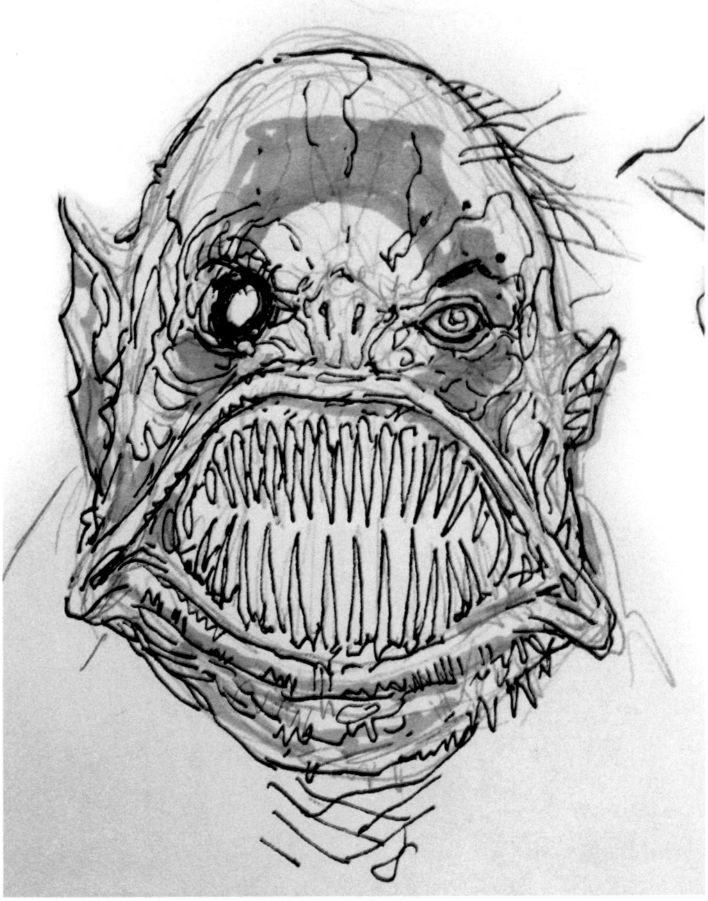

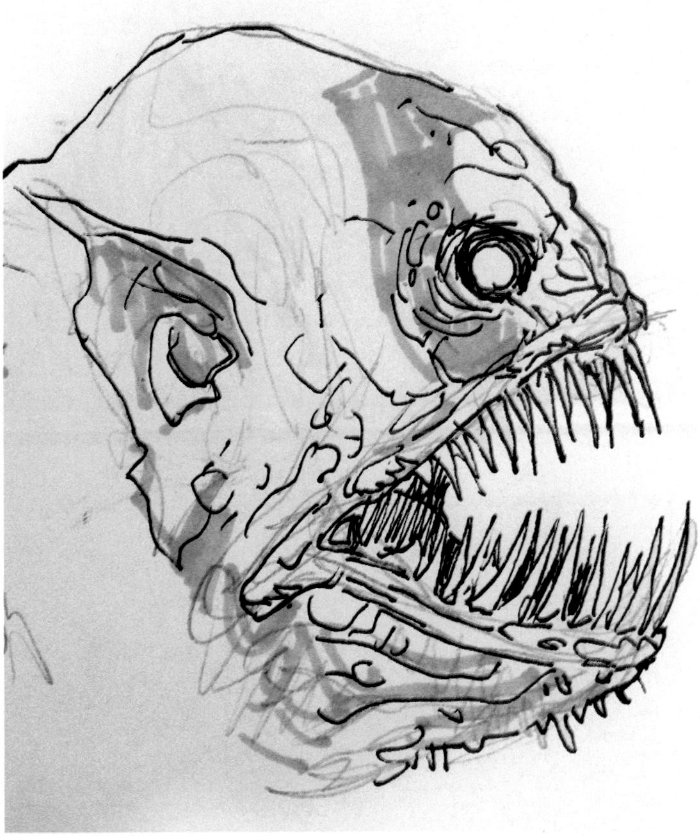

AQUAMAN early concept sketches by RICCARDO FEDERICI

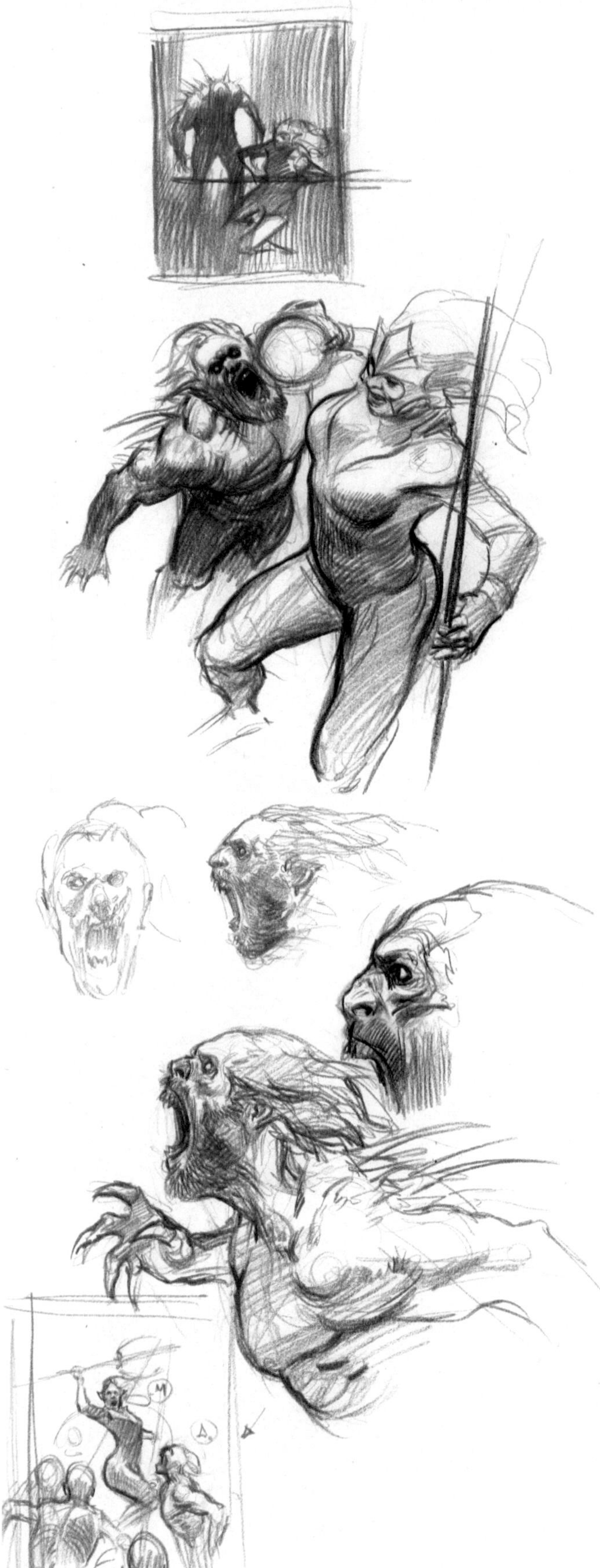

AQUAMAN early concept sketch by RICCARDO FEDERICI
MERA'S OCTOPUS sketch by RICCARDO FEDERICI

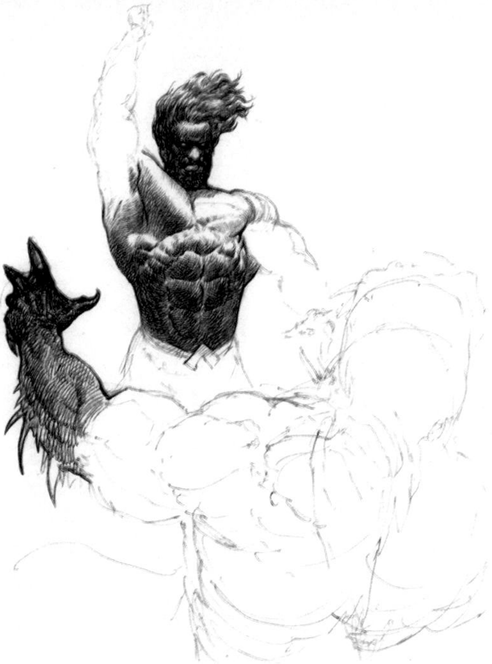

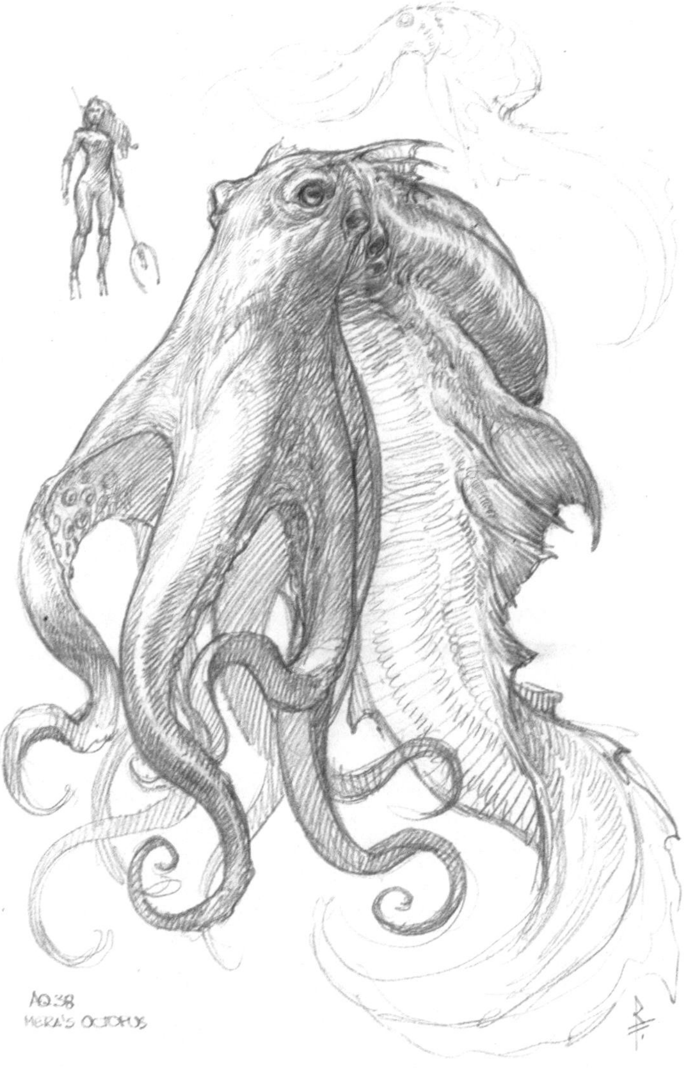
AQ38
MERA'S OCTOPUS

Early layouts for AQUAMAN #38 by RICCARDO FEDERICI

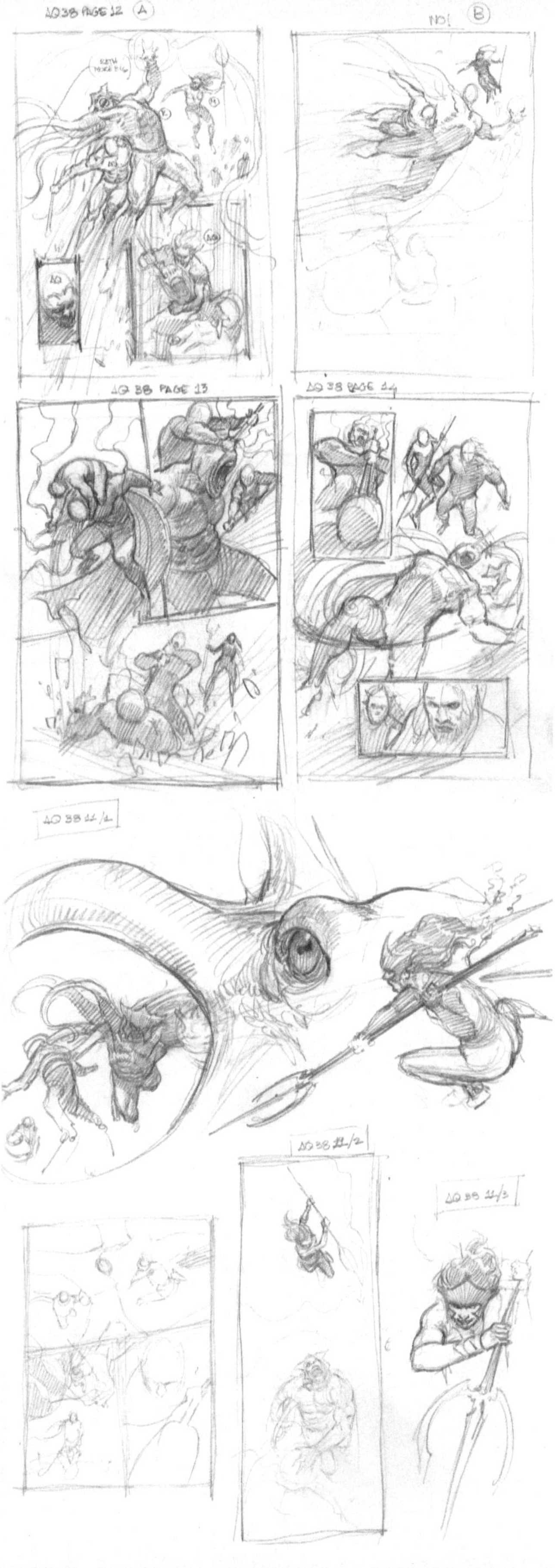
AQ 38 PAGE 12
AQ 38 PAGE 13
AQ 38 PAGE 14

AQ 38 PAGE 6

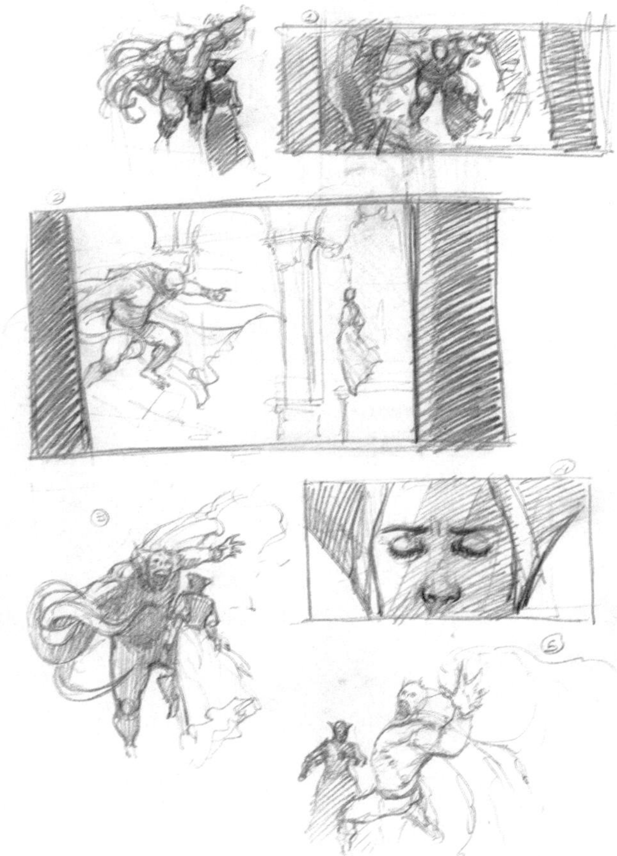

AQ 38 PAGE 1

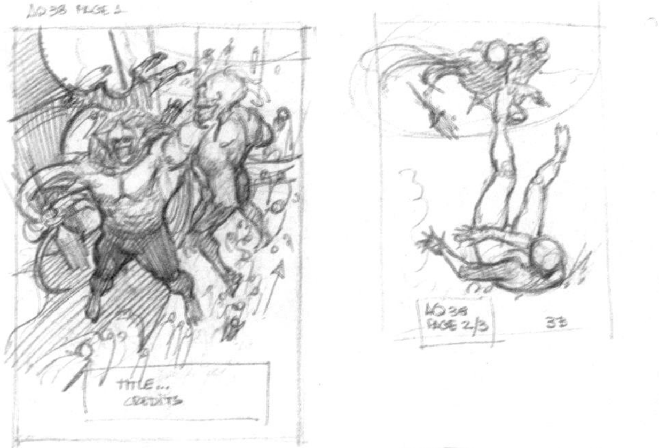
TITLE...
CREDITS
AQ 38
PAGE 2/3
33

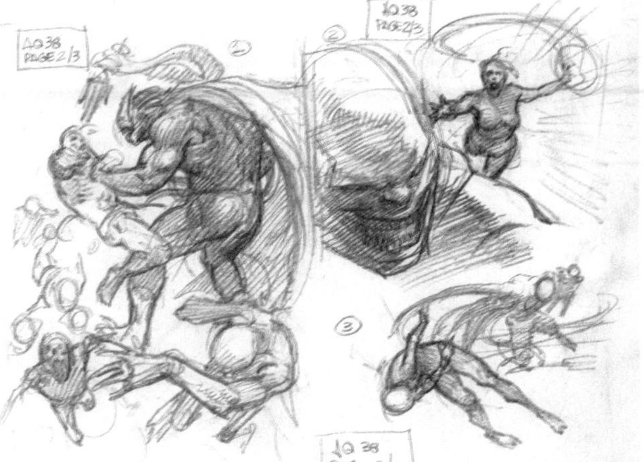
AQ 38
PAGE 2/3
AQ 38
PAGE 2/3
AQ 38
PAGE 2/3

AQ 38 PAGE 16

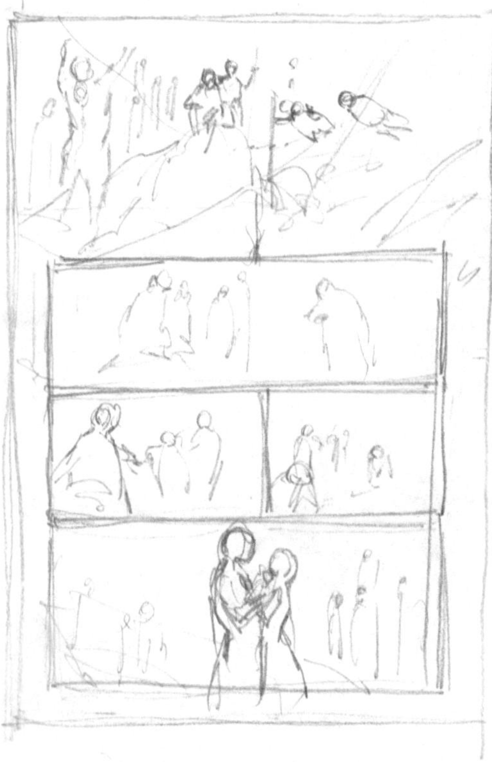

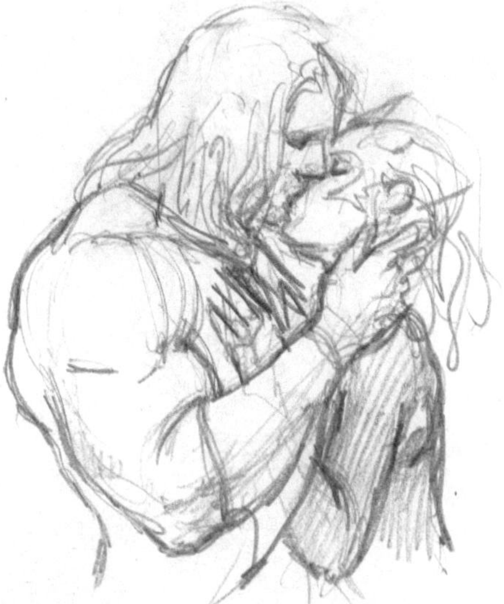

AQ 38 PAGE 17 A

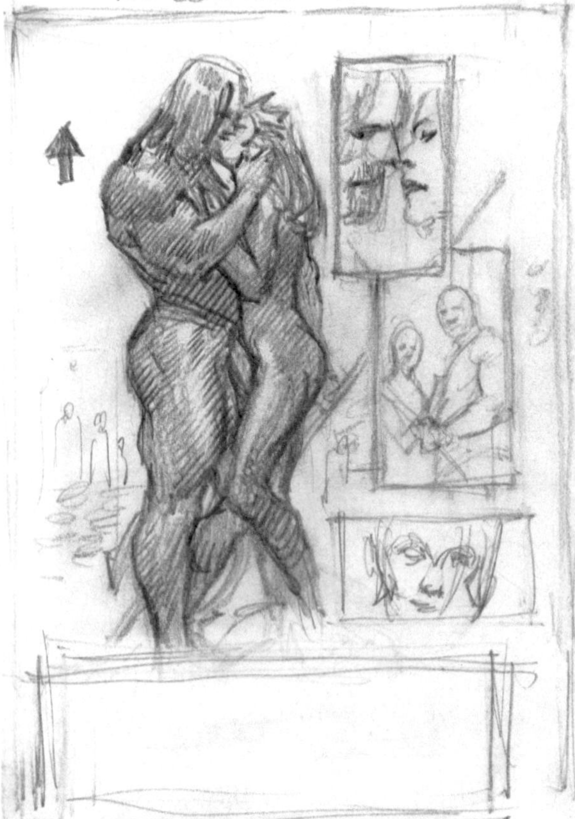

AQ 38 PAGE 17 B

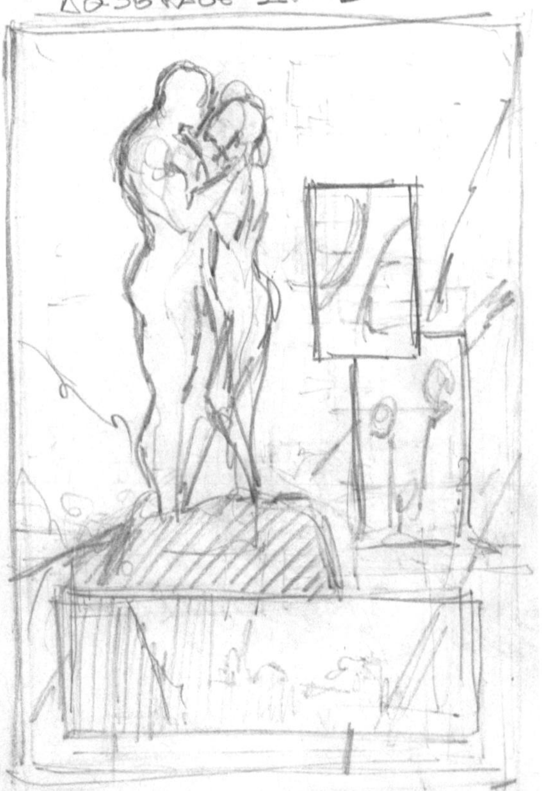